DESIGNING AND PRODUCING THE TELEVISION COMMERCIAL

LARRY ELIN

Syracuse University

ALAN LAPIDES

Leo Burnett USA, Inc.

PEARSON

Boston ■ New York ■ San Francisco
Mexico City ■ Montreal ■ Toronto ■ London ■ Madrid ■ Munich ■ Paris
Hong Kong ■ Singapore ■ Tokyo ■ Cape Town ■ Sydney

Dedicated to the memory of
Hooper White

Series Editor: *Molly Taylor*
Editorial Assistant: *Michael Kish*
Marketing Manager: *Mandee Eckersley*
Production Administrator: *Michael Granger*
Editorial-Production Service: *Omegatype Typography, Inc.*
Manufacturing Buyer: *JoAnne Sweeney*
Composition and Prepress Buyer: *Linda Cox*
Cover Administrator: *Kristina Mose-Libon*
Electronic Composition: *Omegatype Typography, Inc.*

Library of Congress Cataloging-in-Publication Data

Elin, Larry.
  Designing and producing the television commercial / by Larry Elin and Alan Lapides.
      p.   cm.
  Includes bibliographical references and index.
  ISBN 0-205-36538-8 (alk. paper)
    1. Television advertising.   I. Lapides, Alan.   II. Title
  HF6146.T42E43 2004
  659.14'3—dc21   2003044417

Printed in the United States of America
10 9 8 7 6 5 4 3 2 1   08 07 06 05   04 03

CONTENTS

CHAPTER FOUR
Creative Development   75

CHAPTER FIVE
Selecting the Director   108

CHAPTER SIX
The Client Estimate   125

CHAPTER SEVEN

Preproduction   143

CHAPTER EIGHT

Shooting the Commercial   166

CHAPTER NINE

Sound, Graphics, Special Effects, and Animation   194

CHAPTER TEN

Postproduction   217

CHAPTER ELEVEN

The Wrap   238

PREFACE

"Every frame is a poster." That is how Tony Viola, senior art director at J. Walter Thompson Advertising and twenty-five-year veteran of television commercial design and production, describes the typical thirty-second spot he creates for his clients.

Every frame is a work of art, carefully designed, skillfully crafted, and meticulously fine-tuned before it goes on the air. And, that is how it should be, considering the extraordinary amount of time, effort, and money invested in every nationally televised commercial. Some commercials cost more than $1,000,000 to produce, which means that every *poster* in the commercial—each of the 720 film frames or 900 video frames—costs more than $1,000. Factor in the costs for research and design at the agency, and for media time buys on television networks and cable channels, and nationally televised commercials represent investments in the hundreds of millions of dollars. Every frame had *better* be a poster.

As compelling as the high costs of design, production, and distribution are, the importance of the effectiveness of the commercial for everyone involved is the main driving force behind the quest for perfection. Simply put, the commercial must do its job. The stakes are extremely high for a commercial client, a multibillion dollar soft drink company, for example, that puts its sales goals on the line with an advertising strategy orbiting around a particular television commercial campaign. In an increasingly cluttered media environment, the commercial has to grab and hold on to the attention of an ever-more jaded and discriminating audience. It has to cut through the multitasking attention of its target market—make people look up from their pizza, turn away from their Internet surfing, or shush their children for a moment. Watch. Listen. Be convinced. Be motivated. Buy. An advertiser's entire marketing plan could hang in the balance—its quarterly profits, its regard on Wall Street, and certainly the careers of a few people closest to the commercial. It should come as no surprise to anyone that those with the most to gain, have the most to lose and insist that every frame be a poster.

Over at the advertising agency, an important account is at stake, perhaps its biggest account and perhaps billions in annual billings. For the individuals involved, there are promotions, stock options, and bonuses. For executives, creatives, researchers, and media buyers at the agency, reputations are built and, as a highly regarded commercial producer, Dan Fitzgerald, once said, "All you really have in this business is your reputation." Agency people take their work very seriously, and every frame must be a poster.

A director and his or her production company will be hired to shoot the commercial. A postproduction house, various subcontractors, crew, talent, music composer and arranger, special effects experts, computer animators, and others will be hired. Every one of them is hired based on the skills and talents they demonstrate on their show reels, and on the word-of-mouth about their work and what it's like to work with each of them that circulates in the production community. Often, they are hired for their taste and sense of style. Even though any single commercial may be one of a score or more that they work on in a year, for a variety of agencies and their clients, every commercial is evidence of their professionalism, creativity, and value. Every frame must be a poster.

WHAT THIS BOOK IS ABOUT

This book is about the business, the art, and the technology of the television commercial, and about the three main players—advertiser (or client), advertising agency, production company—who collaborate on it. The book covers the components of the television commercial by tracing the design and production process, which begins with the advertiser's need to reach a target market with a persuasive message and ends with the delivery of the finished television commercial to the media. Every step of the way, the players deal with various creative, business, and technical issues as they begin with a blank piece of paper and a few sketches, and finish with 900 posters on videotape. For more than fifty years, this process has made it possible to create the television commercial to the necessarily high standards that the client, the agency, and the production community expect. Although described in terms of the high-budget, nationally televised commercial, the processes and procedures can be (and should be) applied to all commercials regardless of product or service; national, regional, or local distribution; budget size; or other qualifiers. Some of the must do tasks are clearing rights, paying reuse fees to union talent, and making truthful claims. Throughout the book, we show how the processes are the same and how they differ somewhat.

The design and production process that has evolved is more than a tradition—it has become the industry standard, making it possible for clients, agencies, and production companies to easily work together on commercial projects with little or no reeducation. Every advertising agency and every commercial production company is structured and operates in roughly the same manner. Research, creative development, creative tools, and production procedures are the same or similar from one agency to the next. Parts of the process are even codified in the form of standard contracts, budgeting and bidding templates, union rules and agreements, and other formalized or legal procedures. Other parts, such as job titles and descriptions, are more cultural or systemic, but every bit as ingrained into the industry. A network of interrelated businesses has sprung up around the television commercial, including audience measurement services such as Neilsen Media Research; trade magazines such as *Advertising Age, Shoot, Adweek,* and *Boards & Creativity;* awards competitions such as Cannes, The One Show, and the Clios; trade organizations such as ANA, 4As, and AICP; and hundreds, if not thousands, of vendors running the gamut from caterers to casting agencies.

Throughout the process, various people are responsible for completing certain tasks, meeting milestones, and providing certain deliverables. These tasks, the milestones, and the roles and responsibilities of the people involved are arranged along a timeline and described in depth.

WHO SHOULD READ THIS BOOK

In the broadest sense, students should read this book—students of the television commercial. It is written with college television, film, and advertising students in mind; however, professionals at the client, in advertising departments or at advertising agencies, and in television or film, who may not be acquainted with the design and production process, should read this book. The book clarifies the business, the art, and the technology and provides a breadth and depth of knowledge about all three. Although there is no substitute for direct, meaningful, hands-on experience, this book provides the reader with an accurate view of how professionals design and produce television commercials and provides valuable industry insight and orientation. Much of the book is necessarily written in a way that describes *how* things are done in the industry, and we try hard to convert this message to *how you can* do it. The book suggests exercises that put the reader in the position of the professional and discussion questions that ask the reader to think critically.

HOW THE BOOK IS ORGANIZED

The book has three parts. Part I provides foundation and background—the big picture about the television commercial itself and the businesses that surround it. In chapter 1, we discuss television commercials and the people who make them. We describe the elements addressed in the design and production of the commercial—the message, the audience, the concept, the theme, and the visual language. We talk about the social and cultural impact that the commercial can have, and the responsibility commercial makers have to be forthright and ethical. Chapter 2 is a broad overview of the television commercial industry. We discuss the business model that drives advertiser-supported broadcasting, the history of broadcast advertising, and the rules and regulations that govern what is permissible in television advertising. The best source for current advertising trends and news are the trade magazines and Websites, lists of which we provide at the end of several chapters. Chapter 3 covers the role of research in advertising, and how it is used to direct the purchase of media, the identification of the audience, the development and testing of creative concepts, and the evaluation of performance.

There is a chronology to the design and production of television commercials, and the rest of the book follows this step-by-step process in the order in which these events should occur.

Part II discusses the design process, which is driven by the goals of the client, guided by research and the advertising budget, and challenges the creative ability of the advertising agency. The design process actually begins with the client, when it evaluates its marketing goals and its need for an advertising agency. During the design phase, the agency develops an advertising plan, part of which is the creative development of the television commercial. The plan is pitched to the client who then approves the concept and the budget. The design process continues when the agency creates copy and storyboards to be shared with commercial directors who add their creative touch and then bid on the production.

Part III covers the production process, which begins when the agency and its client settle on a commercial director, and the agency and the production company begin preproduction. This part discusses the production and postproduction processes through to delivery of the final commercial.

We've done our best to make sure that the contents of this book aren't dated before the book is even published. We focus on the processes that seem to be permanent fixtures after fifty years of commercial production. Current practitioners at agencies and production companies helped us sharpen our descriptions of how things work in this exciting field and gave us some good ideas and predictions about where things are headed. As a result, this is a book that will benefit both students and professionals.

A WORD ABOUT NOMENCLATURE AND PROCESS

To make the reading of this book, not to mention its writing, simpler and more pleasant, we avoid constantly qualifying that a person—a commercial director, for example—may be either a *he* or a *she*. Everybody knows this already. Instead, we variously use either *he* or *she* but not both, and we have tried to use them equally. Almost always we refer to *filming* the commercial, even though commercials are also *shot* on tape.

We also want to say one *more* time, for the record, that although much of this book describes processes and procedures peculiar to the major, national, high-budget television commercial, the process is applicable to the low-budget spot shot by a local television station. We are certain of this from our own combined fifty-plus years of experience in the field and from a conviction that it is much better for the student to know the right way to do things, and to apply it to the low-budget sphere, than the alternative.

ACKNOWLEDGMENTS

Many people helped to make this book possible. We'd like to thank Karen Bowers at Allyn and Bacon for agreeing to publish the book, and Molly Taylor and Michael Kish for their hard work keeping us focused and on schedule. Professor Amy Falkner graciously contributed Chapter 3, Advertising Research and Strategy. Jim Longstaff provided terrific feedback on Chapter 4, Creative Development. Tony Viola at J. Walter Thompson was an early advocate for the book and reviewed early drafts. He provided valuable insight into the creative process. We'd like to thank our other reviewers: Fred K. Beard, University of Oklahoma; Nancy Mitchell, University of Nebraska; and Ron Stotyn, William Patterson University. They'll all notice we really read their reviews and took their advice.

Scot Byrd at Rhythm & Hues, Pennie Gorney at Eric Mower & Associates, Vicki Wilson at Romanelli Advertising, Talia Kipper at J. Walter Thompson, Lorraine Koury at Boom Babies, Roy Schecter at IBM, McCay Brown at Novell, and David Herdman and Kristen Meade at Kellogg all provided images and valuable information for the book. Stu Lissit and Robert Gerbin helped us capture images and Andy Breyer did some sketches for the book.

We interviewed many people and each one provided valuable information and ideas for the book, including Bill Kroyer, Elise Kleinman, Danielle Teschner, Pete VonDerLinn, Kevin Tripodi, Andrew Donovan, Jeffrey Hammond, Scot Kaitanowski, David Thomson, Carla Lloyd, Fiona Chew, Bud Carey, Mike Sweeney, Crystal Anderson, Cindy Tsai, and Spencer Baim.

In addition, all these industry people helped a great deal: Steven Novick, Brian Crotty, Kathy O. Ring, Ken Gilberg, Kathy Ring, Michael Sirota, Peter Keenan, Bonnie Van Steen, James Wahlberg, Ron Nelken, Jonathan Davis, Glant Cohen, Chris Rossiter, Rudy Behlmer, Bob Carney, Bob Harley, David Moore, Tom Duff, Blair Stribley, Kevin Smith, Paige Miller, Mimi Mayer, Craig Colvin, Stewart Skelton, Barbara Rowan, Diane Pidrak, Barbara Dent, Stephaine Ross, Mike Shanahan, Randi Petrakis, Miffie Gardner, Jovita Pacheco, Shirley Costa, Laura Bratu, Susan McGarrigle, Leslie Meeds, Joyce Stevens, Sergio Lopez, Vicki Buttens, Marsha Kabb, Steve Wolff, Carol Hurlburt, Sid Hurlburt, and Carla Michelotti.

And, of course, we thank our wives: Fran Lapides who "understands" and lovingly puts up with most of Al's idiosyncrasies, and Katy Benson who does the same for Larry.

CHAPTER ONE

TELEVISION COMMERCIALS AND THE PEOPLE WHO MAKE THEM

In 1964, President Lyndon Johnson faced Republican challenger Barry Goldwater in a presidential election that, by Election Day, seemed to revolve entirely around the issue of how best to win the war in Vietnam. Goldwater had chosen William E. Miller as his running mate, an outspoken proponent of winning the war at all costs, and Goldwater had made public statements that suggested he might use "the bomb" to end the war quickly (although he never actually used those precise words).

New York advertising agency Doyle Dane Bernbach (DDB) had been handling television advertising for the Johnson campaign, and it hired veteran sound man Tony Schwartz to create the sound for spots they were already working on. He worked on the sound for a number of them, and then, all on his own, pitched an idea that would stress Johnson's reluctance to use nuclear weapons. Political consultant Joseph Napolitan, a close friend of Schwartz, recalls what happened next:

> Tony played them a sound track of a spot in which a little girl is counting from 1 to 10. When she reaches 10, her voice fades away and is replaced by a militaristic male voice counting backward from 10 to zero. We then hear an explosion that sounds like (and was) an atomic bomb. A decision was made to produce a visual version of the spot. Tony suggested using a little girl peeling petals off a daisy, and found a little girl he thought would be good for the spot. DDB shot the film from Tony's concept, and Tony did the sound. He added part of a speech made by Johnson to the end that goes, "These are the stakes...to make a world in which all God's children can live, or to go into the darkness. We must either love each other, or we must die," and a the tag line, "Vote for President Johnson on November 3. The stakes are too high for you to stay home."[1]

The commercial known as "Daisy" ran only once, on *Monday Night at the Movies,* and was pulled (see Figure 1.1). Even though Goldwater was never named, and no accusations were made, the viewers themselves connected the central message of the spot to Goldwater. The spot, as Schwartz would say later in his book *The Responsive Chord,* simply confirmed what the audience had already come to believe.[2] The Goldwater campaign slogan, "In your heart you know he's right" was transformed into, "In your heart you know he *might*." The chilling notion that the Republican ticket was capable of taking us to

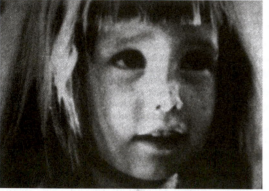

FIGURE 1.1   In the "Daisy" commercial created by Tony Schwartz for Doyle Dane Bernbach and the Lyndon Johnson campaign, a little girl is shown plucking a daisy and counting to ten. The camera zooms to her face while another voice counts down to zero. Then a nuclear blast fills the screen. The images were frightening, and helped to label Barry Goldwater and his running mate, William E. Miller, as dangerous, even though they were never mentioned in the spot.

Courtesy of Tony Schwartz.

a nuclear holocaust was more than a generation of jittery cold war veterans could take. Johnson won the election by a landslide.

The commercial alone did not determine the outcome of the 1964 election—there were many other issues on which Johnson ran, including a strong domestic record that included the Equal Opportunity Act, The Civic Rights Act, and the War on Poverty. However, the impact of the commercial made a lasting impression on every advertisement maker in the country. It continues to be shown in advertising classes and political science classes as a prototype for political advertising. It proved that image messages—reaching the viewer with visual and aural associations—can be powerful, particularly when dealing with emotional issues.

In an ironic twist, Goldwater's running mate William E. Miller dropped out of politics after the 1964 election, but later surfaced as one star in an American Express commercial campaign in 1975. In this campaign, the once-famous politician appeared on camera using the opening line, "Do you know me?" The celebrity would then say, in not so many words, that the viewer probably didn't, but the American Express Card made it possible for one to continue to be treated in the manner to which he had been accustomed. The spots ended with the celebrity's name being imprinted on a card. Miller once told a reporter that he was more famous for appearing in the commercial than for running with Barry Goldwater.[3]

The brief, a half century of television commercial history has given us many such examples of success (and others of failure). In fact, everything we know about commercials comes from the experience of making commercials like "Daisy" and learning from the process and the results.

Used as a communications tool within the advertiser's overarching marketing strategy, the commercial has helped to create brand names for products and services, and groom generations of product loyalists. Public service announcements have helped to turn Americans into environmentalists, nonsmokers, and seatbelt wearers. Political ads have gotten some candidates elected, often because of what they say about the other guy. In the process of entering our homes, the commercial has affected our society and popular culture in some profoundly positive ways, and in some negative ways as well.

Here, we discuss the basic elements that comprise the commercial, the people who create and produce the commercial, and the overview of the process of creating and producing it. We discuss the effect that commercials have had on society, which should give current and future television commercial designers and producers pause, as you consider the enormous power you wield and the ethical responsibility you must accept.

In this chapter, you will learn the following:

- The television commercial is only one part of an advertising plan, which in turn is a part of a promotional mix. Both derive from the advertiser's marketing strategy. Because of this "chain of command," the commercial must be conceived as something to help achieve a specific marketing objective.
- The television commercial is an art form, a film genre, and a social and cultural phenomenon. It is a powerful form of communication.
- Advertisers, ad agencies, and production companies collaborate on the design and production of commercials and have specific roles and responsibilities in the design and production of the commercial; they follow a time-tested process to design and produce commercials.
- There are three basic types of commercials—selling, image-making, and public service announcements.
- Commercials are aired nationally, regionally, or locally.
- The central message of the commercial is the idea that must be left with the audience after it is viewed.
- When designing the commercial, it is important to determine and examine the target audience and use that knowledge in the creation of the concept and theme.
- The concept and theme is the creative approach that carries the message.
- The visual language is the set of techniques filmmakers use to interpret, or execute, the creative approach.

The basic concepts discussed here should provide you with the foundations for learning how to make commercials using the step-by-step process detailed in the chapters that follow.

WHAT IS A TELEVISION COMMERCIAL?

A television commercial is a very short persuasive film, shown to the audience during interstitial minutes between programs, or at times when the program is interrupted specifically to show commercials.[4] There are three basic types of television commercials:

1. *The selling commercial*—the focus is on specific attributes of the product or service; the goal is to stimulate preference for the product and a desire to buy it.
2. *The image commercial*—the focus is on creating an aura, or image, for the product, service, or company; this kind of advertising is also thought of as selling an idea.[5] The goal is to leave the consumer with positive feelings toward the company, product, or service, which will eventually lead to sales.
3. *The public service announcement*—the focus is to inform or persuade the public about something that is in *its* self-interest; commerce usually is not the goal.

All commercials are designed to inform, to persuade, and ultimately to motivate the audience to action—most often to buy a product or service. The most pervasive local commercials are selling ads, with which we are all familiar. Furniture, grocery, clothing, and automotive retailers fill commercial timeslots with spots that announce clearance sales, new inventory, two-for-one specials, and so on. The message is clear: "We are located here, this is our phone number, we're open at 9 A.M., and there has never been anything like this sale before." On the national level, ads for skin creams that *show* the difference that using the product can have, or for antilock braking systems in which the benefits are demonstrated on an icy patch of road, are selling ads.

Some commercials are designed to help establish an *identity* for an advertiser, or an *idea* about the product or service. Image ads have little to do with advertising specific product qualities. The goal instead is to align the company or the product with a particular consumer group, lifestyle, trend, or current event, and the end goal is to increase awareness of and positive feelings toward the advertiser or its products. The theory is that this eventually leads to increased sales or positive feelings toward the company. It is often used to counter bad publicity, which may be afflicting the company. There are more dots to connect in the mind of the consumer, but image ads are overtaking selling ads, particularly on the national level.

In a commercial for Pringles potato chips—the ones that come in a can—a room full of trendy, attractive, and happy teens and some twenty-somethings dance and grind to techno-industrial music. Some of them are bouncing up and down on a trampoline. Laser lights are everywhere. Suddenly, the last chip is taken from what appears to be the last can of chips, and the music stops. Oh no! The party's over! But then the sound of air escaping from another airtight can makes everybody realize there are more Pringles! The party picks up where it left off. Bounce and grind.

The goal of this ad is to align a product with a consumer group that otherwise might not associate itself with the name and package design that features a sort of Gay '90s (that's 1890s) theme. The message of this image ad seems to be, "Don't look at our package, look at who eats us."

On the national and the local level, many political commercials are primarily image ads designed to portray the candidate in a particular light[6] but not necessarily highlight specific proposals.[7] Ads such as these might aim to establish a candidate as "tough on crime," or "fighting for the working family," the end goal being to win the viewer's vote. Stephanie Miner won a seat on the Syracuse, New York, common council—essentially the city's ruling body—by using a pool of ads underscoring that she will be a "real fighter" on issues such as job growth, improving neighborhoods, and education (see Figure 1.2).

Park Row Campaign Management, which designed and produced the spots for Miner, developed the creative and media approach this way because:

- "Real fighter" slogan—Stephanie is young, so we wanted to portray her as someone who could do the job effectively.
- Using real people—Stephanie has real supporters whom she had made contact with regarding the very issues highlighted in the ads; we felt that using these residents would lend the spots authenticity and punch.
- Fifteen-second spot—The message we had was simple. It could fit into a :15 effectively, and the shorter spots would make the most of her budget. They also stood out among the tedious :30 and :60 spots many politicians use. Bookend placement completed the originality of using the :15.
- "Paid for by friends of Miner…Like me"—We have to tag the spots with the "paid for" (by law) so why not make it work for the spot? The people featured were real friends of Miner, so we identified them as such. No other ad we know of has taken this approach.
- Lastly, Stephanie has natural energy, ambition, intelligence, and compassion. No matter when you meet her or where, these traits are apparent. We knew she would play well on television, and for this reason, we needed voters to see her—that's why we did television.

Some commercials are public service announcements (PSAs), which differ from the typical product pitch, or image ad, in that the message is generally for the public good and is not self-serving on the part of the advertiser. PSAs may promote getting flu shots, voting, attending a charitable event, literacy, or caring for the environment, for example. PSAs are often created by nonprofit organizations devoted to these projects or movements with funding generally provided by individuals, members, foundations, and corporate gifts. On a local level, PSAs are sometimes aired at no cost by broadcasters who must demonstrate to the Federal Communications Commission (FCC) that they have been acting in the public's interest in order to acquire or to retain their broadcasting license. Unlike paid commercial time, public service announcements are not scheduled by the advertiser, but run at the discretion of the media, usually during unsold time.

Marketing, Promotion, and Advertising

A television commercial is only one part of an advertising plan that, in most cases, includes other forms of advertising, including print, outdoor, transit, and Internet advertising.

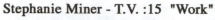

Stephanie Miner - T.V. :15 "Work"

Man: Thomas, Katie... none of them live here...

We need somone who'll fight for opportunities for our children and their children.

Stephanie: I'll work to give young people a reason to come home.

Narr: Stephanie Miner, elect a real fighter to the common council

Man (V.O.) Paid for by the friends of Miner

PARK ROW Campaign Management

...Like me

Synergistic Productions

FIGURE 1.2   Political ads are often image ads designed to leave the voter with an idea or sense about the candidate.

Courtesy of Park Row Campaign Management of Clinton, New York, and Synergistic Productions of Syracuse, New York. Reprinted with permission.

Advertising itself is one form of *promotion,* which also includes sales promotion, personal selling, public relations, and publicity. In what is called the promotion mix, advertising is the form of marketing communication in which media exposure is planned, created, and paid for. Public relations and publicity are forms that are not.

Promotion, in turn, is one of the famous four *P*s of marketing: product, place (distribution channels), price, and promotion. The design and production considerations for a television commercial, particularly for a major consumer product, take place long after a grander scheme for the branding and marketing of the product has been determined. Figure 1.3 shows the hierarchy of the marketing plan.

The typical consumer products' manufacturing companies—the leading advertisers in all media, including television—develop an annual marketing strategy for each of their brands. Johnson & Johnson, Procter & Gamble, General Motors, Microsoft, Nabisco, and Philip Morris are household names in this category, each with many product brands. The company begins with a review of a particular brand's past and current performance. Sales growth or decline, growth rate over time, and pricing data are evaluated. The brand consumer is profiled demographically, enthographically, and psychographically. Consumer trends are followed. Competitors' past spending and strategy are considered. The company's

The Marketing – Advertising Hierarchy

FIGURE 1.3   The television commercial is part of the overall advertising mix, which is determined by the marketing plan.

own manufacturing capacity, capital investment, distribution channels, and production/ purchasing systems are studied. The product itself is put under the microscope—what are its unique attributes, sizes, varieties, and margins. Product and market research of all kinds, from many sources, are included in the evaluation.

From this review, the marketing department can see potential opportunities for the brand in the coming year, and it identifies potential problems. This takes it to a set of recommendations, in terms of units and sales, and expenditures to achieve those sales, about the brand's basic objective for the year. A brand marketing strategy emerges for positioning the product, distributing it, pricing it, and promoting it. The strategy, which could be thought of as big picture, high-level objectives, guides decisions that are made on the more tactical level of the promotional mix.

A product's promotion mix includes sales promotion; examples are cross-promoting with other products, product placement in movies and television programs, store displays, contests, coupons, and so on. The McDonald's "Happy Meal" is the physical, edible embodiment of cross-promotion because it is often in a box covered with characters from a current children's film release and contains toys, coupons, and free samples designed to promote the film. The promotion mix includes personal selling, public relations, publicity, and advertising. An advertising plan may include plans to advertise on television and radio, in certain print publications, on billboards, via direct mail, and/or over the Internet, depending entirely on the marketing strategy.

CASE STUDY
SERVICE IMPROVEMENT ADVERTISING CAMPAIGN

In Syracuse, a city of 150,000 within a county of 350,000, bus service is provided by the Central New York Regional Transportation Authority, or Centro. Centro must increase its ridership while adjusting service to certain areas in order to raise revenue and cut costs—a fact of life for nearly all public transportation systems. Centro developed new routes and schedules and had to get the word out. It worked closely with its agency, Eric Mower & Associates (EMA) to develop the marketing objectives from which the creative concepts and media plan were derived. EMA produced the following plan.

MARKETING OBJECTIVE...INTRODUCE ROUTE AND SCHEDULE CHANGES
Rationale: Centro is making major improvements to its routes and schedules in November 2002. These changes, which focus on making routes more frequent and more direct to key retail and employment locations in the community, will make the system more convenient for riders. These enhancements provide a major opportunity for Centro to generate new ridership. They also give the Authority the ability to highlight the important role that the Centro system plays in the community.

A significant advertising program is required to ensure that as broad a cross section of the community as possible is aware of the improved routes and schedules. Advertising will successfully reach current riders, prospective riders, and community opinion leaders with important messages about the Centro system.

Objective: Generate increased ridership.

Strategy: (1) Use paid, mass media vehicles to reach riders, prospective riders, and the community at large. (2) Support with public relations. (3) Time advertising to avoid clutter with gubernatorial election.[8]

Program Elements:

- Television advertising—:30 television commercial focusing on the increased convenience of the Centro system
- Radio advertising—:60 radio commercials focusing on the increased convenience of the Centro system
- Newspaper advertising—quarter-page ads focusing on specific route and schedule changes; ads will be placed in weekly publications that can be targeted to specific geographies (see Media Plan for details):
  –Scotsman Pennysavers
  –Syracuse Newspaper Neighborhood Editions

Timing (To be confirmed based on actual launch of service):

- Television and radio:
  –First flight: November 18 to December 2
  –Second flight: December 2 to December 16
  –Third flight: December 30 to January 13
- Newspaper: Ongoing from October through March

Similar plans were written for the public relations and direct mail efforts. Short, concise, and to the point, these two-pagers are used by media buyers and researchers (see chapter 3) and the creative team (see chapter 4) to direct their activities.

The brand's advertising agency usually develops the details of the advertising plan. The marketing plan gives direction to the agency in the form of brand objectives, research information about consumers, the brand's unique attributes, information about the competition, and what other promotional activities are planned. The agency then recommends the creative approach and the media buy to achieve the objective.

The important thing to take from this brief discussion of the marketing plan is that the television commercial is not designed and produced in a creative playground, separate or divorced from marketing and sales objectives. It is closely tied to other forms of advertising and promotional activities, all driven by very carefully considered marketing objectives.

National, Regional, and Local Spots

Advertisers that sell products or services on a national scale, such as automobiles, breakfast cereals, and airline travel, need to reach the mass audience. Nationally televised commercials appear on major networks—ABC, NBC, CBS, Fox, UPN, WB, PaxTV—which collectively reach nearly 100 percent of the viewing public. In terms of media expenditures, national network spots are the largest category of television advertising, accounting for approximately $18 billion of the $45 billion spent in 2001 on advertising.[9] National spots also appear on cable channels, which now reach approximately 80 percent of the viewing public, and through national-spot media buys in which an advertising agency buys time on a number of stations that provide, collectively, national coverage (or coverage of specific areas, such as the top-20 markets, only). National spots are generally designed and produced by advertising agencies for major clients and have considerable production budgets and high production values. It is not unusual for a major brand's nationally televised commercial to cost $500,000 to $1,000,000 to produce.

Advertisers that sell their products or services on a more local or regional level advertise on local broadcast stations and on cable channels through a local cable carrier. A regional advertiser is one who needs geographic coverage beyond a single city and its hinterlands. There are regional beers, breads, and other consumer products unique to New England, the southeast, and the northwest, for example; and the commercials must air in many different cities. Because they advertise over a large and contiguous area, which may have a regional identity, regional advertisers tend to use mid-size ad agencies that know and understand the market. The commercials are typically produced for much lower budgets than network spots, but they have good production values. Regional ads may cost in the neighborhood of $15,000 to $100,000 to produce.

Other advertisers are small retailers that serve their immediate community, and they would be wasting their money if they advertised outside the local area. Their commercials are known as local spots, which are sometimes created by the television station or small production companies directly for the advertiser without involving an advertising agency. A car dealership, for example, may approach the local station and work out a media buy to pitch an inventory clearance. A producer at the station writes the copy and a small camera crew goes to the dealership to shoot video scenes of the lot, the showroom, and a stand-up presentation by the owner. Graphics may be added later at the television station using the same equipment used to edit local news stories. These commercials are generally inexpensive and produced quickly and efficiently; because of this, they may lack the sophistication and production values of big-budget national commercials. With creativity and a sound production process, however, even low-budget commercials can look quite good.

It is important to understand that even though budgets vary for the design and production of the commercial depending on how widely seen it will be, all commercials have the same basic components. The number of people involved, their job titles, and what organization they are with differ greatly between network and local commercials; but, they must all be written, produced, and directed using the steps described throughout this book.

COMPONENTS OF THE COMMERCIAL

There are five basic components of all commercials whether they are national, regional, or local; and whether they are selling, image-making, or public service announcements. All commercials have a central message that is targeted at a specific audience. The message is presented *thematically*—imbedded in a story or format of some kind. The theme grows out of the creative concept and, because commercials consist of visuals and sound, the story is told using the visual language—the skillful use of framing, composition, camera angles, lighting, movement, editing, pacing, sound, and other aesthetic techniques. The use of visual language is usually referred to as the *interpretation* of the concept, or the *execution* of the concept.[10] Hang on to these components, because we return to them again and again throughout the book. We cover these important commercial elements briefly in this section and in more detail in subsequent chapters.

The Target Audience

Of the several criteria used by an advertiser when it decides to advertise at all, much less on television, one of the most important is the *target audience*—the group of people whom the advertiser has determined is the primary consumer of its product or service. Other criteria are the nature and benefits of the product itself, branding strategy, the competition, current market forces, and the general social and economic climate. Even the season (Christmas, for example) is a criterion used by the advertiser for creating its commercials. It cannot be emphasized often enough, however, that commercials are created to reach specific target audiences and that the advertiser must begin with a clear understanding of the age, sex, education, income, likes, dislikes, motivations, and other characteristics of that audience. The target audience not only drives decisions about the basic message, the creative concept and theme, and the execution of the visual language, but the media buy— when and where the commercial will air.[11]

In the case of the politician, for example, the target audience might be undecided, independent voters in her district. Members of the other political party may be unlikely to be swayed by her appeals, and members of her own party may already be onboard. The election may hinge on capturing the independents. Research might tell the politician what the undecided voter's profile is—the demographic and psychographic descriptors of this particular voter—and this would lead to a decision about what message the target audience would respond to most positively. In chapter 3, we talk a great deal more about the audience and the research that helps the advertiser design the message for its target.

The Message

Every commercial has a single, overarching message that at one time was referred to as the *unique selling proposition,* or USP. The USP is, as author and advertising expert John Phillip Jones says, "more concerned with what people take out of an advertisement than what the writer puts into it."[12] Even though the term isn't used much any more, the idea that a single important message is at the core of every commercial is an important one. The message is not the story, or the presentation of the argument; it is the central idea the audience must have after viewing the commercial.

Consider, for example, a candidate's political image ad targeted at the undecided voters who are young, affluent, and have young children. *Surveys* and *polls*—types of research often used by politicians—may reveal that voters are concerned about the environment in which they raise their children, and they are concerned about education, recreation, health, and safety. Some of the things that they want for their children they can control themselves, such as whether they attend a private school or go to music camp in the summer, but other things are provided by others as part of the public trust. Those are things that are, at least partially, out of their direct control; police and fire protection, or the location of the public library, are examples. The message that the candidate's strategists determine will engage this voter is: "The candidate is a strong proponent of safe neighborhoods." But how does the candidate get this message across? For every message, there are hundreds of possible concepts that the message can be carried in.

The Concept

The *concept* is the creative starting point for developing the theme, writing the script, drawing the storyboard, and later shooting and editing the final commercial. The concept drives everything. Think of the commercial described in this chapter's opening anecdote. The message the Johnson camp wanted to establish was a distinction between his Vietnam policy and Goldwater's, which was simply that his was more moderate and thus less risky. The concept may have been, "Your children are at risk," which is certainly the idea the audience was left with, and it resonated with them on a personal level. Think of the concept as the link between the basic message the advertiser wants to deliver and the commercial the audience will watch with interest.

The Theme

The *theme* of the commercial is the creative approach—the presentation of the concept in terms of style, story, and structure. Based on the creative concept, it is how the message will be communicated to the audience. The theme of the commercial must resonate with the audience intellectually, emotionally, or intuitively (the head-heart-gut approach), ideally all three. The audience must identify with the basic premise, the style of presentation, and the underlying truth of the message.

In his book on producing television commercials, the late Hooper White lists eleven different themes, which include testimonials, slice-of-life, stand-up presenters, demonstrations, animation, and celebrity endorsements, among others.[13] These and other thematic approaches are familiar to all of us. We have watched basketball legend Michael Jordan wearing Hanes underwear in a celebrity endorsement, and we've watched an average housewife (an actor) get a stain out of her child's play clothes with Tide in a slice-of-life.

In a combination live-action and animated commercial for Lubriderm, a computer-generated alligator gets a real-life massage in a live-action setting, acting as the visual representation of the dry skin the product remedies (see Figure 1.4). On almost any local station, one can see a spokesperson pitching the arrival of new car models at a local auto dealer in a stand-up presentation.

Class Exercise

As a class exercise, brainstorm various thematic approaches for the hypothetical politician to reach a young, affluent, child-rearing couple with the message that she is the best candidate to ensure safe neighborhoods. Come up with a slice-of-life scenario, a testimonial, and a man-on-the-street opinion concept. Which of these concepts would resonate with the audience? Why?

Do the same for a consumer product, such as an automobile, that promotes safety, convenience, and economy. Use the same audience profile—the young affluent family.

FIGURE 1.4   In this commercial for Lubriderm, a computer-generated alligator gets a massage by real people. The 'gator represents the dried-out skin that Lubriderm can treat.

Courtesy of Pfizer, Inc., permission granted by J. Walter Thompson U.S.A., as agent for Pfizer, Inc.

The commercial's creative approach is arrived at based on a number of consider-ations, the most important being what is the product or service, what is the message, who is the audience, and what kind of creative approach will the audience most positively react to. Cost, time, research, available production resources, and the creative team's strong in-stincts play a major role in determining how to design and produce the commercial. Chap-ter 4 covers the creative process in more depth.

The Visual Language

Creative people at the ad agency and filmmakers hired to make commercials are experts in the *visual language:* the proper use of framing and shot composition, camera angles, focus and depth of field, lighting, color, texture, motion, pacing, editing, special effects, and sound. For example, they know that in a *low-angle shot*—the camera is positioned lower and is pointed up—a subject looks superior and dominant.[14] They know that soft-focus and eye lighting on a woman's face can result in what is known as the *glamour shot.* Fast-paced editing and using cuts rather than dissolves can give a frenetic and high-energy feeling to the commercial. Creative people use these techniques while designing and shooting the commercial, knowing that each technique, in combination with others, contributes some subtle piece of information or idea to the storytelling.

In filmmaking, the decision about *how* to communicate a concept is called *interpretation,* and in the commercial production business, it is the director's job to interpret the concept for the screen and to meticulously apply the visual language to the execution. In fact, the main difference in production value between the high-budget and low-budget commercial, alluded to earlier in this chapter, is the time and talent of the director, *not* the technology used by the crew. A student who takes the time, and practices the skills of a director, can create a commercial with high production values on a shoestring budget.

The design and production of the television commercial is largely a matter of understanding the audience, determining the message, creating the theme, and executing the visual language. Each of these four essential steps is covered in subsequent chapters. Here we acknowledge that advertising professionals have mastered these art of persuasion elements. As a result, the commercial has not only bolstered sales, established brands, and gotten more than a few people elected but has also had a profound effect on society and our culture. The following section covers this notion.

THE TELEVISION COMMERCIAL IN SOCIETY

For most American viewers, the television commercial has always been part of the viewing experience, and they have come to accept the fact that during almost any program, and sometimes at the peak moment of dramatic, romantic, or comedic interest, a commercial will suddenly appear. The commercial is so ingrained in television programming that its appearance at specific times actually provides a kind of rhythm to the storytelling that takes place around it. The dramatic structure of made-for-television programs is different from the structure of theatrically released feature films precisely to accommodate the fact that commercial breaks will be inserted here and there.[15]

Commercials are an integral part of television programming, reaching millions of viewers. Unlike the shows they interrupt, national television commercials are shown on several networks or cable channels at the same time, day after day for several weeks or months. Some commercials are so pervasive that it is easy to imagine how people with very different viewing habits can hum a bar from the jingle together, or easily recall the tag line.

It is the rare babyboomer indeed who cannot finish these sentences—all famous tag lines from commercials of the past:

- Winston tastes good, like _____ .
- See the USA in _____ .
- (Swedish accent) Take it off _____ .
- Ace is the place _____ .

Plus, nearly all of us have finished a difficult or time-consuming project with a friend and have remarked, "Well, it's Miller time," even when it was really time for a cup of coffee. The question for today's college student is: What commercials will you remember twenty years from now? Why? Are any of them changing the way you think, behave, or see yourself?

Some commercials are made for a single appearance, such as during the Super Bowl when as many as 300 million people worldwide will see them.[16] The unofficial Super Bowl commercial competition has become as storied as the game itself and is sometimes more entertaining; newspapers and television shows actually have experts review the spots the following day.

A Social and Cultural Phenomenon

Television commercials are a social and cultural phenomenon. Whether the net effect of commercials on society is positive or negative, great or negligible, is an ongoing debate. Proponents claim that commercials are informative and educational. They point out that advertisers, acting in their own self-interest, position their products in socially acceptable, even socially ideal situations, and that children exposed to these scenarios learn proper behaviors. Detractors counter that commercials cause harmful, illogical consumerism by creating a desire for goods most people really don't need. Both arguments may be giving more credit, in terms of the power to persuade and effect change, to commercials than they deserve.

However, much of what commercials are capable of and have accomplished is self-evident. In the introduction to his book, *Visual Persuasion: The Role of Images in Advertising,* Paul Messaris describes a domestic scene in which his then eleven-year-old niece and a girlfriend were watching television when Luke Perry appeared in a Mars Bar commercial. The girls went crazy, and one of them actually kissed the screen. In the store later, both children gravitated to the Mars Bars in the candy section.[17] We have all been there ourselves, either grabbing for the candy, toy, or brand new BMW or watching others succumb to a television commercial's power of suggestion. But there are other effects, as well.

Commercials both reflect society's cultural mores and extend them to the mass audience.[18] Commercials document fashions, music, dance routines, colloquialisms, and social behaviors that are popular and trendy in urban areas or in certain regions of the country. In many instances, people in other geographic areas or from other socioeconomic groups are exposed to some elements of popular culture for the first time by seeing them on nationally televised commercials.

Because commercials can be designed and produced within relatively short time frames, they act as nearly instant barometers of our national temperament. Commercials requesting relief aid that featured firefighters and rescue workers at the World Trade Center appeared within a week of the disaster, for example. Flags, slogans, and other patriotic material and themes soon followed in commercials for airline travel, Broadway shows, and investment services.

Television commercials often break new ground and, in the process, break down old social barriers. Commercials featuring interracial couples; gays; positive African American, Hispanic, and Native American role models; and women and men in nontraditional roles appeared before these portrayals were common. It was a PSA developed by Young & Rubicam's Marsteller Inc. in 1970, featuring Native American Iron Eyes Cody, that is often credited with awakening the whole country to the environmental movement (see

Figure 1.5). In the spot, Cody paddles past factories belching smoke, industrial sludge, and household waste, and lands his canoe on a beach covered with litter. A car goes by on a nearby road, and somebody tosses more trash at his feet. In a dramatic close-up, a tear rolls down his face while the announcer says, "People start pollution. People can stop it." Created for the Keep America Beautiful advocacy group, the spot became the most watched and remembered television commercial of all time, registering more than 24 billion household impressions during its ten-year run.[19]

In his book, *How to Create Effective TV Commercials,* Huntley Balwin reminds us of commercials that aired during the women's movement that not only showed women keeping house with products from Procter & Gamble, but of women taking men out to dinner with their American Express cards.[20] Commercials for health, beauty, or intimate products, featuring talent in believable states of undress, have further stretched if not undone some of our social taboos. At one time, advertisers were not allowed to show a woman wearing a bra, *in a bra commercial,* on her bare skin. The model had to wear the bra *over* some clothing, or it could be displayed on a mannequin. It looked absolutely ridiculous, and advertisers (Playtex, in particular) eventually fought for and won over the network restrictions to show life as it really is. By comparison, the current commercials for Victoria's Secret demonstrate the dramatic shift in social mores.

Lessons about Persuasion

Over the years, the television commercial industry has matured and lessons have been learned about what kinds of themes and creative concepts are effective, and how to use the visual language to best advantage to communicate those concepts. Researchers study and attempt to quantify the effectiveness of commercials, and academics have developed theories about the effects of the visual language as persuasive elements based on the study of

FIGURE 1.5   The Crying Indian PSA from Keep America Beautiful was one of the most memorable commercials ever.

Courtesy of Keep America Beautiful, Inc. Reprinted with permission.

viewers' reactions to certain visual elements. A group of researchers, for example, found that sharp-angled shapes used as design elements were rated high by respondents as being hard, strong, potent and action-oriented while curved shapes were rated low. In fact, the star shape ranked the highest among sharp-angled shapes for positive response.[21] How might an advertiser use this information? The art director of the commercial could see to it that hard, sharp angles are used in the design of the set for a product that must have notions of strength, potency, and action associated with it, such as power tools or home security systems. Concepts such as these go beyond advertising and are used in product design, packaging, and all other graphic representations.

The Potential for Misuse

The power of the commercial to reach and persuade a mass audience is so well understood and documented that there is the possibility for abuse. Unscrupulous, but talented, advertisers can dupe the public, and there are many current and historic examples of this. In 2002, an attorney who advertised that he "won millions" in compensation for his clients and advised, "Don't bring a knife to a gunfight," was found guilty of malpractice and false advertising by a New York State Supreme Court jury in Rochester. The plaintiff in the case, a former client, won a $1.5 million judgment. The attorney had promised to collect "every last dime" owed to his clients. It was revealed that he had never personally appeared in court and that his firm talked the former client into a settlement for a fraction of what he would have won had the case gone to trial.[22] It was found that the attorney *knowingly* made false claims in his advertising, a serious breech of the public trust.

There are other forms of misleading advertising that are not intentional, but nevertheless they can confuse the public. In early commercials, clever devices or techniques were used to improve the appearance of products that were shot under hot lights, or did not look good in black-and-white photos.

A classic case that set the stage for government regulation of commercials' content was the "Sandpaper Case." Prior to this particular commercial, advertisers could use props to represent how things *appear* to perform. Rapid Shave wanted to demonstrate that with the lubrication provided by its shaving cream, a razor could shave the sand off sandpaper. For the purpose of photography, however, they glued sand to glass, then placed the shaving cream on the surface and shaved it off. Photographically, the effect was very pleasing, *and* convincing. The Federal Trade Commission (FTC) objected to the use of these props to demonstrate the product. The agency claimed that this was an accurate demonstration of what would happen if they had used real sandpaper. The FTC argued that this was not an accurate demonstration and pressed the issue. The case went all the way to the U.S. Supreme Court.[23]

Basically, the Court ruled that "demonstrations must be what they seem to be." Photographic problems or shortcomings cannot be used as a rationale for modifying a product demonstration. Faking it is permissible under some circumstances, however; for example, you can use mashed potatoes to represent ice cream in a shot if you are not selling the ice cream. In such a situation, the mashed potatoes are simply props or set dressings. In an ice cream commercial, you must use the real product even if you have a hard time keeping it frozen.

In the late 1960s, the agency for Campbell's Soup photographed a "beauty shot" of a bowl of vegetable soup—basically attempting to make the product look appetizing and hearty. However, the vegetables sank to the bottom of the bowl and the soup looked like a pool of gray liquid (ah, the days of black-and-white television). Marbles were added to the bowl to force the vegetables to the top. This violated both FTC directives and the Supreme Court decision. It was not an acceptable demonstration since the product was not presented as it actually performed.

We often see shampoo commercials in which a model with beautiful hair swirls her mane in glorious slow motion in the "swish" shot. Her hair must be washed according to the instructions on the bottle before being photographed. If you are selling detergent and showing a pile of washed towels, those towels have to be washed with the product according to the instructions. If you are demonstrating stain removal, the clothes must be laundered, without any additional assistance, in the product being sold. A complete affidavit of demonstration must be prepared on the set and signed by an authorized representative attesting to exactly how this demonstration was accomplished.

Professional organizations, watchdog groups, and various government agencies have all weighed in with codes of conduct, public policy, and rules and regulations designed to prevent the possibility of deceit in commercial messages, whether intentional or not. This subject is covered in more detail in the next chapter; however, it is incumbent on all of us in the industry to approach our jobs with a sense of awe and caution about our power to communicate to a mass audience. We alone are responsible for approaching our vocations with integrity and sound judgment.

An Art Form

The television commercial has emerged as an art form; it is a *genre* of film, along with documentary and narrative. Hundreds of articles and books have been written about commercials. Professional organizations have sprung up around commercials, and sponsor competitions, such as the Cannes Gold Lion, the Clio Awards, and the One Show, reward excellence in commercial design and production. Many commercial directors are regarded as artistic masters of the film craft, and go on to long-form filmmaking—for example, Ridley Scott (*Alien*), Bill Kroyer (*FernGully*), Steven Lisberger (*Tron*), David Fincher (*Seven, Fight Club, Alien 3, Panic Room*), Michael Bay (*Armageddon, Pearl Harbor*), Tarsem (*The Cell*), and Mark Pellington (*Arlington Road, Mothman Prophesies*).

The Commercial Challenge

Despite the commercial's stature as an art form, as a social and cultural phenomenon, and its place in the mass media, television advertisers have an uphill battle. Commercials are produced in industry-standard lengths of :15, :30, and :60 seconds. During this very brief time period, the advertiser attempts to get the viewers' attention, hold their attention, convince them with some message, and motivate them to some action. The advertiser must do this even though the raw materials of the commercial—pictures and sounds—are exactly the same as the raw materials of the program it has just interrupted. Complicating this is the fact that the audience is sometimes annoyed when interruptions take place. Furthermore, it is the rare product or service that is of interest to the entire audience, especially when the commercial plays in front of the *general audience*—one that would include males and females or adults and children, for example. A commercial is often shown during breaks in programming, along with several other commercials, creating a clutter of messages that further frustrates the advertiser's intentions.

Advertisers overcome some of these obstacles by being very careful about when a commercial is shown and during which programs. Intelligent, well-researched media buying is just half of the advertising strategy. The other half—the focus of this book—is the creative approach; that is, what the commercial sounds and looks like and how it is produced.

WHO MAKES TELEVISION COMMERCIALS

Advertisers (henceforth referred to as *clients*), advertising agencies, and commercial production companies collaborate on the design and production of high-end television commercials. On the opposite end of the spectrum, many local television spots are written and produced by the stations that will air them, working directly with the advertiser; or, local production companies or independent videographers can produce commercials for local advertisers. There are, of course, variations between these extremes. Ad agencies in medium-size markets provide creative and media buying services for clients and produce commercials with moderate budgets using local talent and production resources. The roles and responsibilities listed briefly in the following sections, and in more detail in later chapters, could shift around from one party to another depending in large part on the budget and market for the commercial.

Advertisers/Clients

Advertisers are companies or individuals with something to sell or promote. They are local restaurants and insurance agents, regional sports teams and shopping malls, and national and international automobile manufacturers and breakfast cereal makers. They are in a competitive, capitalistic economy in which the microeconomic concept of *consumer sovereignty* governs. Consumer sovereignty recognizes that consumers, whose discretion determines what products and services they want, ultimately control demand and demand determines supply. Advertisers attempt to influence demand with persuasive messages about their products and services.

Advertisers have to reach customers, as part of an overarching marketing strategy, and convince them to buy their products or services rather than those of competitors. They try to establish an image for themselves and a brand identity for their products. Clients know that advertising is an essential vehicle for communicating messages to consumers, and they acknowledge that advertising agencies have the expertise to help them do so—to differentiate their product or service and to demonstrate its superiority over the competition. Clients know their products and their customers and that their role in the commercial design and production process usually involves the following:

- Communicating product information and facts to an ad agency
- Communicating consumer data—both hard data and anecdotal information—to the agency
- Setting the budget criteria for commercial production and media buy
- Reviewing and approving the commercial's basic message, creative approach, and later the final execution of it
- Providing products and sometimes other materials (for example, graphics or props) for use in the commercial production
- Paying for everything

Advertising Agencies

Advertising agencies provide audience and media research, creative development, production supervision, media buying, and sometimes marketing services to the advertisers who become their clients. Agencies specialize in analyzing clients' needs and recommending a comprehensive creative and media strategy that will put the right message in front of the right audience at the lowest cost. Agencies act as the liaison between their clients and the production community that produces the television commercial and the media that distribute it. The agencies conceptualize innovative and attention-getting visual stories, evaluate and hire outside production talent, and supervise the production of commercials. They conduct and/or interpret research; process data; and then buy time on television networks, stations, or cable channels.

The job at the agency is to maximize the net effect of their clients' advertising investment. During the design phase, the agency generally does the following:

- Creates and proposes the basic *message* of the commercial; often, this comes directly from the marketing strategy that drives all of the advertising, promotion, and other marketing activities.
- Creates the *concept* and *theme* of the commercial and presents this to the client in the form of scripts, storyboards, and/or other illustrative materials.
- Determines what the commercial is likely to cost to produce.

During the preproduction, production, and postproduction of the commercial, the agency is generally responsible for the following tasks:

- Selecting and hiring the director and production company from among a number of individuals and companies they invite to bid
- Determining the total final cost of the commercial and getting the client's approval

- Providing the music, either by hiring a composer/arranger to create original music or by licensing existing music
- Casting talent
- Obtaining various affidavits and clearances for legal purposes
- Hiring other contractors, such as animation and special effects houses
- Supervising editing and postproduction work at a postproduction house
- Managing the entire process and watching costs

Production Companies

Production companies shoot the commercial for advertising agencies. Again, in low-budget local situations, the television station or cable company may provide production services, such as shooting and editing the spot, as well as broadcast it. In the national commercial arena, production companies are often led by a single film director[24] whose special talent is interpreting the creative concept designed at the agency and plussing it. *Plussing* is an idiomatic term that means the director takes the basic concept and interprets it by suggesting the specific visual language techniques to be used. Earlier in this chapter, we described the difference between the message, the theme and concept, and the interpretation—how there are many ways to conceptualize a message and many ways to visualize the concept. Whereas it is the agency's job to arrive at the core message and the creative concept, it is the director's job to employ the visual language to interpret, or execute the concept—the director determines how to shoot the spot.

The director's company bids on the commercial based on the overall creative concept developed by the agency, and the ideas about how to shoot it provided by the director. If the production company is awarded the contract to produce the commercial based on its proposed execution plan (as well as the cost), it takes on the responsibility for a number of production tasks, which we will cover in much more detail in later chapters, including the following:

- Plan all details of the shoot
- Find locations, design and build sets
- Assist with casting talent
- Hire a film and/or video production crew and others
- Rent or buy props and equipment
- Shoot the commercial
- Deliver the footage to the agency

Although it may sound as though the roles and responsibilities of the parties are parsed out, and it may appear that there is a hand–off of involvement from client to agency to director during the design and production process, there is actually quite a bit of overlap. Because the client is ultimately paying for everything and has the most at stake, the client has the final approval authority over the concept, creative changes, and budgets. The client approves numerous other creative elements and production milestones before and during the production process and postproduction.

In the intimate local commercial production setting, clients can be very hands-on. It is not at all unusual to find the client in the edit suite asking for last-minute details, changes, or color-corrections even when these changes drive up the cost beyond the original bid. Most certainly, the client is sometimes the star talent in local commercials, hawking his cars or her tax preparation service.

When the commercial is complete and has been approved by the client, it is released to media—the local television station, the broadcast networks, the local cable provider or channels. Some commercials are also released theatrically and/or internationally, and some are even used as point-of-sale vehicles in retail outlets or formatted for streaming on the Internet.

OVERVIEW OF THE PROCESS

Like many things that are built from the ground up and are unique unto themselves, television commercials are designed first and then produced. Buildings are designed and then constructed. Feature films are written and then shot. However, even before the commercial is conceived, a certain amount of research drives the development of the creative concept. The client does initial research to determine marketing and sales goals and whether it even needs to advertise. The client introspects: What is our marketing goal? What is the target market? Is television the best way to reach this audience? What is the advertising budget? It determines if it needs an advertising agency at all, and if the client does, whether it needs a full-service agency.

Choosing an Agency

If a client determines that it needs an agency, it will look for one that has the credentials, experience, and staff to service its particular needs.[25] In an effort to land a new account, an agency may staff-up specifically to attract a specific new client. To win the account, the agency researches and analyzes what it believes are the client's needs and prepares an elaborate "pitch," replete with suggested creative approaches and media strategies. The client may ask several agencies to make such a presentation, and sometimes pays them for it. Other times the agency views the effort as an investment to get new business, and puts together a gratis presentation. This "mating" ritual can include events to bring the parties together socially. The client wants to feel comfortable with the agency on many levels, and trust and confidence is often won over dinner, on the slopes, or on the fourteenth green just as it can be in the corporate conference room.

The client nearly always makes the decision about which agency to choose based on a mysterious formula that includes the difficult-to-define creativity of the agency (usually most important), its media plan, the interpersonal relationships that develop (or previously existed), the agency's track record or location, and some intangibles that vary from one client to the next. Clients look to make sure the agency will have no conflicts of interest. Many clients hire consultants to assist with the agency selection process.

PROFILE OF ACCOUNT EXECUTIVE PENNIE GORNEY

In one of those unusual, serendipitous moments that sometimes transform your life, Pennie Gorney morphed from AAU swimming coach into the go-to woman at one of the largest ad agencies in central New York, and in between enjoyed a twenty-year career in advertising. She's currently a management supervisor at Eric Mower and Associates, a Syracuse-based agency with numerous clients such as The American Red Cross, Arby's, Bristol-Myers Squibb Company, Bruegger's Bagels, The Buffalo Sabres, Corning Inc., DuPont Pharmaceuticals, Eastman Kodak Company, Honeywell, Starbucks Coffee Company, and The United Way. Along with her other accounts, Gorney is account executive for the Central New York Regional Transportation Authority, or Centro.*

Like many people in the industry, Gorney did not set her sights on becoming an ad person, but kind of dove into it (pun intended). Born and raised in Coatesville, Pennsylvania, Gorney went to Syracuse University to study social work but wound up with a degree in special education, majoring in speech pathology. She was also a varsity swimmer, and when jobs in her field didn't materialize, she became coach of an AAU swim team and was heavily involved in recreational sports. The father of one of her young swimmers was the vice president of a large Syracuse ad agency that handled clients like Keepsake Diamonds and Oneida Silver—"back in the heyday of all that consumer advertising in Syracuse," as Gorney put it.** He offered her a job at the agency, filling in wherever necessary when people went on vacation.

"I caught the bug," Gorney said. "I thought, 'This is great, this is what I want to do for the rest of my life. This is so wonderful. Commercials. Advertising.' The world was just so exciting." She bounced around from one department to another, and the exposure gave her a broad, eclectic view of how an agency functions. Eventually a position opened up in the media department, and she got it. She went back to school—Syracuse University—and took graduate-level courses in advertising—"Just so I could have the knowledge behind what I was doing too," she added. Once in the advertising network in Syracuse, "Where everybody knows everybody else," Gorney said, she moved from one agency to another as her résumé, experiences, contacts, and reputation grew. She worked at a small agency, where she had a hand in everything, as a vice president for about fifteen years, then worked for one of the very first home cable shopping shows; that lasted only a couple of years. She wanted back into a big agency and took a job at EMA as a management supervisor, which is essentially an account executive—the liaison between the client and the creative team.

Gorney handles an assortment of clients, half of them consumer advertisers and the other half business-to-business. Her clients, for example, include Centro and a large software company, which serves financial institutions, outside of Philadelphia. "Your function as an account person is to lead the strategy of your client at the agency. So on a day-to-day basis, I

---

*In this book, we return again and again to a commercial pool designed and produced for Centro in which Gorney played a major role.
**Syracuse was once a major test market for new products and ad copy.

CONTINUED

make sure that the client's strategy is being met, marketing objectives are being met," she explained. "Here at EMA we use the term *thought leadership,* which is a real important term when you're an account person. You're doing more than the tactical analysis—making sure that things get done and schedules are met; you should be *leading* the strategy with the client, working in tandem with the client."

On a day-to-day basis, Gorney might meet with her clients to discuss their overarching marketing strategy, to study research results, or to evaluate the campaign. She might be running a creative brief, which is a meeting with the creative staff to help them understand "What is the single most important point of this campaign, what are we trying to achieve, who is the market, what are the influences that might take this campaign astray," she explained. "That's part of my job—to get this information and share it with the team." She also meets with the creative team to discuss the ideas they come up with, and to make sure they are on target.

It takes more than years of experience, and a breadth and depth of knowledge about your client, about advertising, and about thought-leading, to be an account executive. At the top of Gorney's list of three personal traits an account executive should have is business ethics—do what is right, have integrity. "You should not be afraid to tell a client, 'That's not a good idea,'" she laughed. "The old days of *Bewitched* and what Larry Tate was all about—that cracks me up—but it isn't like that and shouldn't be." Second, Gorney said, "You really must have a passion. It's a tough business. It's a deadline business. And if you don't have a passion for it, you'll be unhappy, and lost." "Finally," she noted, "the thought-leader thing. You have to be a leader. You have to be creative. You have to think beyond the project's parameters."

Initial Research

Once an agency has been selected, it is responsible for conducting even more research. Keep in mind here that advertising is only one part of a client's marketing plan, and television commercials are usually only one part of the advertising plan. The agency's media department conducts exhaustive research to match the right media with the target market; they research the customers' demographics and psychographics and create a profile of the typical buyer of the product or service. Although media research directs the *media buy*—which media will be host to print and broadcast advertising and when—audience research is offered to the creative department as a starting point for creating the concept that will resonate with the target consumer.

Creative Development

The creative department develops a creative strategy that incorporates all of the media—print, electronic, and new media. Audience research often provides the rationale for the creative approach—a central theme that all ads and commercials spring from. The combination of the media buy and the creative materials—print ads and commercials—is called the *campaign.*

The creative department writes and designs the commercials. The writer writes a script, and the art director draws storyboards that are pitched to the client and supported by the strategy. The staff adds sound to the storyboard and shoots an animatic or test commercial, which they focus-test with consumers. Focus-test results sometimes lead the creative team to modify or change the concept entirely; when they are satisfied with their approach, and the client has approved it, the agency begins a search for directors, to bid on the commercial. Figure 1.6 shows the creative approach for the television spot shown in Figure 1.2.

Bidding the Commercial

The *bid* is a proposal from a director's company to produce the commercial in a certain way, usually for a fixed price,[26] by a specified date. Agencies have relationships with directors and often use the same reliable talent over and over. Directors' representatives provide agencies with demo reels—videotape or DVD samples of the director's work—which are kept available in the agency for review when a concept is ready to bid out. By looking at demo reels, agencies identify directors who seem to have the right talents and skills for the commercial that has been designed and invite them to bid on the project.

The agency provides each company with a bid package that contains a storyboard, script, and other materials in which the rationale and the creative concept are described, sometimes along with budget and time parameters. Then the agency has a series of conference calls or meetings with production companies. The directors and their producers ask a number of questions to be certain about what they are bidding on so that they can return with a bid. Because agencies hire directors for their ability to create the most outstanding, creative commercial (one full of posters—to use the opening metaphor one more time), the bid always includes the director's ideas about how to shoot the agency's concept: her interpretation of the concept, which is called the *treatment.*

Preproduction

The agency and the production company that is awarded the job then begin the first phase of production—preproduction. During this phase, the director generally creates a tighter storyboard—one that shows every shot—and works with the producer to *break it down,* analyzing what it will take to shoot each scene of the commercial. The director and producer identify talent, locations, props, special effects, animation, music, and other components for every shot. This thorough breakdown of the script or storyboard results in a list of resources to be assembled, other contractors to be hired (sometimes by bidding out portions of the commercial), talent to be cast, crew to be hired, locations to scout, and so forth.

There are permits to get, contracts to sign, and insurance with all the necessary riders to be obtained; basically, a hundred small details to attend to and arrange in the form of a production plan, or schedule. The experienced production company producer has a backup plan for everything including a budget estimate for weather delays. Every aspect of the production plan has to be priced out ahead of time, and the entire commercial should be produced on-budget, or for less than the budget approved by the client. What is striking about the amount of work involved in preproduction is that it often takes place in the course of only a couple of weeks or so.

PARK ROW
Campaign Management

Copy

Date: _____

Job Number: _____

Job Description: _____

Proof Number: _____

Copy: _____ Proofread: _____

Traffic: _____ AE: _____

The foregoing is approved in all respects:

Approved by: _____

Date: _____

Stephanie Miner - TV :15

"Work"

(Open on a photo of a big family reunion with a hand holding the frame and pointing to children.)

Man (VO): (voice begins as if he's been listing names.) Thomas, Katie...and none of them live here.

(Cut to man.)

Man: We need someone who'll fight for opportunities for our children and their children.

(Cut to a "For Sale" sign and Stephanie.)

Stephanie (VO): I'll work to give young people a reason to come home.

(Cut to logo.)

Narr. (VO): Stephanie Miner, elect a real fighter to the common council.

(Cut to Stephanie shaking hands with man.)

Man (VO): Paid for by the Friends of Miner.

(Cut to man facing camera.)

Man: Like me.

13151 853.3944 | 2 College Street
18001 761.3944 | P.O. Box 227
FAX 13151 853.3946 | Clinton, New York 13323

info@parkrowcampaigns.com
www.parkrowcampaigns.com

FIGURE 1.6   This is the script for the political ad discussed earlier in this chapter; note that the final commercial has some subtle differences.

Courtesy of Park Row Campaign Management. Reprinted with permission.

Production

The production phase begins when all of the foundations have been laid during preproduction. The director directs the talent, the crew, and the cinematographer to shoot the film or video and may work with special effects specialists and others to create images and sounds. He directs them all so that their individual contributions will come together to create the live-action portion of the commercial. Other pieces are simultaneously produced or acquired by the agency; for example, the agency arranges for music to be produced or acquired through licensing, and a logo or animated end tag is produced, perhaps at a computer graphics company. The director then turns the finished film or video over to the agency producer who arranges for a postproduction session.

Postproduction

The various film and sound components are assembled at an editing and postproduction session, which is usually supervised by the advertising agency creative director and the agency producer. Today's digital tools enable the editor to construct the final commercial during postproduction using layering, compositing, color-correction, special effects, computer animation, and other techniques, taking the work produced in the camera to a whole new level. In this final production phase, the agency creative can direct a digital artist who can practically "paint" every last frame of the television commercial. After approval by the client, the final commercial is ready to air.

The rest of this book is based on the chronological process of making the television commercial as just outlined. Each chapter focuses in on one or more of the steps and describes how you would perform these tasks if you were with the client, the agency, or the production company.

SUMMARY

The television commercial is only one element in an advertising plan, which in turn is a part of a promotional plan; both derive from the marketing strategy. It is important to keep in mind that a commercial is not an isolated, free electron, but is part of a much larger marketing scheme designed to achieve a predetermined, high-level objective. Television commercials are very short persuasive films, which are designed and produced by advertising agencies for their clients. Commercials come in three types:

- Selling commercials are designed to demonstrate specific attributes of a product or service and to motivate a buy decision.
- Image commercials are designed to sell, or put forth, an idea about a product or a company rather than a specific product.
- Public service announcements are designed to convince the audience about something that is in *its* best interest rather than the self-interest of an advertiser.

Depending on how wide a geographical area the commercial airs in, it may be regarded as a national, regional, or local spot. Nationally televised commercials tend to have high production values because they are designed and produced by ad agencies for major clients and are shot by talented, skillful directors. Regional spots have lower production budgets and local spots lower still. Even though budgets can be as high as $1,000,000 for a nationally televised spot, and as low as $500 for a local commercial, writers, producers, and directors of all commercials follow the same basic step-by-step process.

The commercial has five component parts: (1) It is important to determine and examine the target audience for the commercial and to use its profile in the development of the commercial message. (2) The central message of the commercial is the idea that must be left with the audience after it views it. (3) The concept is the basic creative approach that carries the message. (4) The theme is the story or format, such as a stand-up presenter or a slice-of-life-vignette. (5) The visual language is the set of techniques filmmakers use to interpret, or execute, the creative approach. These key elements are true of all commercials—selling and image commercials and public service announcements.

The television commercial is an art form and a film genre. It is a powerful form of communication that has had profound effects on some social and cultural movements during the past half century, including the women's movement, the use of seatbelts in cars, the antismoking campaign, and the environmental movement. Commercial creators must approach their work with the knowledge that they may have a great deal of influence on a mass audience, so they need to bring a sense of caution, fairness, and ethics to their jobs.

Advertisers, ad agencies, and production companies collaborate on the design and production of commercials, and each has specific roles and responsibilities. The advertiser, or client, is responsible for providing marketing plan details, such as the objective, the customer, the budget, and information about other promotional activities. During production, the client approves and pays for the commercial. The ad agency develops the creative concept and storyboards and scripts. The agency also conducts or acquires additional research about the customer to instruct its creative thinking and to guide the media buy. Then, the agency supervises the entire preproduction, production, and postproduction process. The production company interprets the creative concept and shoots the live-action portion of the commercial.

DISCUSSION QUESTIONS

1. The class should review a collection of videotaped commercials from the Clio competition, The One Show, or any of the other television commercial competitions or festivals. A wide selection of commercial directors' demo reels is also available. Select one commercial and deconstruct the spot based on what you see and hear, then answer these questions: Who is the apparent audience? What is the underlying message? What is the creative approach? What is the intended result of the commercial and is it successful?

2. Select a commercial and discuss the visual language used by the filmmaker. In what way did the use of close-ups, casting, music, editing, lighting, or other visual elements help to get the basic message across?

3. Compare a national spot with a local commercial. Is there a noticeable difference in production value?

4. Select a commercial and contact the advertising agency that designed and produced it. Find out what other media the agency used for this client, and then find their print ads, Internet ads, or evidence of the rest of the campaign. Compare the creative approaches used in the television, radio, and print venues. How are they the same?

RECOMMENDED READINGS AND WEB SITES

Atchity, Kenneth, and Chi-L. Wong. *Writing Treatments That Sell.* New York: Owl Books. 1997.

Baldwin, Huntley. *How to Create Effective TV Commercials.* Lincolnwood, IL: NTC Business Books, 1988.

Burton, Phillip Ward. *Advertising Fundamentals,* 3d ed. Columbus, OH: Grid Publishing, 1988.

Jamieson, Kathleen Hall. *Everything You Think You Know About Politics and Why You're Wrong.* New York: Basic Books, 2000.

Jones, John Phillip. "The Unique Selling Proposition and Usage-Pull." In John Phillip Jones, ed., *The Advertising Business: Operations Creativity Media Planning Integrated Communications.* Thousand Oaks, CA: Sage Publications, 1999.

Kanner, Bernice. *The 100 Best TV Commercials: And Why They Worked.* New York: Random House, 1999.

Messaris, Paul. *Visual Persuasion: The Role of Images in Advertising.* Thousand Oaks, CA: Sage Publications, 1997.

Twitchell, James B. *Adcult USA.* New York: Columbia University Press, 1995.

Walker, James, and Douglas Ferguson. *The Broadcast Television Industry.* Needham Heights, MA: Allyn and Bacon, 1998.

White, Hooper. *How to Produce Effective TV Commercials.* Lincolnwood, IL: NTC Business Books, 1994.

PBS—http://www.pbs.org/30secondcandidate/timeline/years/1964b.html

You can view the "Daisy" commercial in Quicktime or Real Video on this site, as well as other political commercials shown during the '64 and other elections.

NOTES

1. From telephone interviews by the author with Joseph Napolitan and Tony Schwartz, April 15, 2003.

2. Schwartz, Tony. *The Responsive Chord,* Garden City, New York: Anchor Press/Doubleday. 1973. p. 93.

3. McGill, Douglas C. Ex-rep. William Miller, 69, dies; Goldwater's 1964 running mate. *The New York Times.* Saturday, June 25, 1983. Sec 1; page 14.

4. Some commercials created for television are also shown theatrically.

5. Burton, p. 11.

6. Positive image ads are called *advocacy ads* in political science circles.

7. Jamieson, p. 105.

8. This took place during 2002, an election year in New York State.

9. AdAge.com (August 12, 2002); http://www.adage.com/page.cms?pageId=919.

10. Douglass, John S., and Glenn P. Harnden. *The Art of Technique: An Aesthetic Approach to Film and Video Production,* p. 5. Boston: Allyn & Bacon, 1996.

11. Although this book is not about the media buy, it is important for commercial creators to know details about the media plan because it often guides their creative thinking.

12. Jones, p. 250.

13. White, p. 14.

14. Messaris, p. 34.

15. Atchity, p. 61.

16. However, commercials may be only aired in specific markets. Commercials purchased for the U.S. audience are only aired on the U.S. "feed." A "clean" feed is provided to other markets, and through arrangements with the program's owner (the NFL), various commercials are sold and aired in different markets.

17. Messaris, p. v.

18. Many books cover the social and cultural contributions of advertising; however, we recommend the one by Twitchell.

19. Kanner, p. 222.

20. Baldwin, p. 15.

21. Messaris, p. 59.

22. O'Hara, Jim. "Jury Whacks TV Ad Lawyer: Jim The Hammer Shapiro Hit with $1.5 Million Malpractice, False-Advertising Judgment." *The Syracuse Post Standard,* 2002, June 13, p. D1.

23. *FTC v. Colgate-Palmolive Co.,* 380 U.S. 374, 85 S.Ct. 1035 (1965).

24. There are many production companies that have a cadre of directors, each with a specialty such as tabletop, dialogue, action, comedy, children, or fashion.

25. An option growing in preference for many advertisers is the "à la carte" approach—hire a number of agencies. One agency may specialize in media, another in creative.

26. Some commercials are produced on a cost-plus-fixed-fee basis, but this is not common now. It is sometimes used when the cost of certain production elements cannot be estimated accurately at the time of the bid.

CHAPTER TWO

THE TELEVISION COMMERCIAL INDUSTRY

During a panel discussion at the 1998 Electronic Entertainment Expo (E3) in Los Angeles, seven experts from various companies discussed their plans for developing, promoting, and eventually dominating the future of television. Spokespersons from Microsoft, Sony, Sega, a couple of regional Bells, and a set-top box (STB) manufacturer used PowerPoint presentations and screen mock-ups to show the attentive and excited audience what interactive television would be like, and how their technologies would work. The future, they declared, would be two-way, interactive programming.

Consumers would be able to choose everything from camera angles during sporting events to how dramas end, to playing along during game shows. There would be multiplayer games, even gambling. Every one of them talked about interactive advertising that would engage the viewer in not only deciding to buy a product but provide him with the means to do it, right then and there, in what one presenter called *t-commerce*. There was a giddiness among the panelists and throughout the audience that was palpable.

Sitting at the end of the dais, patiently waiting his turn, was a representative from a company nobody had heard of yet. His hair was a little disheveled, and he looked a little like a mad inventor, which, it turned out, he was. He did not have a laptop sprung open in front of him like the others; instead he held onto a smallish appliance that looked like a VCR. Time had practically run out when the moderator suddenly realized he had one more presenter, and called on the guy.

This last panelist explained that he had wanted to demonstrate the device, which he said would indeed be the future of television, but it still had a couple of glitches. It would not make any programming interactive and two-way, but what it would do was allow consumers to time-shift their television watching. They would be able to store their favorite programming and watch it whenever they wanted to. Everybody groaned. The fellow got a little defensive: "I believe in supply and demand, and people don't want interactive commercials, they want a way to skip right past them," were roughly his words. *Nobody* wanted to hear that, and when the panel ended to polite applause, nearly everyone rushed up to talk to the woman from Playstation and the man from WebTV. The inventor from TiVo packed up his device and walked out of the room.

In the years that followed, only TiVo came through with its promise. Currently about 280,000 people use TiVo and a million others use competing devices, to skip past more than 71 percent of all commercials.[1] Although the number of TiVo and other personal video recorder (PVR) users is small, the market is growing by 12.5 percent a year; the cost, now five times more expensive than a VCR, is coming down, and many cable companies are considering putting PVR technology in their STBs.

Most television executives consider devices like TiVo to be a serious threat to television advertising. A report published by the Federal Communications Commission (FCC) cautioned that if cable and satellite operators continue plans to integrate PVR technology into their STBs, within five to ten years there might not be any commercials on television.[2] One television executive said consumers may be asked to pay for programming if the networks lose advertisers. He warned that PVRs could present a real threat to the television industry, translating into a future cost to American consumers of approximately $250 annually per household through cable subscriber fee increases or conversion to "pay-for" services of advertiser-supported basic cable networks.

This, of course, would cause the current advertiser-supported television business model to completely unravel and force all of us to reconsider where the television commercial fits; and, how it should be designed, produced, and distributed. Until that happens, this chapter gives you a picture of the current state of affairs in the commercial industry, which, despite many other problems, is actually a bit more rosy.

The television commercial makes it possible for entertainment, news, and sports events to reach a hundred million American homes at no direct cost to the consumer.[3] All of this is the result of a synergetic relationship between advertisers, ad agencies, broadcast media, content providers, and consumers. This chapter describes how this relationship works and discusses the many ancillary businesses that have sprung up to serve the business model. Included here are some history about television advertising and descriptions of a few of the notable pioneers and their work, current and future trends in the industry, and the rules and regulations that government and industry organizations have instituted to protect the public from false and misleading advertising.

You should get a sense of the basic workings of the television advertising industry, and who the principal players are and how their business relationship is formed and thrives. You will get a picture of how the industry got where it is and where it might be headed. This is especially important for those students who will enter the field soon—you are the next generation of writers, producers, and directors who will pioneer the next wave of award-winning creative concepts. You will understand that there are legal and ethical parameters within which you must work when you design and produce commercials. These fundamentals will provide you with the context for the design and production materials covered in subsequent chapters.

In this chapter, you will learn the following:

- What a business model is
- How the broadcasting business model is fueled by advertising
- Advertiser-supported broadcasting began with radio and was easily adapted to television
- Some technological developments, such as videotape recording, helped move advertising sponsorship of programming to spot advertising

- There are national, regional, and local spot advertising
- What ratings and shares are, and how they are used
- The industry is premised on media research
- Government, the media, and trade and consumer groups have laws, restrictions, and guidelines advertisers adhere to in order to keep television advertising both truthful and tasteful

THE BUSINESS MODEL

A *business model* is the structure of relationships between companies that result in the exchange of products or services for money, to the benefit of all parties. Broadcasting, and to a much lesser extent cable and satellite television, relies on a business model in which advertising is the key component—advertising expenditures provide the finances to create and broadcast all other forms of programming at no direct cost to the consumer. When advertising works as intended, the consumer rewards the advertiser by buying its products or services. This represents the advertiser's return on investment in its advertising.

Advertiser-supported broadcasting is so successful that the new media industry has attempted to adopt the model. From approximately 1997 through 2000, hundreds if not thousands of dot-com Web startups raised billions of dollars in investment capital from venture capitalists and Wall Street investment banks. The founders of these companies convinced investors that the business model, which produced revenue for broadcast media during the twentieth century, would pay off for Internet companies during the twenty-first century. Their pitch: Compelling content placed on the Web will attract Internet users in large numbers, and advertisers will pay to place ads—new forms of interactive, multimedia ads—on the most visited sites. In their business plans, dot-com entrepreneurs projected enormous, rapid growth in the popularity of their sites and a stampede of advertisers waving money. Mesmerized investors took the bait.

Only a small handful of dot-com startups survived what Federal Reserve Board Chairman Alan Greenspan called the "irrational exuberance" that defined the investment orgy. Nearly all of the dot-coms collapsed when their sites failed to attract an audience, and advertisers either failed to show, pulled out, or placed ads so sparingly that the dot-com revenue stream resembled a tiny trickle. Not surprisingly, few of the most viable survivors depended on advertising as the crux of their revenue. Amazon.com and eBay.com, for example, base their income on e-commerce conducted directly on their sites. Other survivors are those that integrated their e-commerce with traditional brick-and-mortar businesses—for example, Barnes & Noble and Land's End.

In hindsight, everybody should have known better. If all of the advertising revenue projected in all of the dot-com business plans had been added together, the total would have easily eclipsed the total amount spent for media placement for all forms of advertising—approximately $247 billion in 2001.[4] *But their instincts were correct.*

The entrepreneurs and their investors had looked at broadcast media and had observed a business model that would seem to have a direct application for the Web. The broadcast model was the one studied most closely because, like the Web audience, the television audience expects to get its programming for free and is happy to watch, or at least tolerate, commercials to get it. Furthermore, to Web entrepreneurs, 1997 probably looked like 1947 did to broadcasters. Fifty years earlier television pioneers also had to build up their businesses, buy new equipment, hire new talent, and lure viewers and advertisers, and they have been phenomenally successful. Web pioneers found themselves in exactly the same position and, quite naturally, thought history would repeat itself. Unfortunately, there are venue, purpose, design, and other differences between television viewing and computer usage that perhaps make it impossible to replicate exactly the television commercial industry business model in the Web universe. One thing that doomed the dot-coms was competition; dot-com startups entered an industry in which the audience was already severely fragmented. Early broadcasters had few competitors, while dot-coms had literally hundreds of thousands.

What makes the business model work in broadcasting is the synergistic relationship that evolved between the advertiser, the ad agency (and a number of related firms), the broadcast media, the content providers, and the consumer. In this model, television networks and individual stations provide programming content (for example, news, sports, weather, entertainment) at no cost to the mass audience who select programs to watch. A critical mass of viewers forms around certain programs, at certain times of the day; broadcasters keep these programs and cull out shows that do not attract a significant audience. Highly regarded shows are not only renewed season after season, but the stars are generously rewarded. The entire cast of *Friends* each received $1,000,000 per episode for each of the 24 current season episodes and will get a 1 percent participation in all future profits from show reruns, which could net each of them many millions of dollars more.

Advertisers, through their ad agencies, pay for commercial time during the programs that have attracted the size and type of audience they want to reach with their message. Ad agencies create the commercials, usually by hiring outside production companies, and buy the media at a discount from broadcasters. Broadcasters use this advertising revenue to produce or buy the rights to the programming that attracts the biggest or most desirable audience. Production companies, Hollywood studios, professional and college sports leagues, and other content providers produce programs for, or license programs to, the broadcasters; and they continuously track audience tastes to create the forms of programming that will attract and hold on to the audience.

In this way, most broadcast television programming is paid for with revenue from advertising (approximately $45 billion in 2001). Were it not for advertising, the cost of television programming would be borne by consumers in some other fashion, such as pay-TV or subscriptions. Many more billions would be spent by advertisers, through their agencies or directly with local television stations, to produce commercials. Accurate estimates for how much is spent on commercial production are not available, but it is well known that thousands of individuals (producers, directors, artists, craftspersons) and hundreds of companies (production, postproduction, animation, sound studios, etc.) are entirely supported by their commercial production work. The cable and satellite industry gets most of its revenue from *subscriptions*—monthly payments made directly to cable operators by consumers—rather than commercial advertising by about a 4 to 1 margin; nevertheless, advertising helps keep a lid on the rising cost of cable services. Revenue from subscriptions and pay-per-view, and from advertising, is called dual revenue streaming.

A LITTLE HISTORY ABOUT BROADCASTING

By the time commercial broadcasting got into full swing in 1948, the idea that the broadcast would be free to the consumer but paid for by commercial sponsors or advertisers was a foregone conclusion. This business model had already been established by the success of advertiser-supported broadcast radio.

Radio Sets the Stage

In the early 1920s, there really wasn't such a thing as broadcast advertising as we know it today. Radio manufacturers like Westinghouse reasoned that they could encourage the sale of radio receivers by providing free programming, so they built experimental broadcasting stations. But this business plan was doomed. Revenue from the sale of radio equipment could not support the creation of content (music, sports, drama, news) and sustain the operations of the stations. At an experimental station in Pittsburgh, literally located in the garage of Westinghouse engineer Frank Conrad, a barter arrangement between his station and a local music shop provided Conrad with phonograph records to play over the air. This solved his content problem. The shop took out ads in the local newspaper telling people to listen to the station and then come to the shop for the sheet music or recordings. Many historians believe that as Westinghouse watched money exchange hands between the shop owner and the newspaper, somebody there conceived of commercially supported radio.

The first radio broadcast sponsored by another party was a ten-minute description of new apartments in Jackson Heights, New York, in 1922 on WEAF, a radio station then owned by AT&T. The persuasive message paid for by the apartment developers cost 50 dollars.[5] Slowly, the idea that businesses unaffiliated with the radio manufacturer would pay a "toll" to broadcast a message to an audience caught on. Within twelve years, there were four radio networks: NBC Red, NBC Blue, CBS, and the Mutual Broadcasting System, all supported by advertising revenue.

The networks were associations of stations located in different cities, some of which were owned by the network and others that were independent and locally owned but *affiliated,* which means stations accepted programs that originated at the network. All supported their operations by having programming provided by the networks sponsored by advertisers or by selling short spot commercials during breaks between programs. In addition to providing programming, the networks had a compensation formula to pay affiliates for carrying advertiser-sponsored programs.

In fact, it was the desire of major advertisers to reach a national audience that played a primary role in the development of broadcast networks. It was economical for advertisers to finance the creation of a single radio show, and then have it aired by many stations that covered the nation, or at least heavily populated urban areas. This became a pattern for media buys for years to come, both in radio and later television because advertisers could reach a national audience with a single purchase of commercial time.

During this time, a close relationship between advertisers and shows' creators developed; at times, the two were indistinguishable. An advertiser whose name was intermingled with the show's name exercised a great deal of control over content. The show became, essentially, one long commercial during which the audience was constantly reminded who the sponsor was. In a memorable scene in the film *The Christmas Story,* based on a story by Jean Sheppard, a young character played by Peter Billingsley is a fan of the radio drama *Little Orphan Annie.* He sends away for the secret decoder ring advertised during the show, and one day it arrives in the mail. In a fit of excitement, and despite the nagging calls from his mother to get out of the bathroom, he hunkers down with the daily list of numbers to decode the secret instructions from Orphan Annie. The final message: "Don't Forget Your Ovaltine."

The public loved radio. Starved for news and entertainment, first during the Depression and later during World War II, people turned to the radio. By far, radio was the most popular pastime, featuring drama, comedy, sports, music, variety, and news. Franklin Roosevelt made regular radio addresses and popularized the "fireside chat" during which he soothed the angst of millions of listeners. It was the first true mass medium and because of advertising, it was free to the public. From 1934 to 1945, the growth of radio and radio advertising was stunning—90 percent of American households had radio receivers by 1945, and advertising revenue reached $310 million.[6] The addition of more stations, as well as a new band (frequency modulation, or FM), further increased radio's reach, popularity, and eventually advertising revenue.

Television Arrives

The first public television demonstration in the United States occurred at the New York World's Fair in 1939 when RCA televised the opening ceremonies to about 200 sets, most of them located within the city. Experiments with television technology—mainly by companies already involved with radio—had been going on throughout the 1930s. England's BBC was on the air with television in 1936. The combination of those successful technical experiments and radio's profitable advertiser-supported business model had convinced RCA, Westinghouse, CBS, GE, and others that television was viable. Although these companies invested heavily in the new medium, sales of television sets to consumers remained sluggish. The start of World War II in 1941 delayed a major, national rollout, but there were other problems too. Competing companies could not agree on certain technical standards, for example; and the FCC was slow to make rules regarding spectrum allocation. Nevertheless, the first television commercial ran in July 1941 on NBC's newly licensed New York station; it was for Bulova watches and cost the advertiser $4.[7]

After the war, the FCC lifted its ban on television station construction, adopted technical standards that had been developed before the war, and made some adjustments to the spectrum allocation, all of which encouraged immediate and rapid growth in broadcast television. By 1948, 108 television stations had been approved for construction and 29 were in operation, owned and operated primarily by the major radio networks—NBC, ABC, and CBS—and by the DuMont Network, which had been started specifically to broadcast television. The first stations were clustered in major cities and attracted large audiences and eager advertisers.

The growth of television's popularity caused the FCC to issue a freeze on the licensing of new stations from 1948 to 1952 while it considered certain other technical issues, which related mainly to color standards, channel and frequency assignments, spectrum space, and the like. This delay caused the eventual demise of the DuMont Network and prevented the others from becoming truly national. It also prevented advertisers from reaching a national audience because only about 34 percent of all homes had televisions or could receive television signals during the freeze. During the next ten years, however, the growth of television was phenomenal. By 1963, television had penetrated 90 percent of U.S. households; the number of stations and the amount of advertising revenue quadrupled during the same period. Today, nearly 98 percent of American households have at least one television.

The three major television networks—ABC, NBC, CBS, each with as many as 200 individual station affiliates scattered all over the country—dominated the broadcasting industry for three decades. Advertisers could reach a mass audience by placing their commercials during network news programs when nearly 30 percent of all households tuned in. In the early 1980s, however, cable television gradually emerged, and by the mid-1980s, about three million households had satellite dishes. New networks emerged, including Fox, UPN, WB, and PaxTV, which has caused audience fragmentation, which we discuss later in this chapter.

THE BIRTH OF THE TELEVISION COMMERCIAL

The look of commercial television during the early days was very similar to the sound of commercial radio in the thirties and forties, with variety shows, soap operas, sporting events, and news. Many early television stars were "recycled" from radio and vaudeville—Jack Benny, George Burns and Gracie Allen, and Fred Allen (*Fibber McGee*) all made the transition. As with radio, advertisers sponsored entire shows. Because most television was broadcast live, most of the early commercials were as well. The host of a variety show, such as Milton Berle or Ed Sullivan, would simply walk to a portion of the television studio where he would pitch the product, sometimes with some assistance, and then go on with the rest of the show. It was impossible to tell when the show stopped and the commercial started because they were intertwined. In fact, much of the early television programming was actually supervised by advertising agencies.[8]

The Decline of Sponsorship

Program sponsorship started to decline in the mid-1950s after Ampex developed videotape recording and Hollywood studios began creating films specifically for television. Videotape recording made it possible to produce television programs more carefully and with greater production values than was possible in a live studio. Multiple locations and scene transitions were possible. Taped productions, many of them dramas that competed favorably with Hollywood films, became disengaged from advertising because it was possible to produce commercials ahead of time and quite separate from the television programs.

Nearly all television stations could run film through their systems, so national advertisers started to produce and distribute their commercials on film. They too started to have a look of their own, with better production values; dissolves, wipes, animation, and special effects could be incorporated. Products could be demonstrated where they were used—out on a highway, for example. Tape and film also gave the television commercial some distribution versatility. No longer bound in time and space to a live television show, it could be physically sent to local stations to air anytime.

Even before the advent of tape, some programming and commercials transitioned from live to film production. *I Love Lucy,* for example, was produced on film and was the originator of reruns. The show set the example for post-network syndicated distribution because the original product, with its original quality, became available for use in perpetuity. *Lucy* reruns are still shown and enjoyed forty years after their original production. Interestingly, there is an anecdote: The writers of *I Love Lucy* were not allowed to use the word "lucky" in any of their scripts because the show was sponsored by Philip Morris, whose competitor was Lucky Strike.[9]

Shooting commercials on film and tape gave advertisers and their agencies more control over production and distribution. They were able to develop a specific look and message, hire specific spokespersons, produce at the quality level they wanted, and buy media in all the markets that their research said they should. Filming allowed the techniques (see visual language section in chapter 1), which had been developed over the past century, to be integrated and used in the commercial to make the message as intriguing and effective as the best Hollywood movie. To this day, motion picture techniques continue to be developed and used in commercial production.

Class Exercise

Ad agency creatives often adopt the "look" of recent Hollywood films in their commercials. Star fields, for example, were prevalent backgrounds after *Star Wars* was released. View a reel of recent award-winning national or international commercials and observe the visual techniques that appear to be borrowed directly from Hollywood films. Watch especially for special effects produced by a computer, lighting, and fashions.

In an effort to improve program offerings and gain a competitive edge against rival networks, television networks turned to the Hollywood studios to produce programming, and the studios willingly obliged. Hollywood studios had been hurt by the popularity of television as people opted for a night at home rather than a night at the movies. The ABC network reached agreements with the Walt Disney Company and Warner Brothers, so *The Mickey Mouse Club* and dramatic Westerns were born. The television network, not the advertising agencies, licensed the programming from the studios, and a final separation between the entertainment and the commercial messages occurred. Advertisers naturally became more interested in a particular show because of the size of the audience it attracted—its rating and share—and who made up the audience—its demographic—rather than in sponsorship.[10]

Advertisers' shift in emphasis—from direct name association with programming through sponsorship to spot advertising on popular shows—placed the responsibility for branding products and establishing consumer loyalty and confidence on the television commercial alone. The advertiser now had 30 or 60 seconds to get the attention of the audience, not an entire 30 or 60 minutes. The creators of commercials were now challenged to design and produce television commercials that would get a persuasive message across in a short period of time, often in competition with other commercials for similar products. This marked the birth of the truly creative television commercial, and a golden era in design and production excellence that continues today.

The Emergence of Spot Commercials

As television commercials became free-floating 30-second or 60-second entities that could be aired at any time, on any station, they came to be known as *spots*. This, in turn, gave rise to the term *spot market,* which refers to the type of media buy an ad agency makes on behalf of the client. The buys fall into three categories:

- Network spot
- National spot
- Local spot

Network spots are aired on a television network and are shown on every affiliate station of that network on the same show, in the same timeslot. A *national spot* is shown in a more selective way—possibly on a subset of network affiliates or on an assortment of stations in order to reach a more specific demographic or geographic audience; for example, restaurant chains, retailers, and certain food products that can be found more or less throughout the country, but may be concentrated in urban areas. A national spot buy is more appropriate than a network spot buy for such a client. The *local spot* buy is even more selective; the agency buys time on individual stations, perhaps only one in the city where the advertiser does business. A local advertiser can buy time on one or more stations, or cable channels, to reach individual areas within a market. Local advertisers produce commercials using a local advertising agency; sometimes they have the broadcast or cable outlet produce commercials for them.

The Importance of Media Data

When television commercials were finally severed from programming, not only did they have to be well designed and executed, but their placement during appropriate shows became critical. No longer in control of television programming and now unable to "weld" product messages to show content, advertisers instead bought time on whatever shows attracted the right audience. The need to determine who was watching what and when gave rise to audience measurement, or *rating* services, currently monopolized by Nielsen Media Research.

Initially, the rating services audited the television audience by taking a sample of 1,200 households, which statistically represented the entire U.S. audience. The reports that were generated were sold to advertising agencies, which used the data to select the programs that would deliver the largest audience at the lowest cost. Television networks used the same data to determine which programs to continue airing, which ones to cancel, and how to organize their shows as a group—the slate or lineup—to reach the largest audience throughout the day, and hence attract advertisers.

Ratings and Shares

Nielsen measures and reports both local and network programming in 210 markets and produces a pair of numbers—a *rating* and a *share*—for each show. A show's *rating* is a number that represents the total estimated number of viewing households expressed as a percentage of the total number of available households. The term *available households* really means how many households have televisions at all, whether they are being used or not. Because there are approximately 105,000,000 U.S. households with televisions, a program that gets a rating of 1.3 probably had close to 1.3 million households tuned in.

A share is different; *share* refers to the estimated number of households tuned in to a program expressed as a percentage of households with televisions turned on at that particular time. The number of households using television (HUT) is the basis for determining share, and the HUT varies by day part; during daytime hours, an average of 25 percent of households watch television and the number climbs to more than 60 percent during primetime.[11] A show's rating is useful to the advertiser because it can determine the size of the audience that has the opportunity to see its commercial. A show's share is important to the programmer because that information tells it how well its program is doing against the competition.

Because of the high cost of collecting data continuously, Nielsen measures all markets during four-week-long periods, four times a year—*sweeps weeks*—and measures large markets more often. During sweeps weeks, television networks and individual stations make extra efforts to attract large audiences through promotions and special programs. Ratings and shares figures determined during sweeps periods help broadcasters set the prices for various timeslots.

Today, Nielsen uses a larger sample—5,000 households—and sophisticated interactive devices to gather viewer data, and that data drives almost every decision made by television stations, networks, cable channels, and advertising agencies. Some say that Nielsen's audience data sets the rates charged for ad placement on every show during every timeslot in every locality in the country. The entire business and financial relationship between advertisers and the television industry is based on a mutual confidence in the audience data gathered, processed, and reported by Nielsen. Even though this method has been questioned over the years, and there have been attempts to improve it, to date no one has come up with a better or more workable method.

The Importance of Consumer Research

As data was collected and compared, certain viewing patterns within the television audience began to emerge; certain kinds of people could be counted on to watch certain kinds of programs. Ratings for programs would rise and fall with subtle changes in cast, music, locales, plots, and stories. It occurred to behavioral scientists, and advertisers, that there was much more to the data than simply aggregate numbers of viewers. There was deeper and more interesting information about the identity of the viewers, and their psychological, emotional, intellectual, and physical needs. As researchers began looking more carefully at the psychographics of each segment of the television audience, a new field of study dawned. What sounds, images, activities, and suggestions resonate with audiences, and why?

It became quite clear very early on that this information could be used by advertisers to design and produce commercials in such a way that they would reach the intended audience on every possible level—emotionally, intellectually, and intuitively. Consumer research is now a thriving, integral part of the commercial design process; results are used by agency creatives to guide their earliest ideas on how to reach the target audience. It is not unusual for a creative idea expressed during a brainstorming session to be referred to the research people with the query, "What does your research say about that?"

Although media research is a critically important component of an advertising campaign strategy, and audience research can assist in identifying the consumers and the message and concept that will reach them, the talent, skills, and instincts of advertising professionals play an equally, perhaps even more, important role. Newcomers and beginners in the field should not be afraid to defend a concept that comes from deep within, or be cowed into silencing inner voices that tell them their ideas are good. Many commercials tested poorly and were nearly scrapped, but the creative people behind the concepts pushed hard to keep them, and they were very successful.

RULES, REGULATIONS, AND STRONG SUGGESTIONS

As a result of the emergence of spot television, and the proliferation of commercials on the national and local level, along came government rules, industry regulations, and public policy determined to put some control on commercial messages. Television commercial producers and creatives must be aware of the many laws, regulations, and other restrictions to keep commercial messages truthful and tasteful imposed on them by the government, the media, and industry groups. Some creative concepts may be brilliant in an aesthetic way, effective as a persuasive message, but illegal or unintentionally misleading. There is a long history of both government and self-regulation of advertising, and the gradual buildup of policing and controls is reaching an even higher level. Many people in the business today cannot believe what their counterparts in the 1950s, 1960s and 1970s got away with.

The government began regulating broadcasting with the passage of the Radio Act of 1912, a minimal set of rules that were not even enforced by the Department of Commerce. At that time, radio was primarily used for communications between ships at sea, and between amateur experimenters. As radio ownership grew and it started to develop into a mass medium in the early 1920s, interference and other technical problems were aggravated.

With the Federal Radio Act of 1927, which established the Federal Radio Commission, Congress tried again. But technology outpaced the government's attempt to establish order, and things only got worse. Finally, Congress established the Federal Communications Commission with the Communications Act of 1934. A permanent body with teeth, the FCC was established to represent the *public's* interest in broadcasting, premised on the notion that the airwaves belong to the people and broadcasters must serve the public's "interest, convenience, and necessity."

The FCC and Television Advertising

The Federal Communications Commission basically maintains order among broadcasters by licensing radio and television stations, assigning frequencies and call letters, and requiring regular reporting from the licensed stations to be certain they are in fact serving the public. The FCC also reviews and approves (or not) major acquisitions and mergers between media companies. During 2002, for example, the FCC declined to approve the merger of Echostar and DirecTV, the world's two largest satellite television companies.

While the FCC is officially an independent government commission, its members are appointed by the President with Senate approval. The commission is made up of five members—three must be from one political party (normally the party of the President) and two from the minority party. In addition to confirmation authority by the Senate, both the Senate and House of Representatives exercise other influences on the FCC through budget appropriations; during the 1990s, Congress appropriated $200 to $250 million per year for the FCC. Individual broadcasters, trade groups, lobbyists, and consumer groups also have some influence over the commission and its actions.

The FCC is specifically forbidden to control content, or programming, including advertising; however, because the FCC evaluates licensees based on their programming, it does in fact exercise a certain degree of oversight. It could deny a license renewal to a station that does not provide equal access to political candidates, including political advertising, for example. The FCC also enforces certain Communications Act sections that affect broadcasters, advertisers, or both; for example, ensuring that all sponsors of programs and commercial announcements are identified.

The FCC investigates fraudulent billing, deceptive promotions, rigged or illegal contests, and lotteries. In its most contentious role, the FCC is charged with enforcing that part of the U.S. Criminal Code specifically forbidding "obscenity, profanity, or vulgarity"; this is what most often winds up in court, with fights over First Amendment rights.

The only form of advertising that the FCC has direct jurisdiction over is the amount of advertising shown during children's television programs. The amount is currently limited to 10.5 minutes per hour on weekdays and 12 minutes on weekends.

The Federal Trade Commission

The Federal Trade Commission (FTC) was originally established by Congress in 1914 to protect businesses from each other, but in 1938 the agency's mandate was extended to protect the *consumer* from unfair business practices. In addition to protecting the public from various forms of business fraud and dangerous products, the FTC protects the public from being victimized by false or misleading advertising. The FTC does this by enforcing a number of requirements on advertisers before their commercials are aired, and by fielding complaints from consumers if something arises afterwards.

For the FTC to take action, there is no requirement that an advertisement contain false or misleading messages, only that the possibility exists for the consumer to misunderstand the message. When advertising deception is alleged, the FTC has a choice of three progressively more serious responses. The first course of action is the *stipulation*—an informal but strong suggestion to the advertiser to voluntarily stop its objectionable advertising. This may be followed by *consent order*—stronger but still carrying no penalties. If these fail, the FTC must issue a *cease and desist order,* which involves proving in court that the advertiser is guilty of fraudulent or misleading practices.

To stop false or misleading advertising before it can occur, the FTC issues rules and orders that all advertisers are required to abide by; for example, there are regulations about substantiating claims made in product demonstrations and regulations about how user testimonials must be given. Celebrity talent must actually use the product they pitch; that is, their endorsement of a product must be true. Responsibility for adherence to FTC regulations that require substantiations and affidavits falls on the advertising agency.

The FTC also issues guidelines to inform advertisers in various industries or trades what practices are acceptable, advises those who submit inquiries about their advertising intentions, and reviews (and approves or disallows) advertising copy and design materials submitted for preapproval.

There are other federal regulations that affect what can be or must be revealed during a television commercial, including rules enforced by the Food and Drug Administration, The Federal Reserve Board, and the U.S. Postal Service. Every state has consumer protection laws, which, in some cases, are tougher than federal regulations, about the advertising of alcohol, cigarettes, lotteries, coupons, contraceptive devices, financial services, real estate, and/or insurance. National advertisers must be aware of the laws in each state where the commercial will air and factor those regulations into the creative formula. Other books covering these and other restrictions on advertising that we recommend can be found in the bibliography. It is important to be aware that lots of regulations exist, and that they very well could directly impact the design and production of your television commercial.

Trade Groups

The National Association of Broadcasters (NAB, the main industry trade association); television networks; local stations; and, to a lesser extent, cable channels have attempted to self-regulate. Some have developed guidelines about which commercials are acceptable for broadcast, how many minutes per hour can be devoted to commercials, and other rules. Although the codes developed by the NAB are no longer enforced, most aspects of the codes are still adhered to by member and nonmember stations, including restricting the number of commercial minutes per hour and using common sense and good taste regarding the acceptability of commercial messages.

Network Restrictions

Television networks enforce a number of restrictions on the content of commercials and require ad agencies to submit substantiations and affidavits that attest to the authenticity of demonstrations, testimonials, and other claims made in commercials. Agency producers and business affairs staff members are well acquainted with all of the rules, regulations, and strong suggestions concerning television commercial content, and they work hard to keep commercials within bounds. Chapter 6 covers the specific concept of network clearance and continuity.

LOOKING TO THE FUTURE

The future of television advertising will parallel the changes that take place over the next decade in media in general, and in television in particular as a result of the following current and future trends:

- Consolidation of companies on both the sell-side (media) and the buy-side (agencies and clients)
- New technologies now available, including digital television
- Fragmentation of the audience
- Globalization of the economy

Large-scale changes are taking place rapidly and will affect television advertising very quickly. The following sections discuss some of the developments and their possible effects on the future of the television commercial.

Consolidation and Vertical Integration

There has been consolidation (mergers and acquisitions) on both the sell-side and buy-side of the media industry. The *sell-side* is the media—television and radio networks and stations, cable providers and channels, film studios, the Internet, and print media. The *buy-side* is the agencies and their clients. Due largely to a relaxation of FCC rules related to media ownership, a small number of very large companies dominates the media (for example, GE, Disney, Viacom, AOL Time Warner). These companies and others own television networks, many independent television and radio stations, cable providers and channels, and production companies and film studios. Company mergers, purchases, restructurings, and adjustments in the law or FCC policy lead to constant changes in this area.

Media companies are also vertically integrated, which means that they own the intellectual property (Mickey Mouse, for example), the means of production (Disney Studios), and the means of distribution (ABC television network, and cable providers and channels). This consolidation of ownership and the integration of the business chain has occurred even while the audience has been fragmented and spread out over the television (and new media) landscape.

An equally small number of holding companies—WPP Group, Interpublic Group of Companies, Publicis, Omnicom Group—own a lion's share of the world's advertising agencies, and thus control the major accounts. These major consolidated ad agencies have been able to offer clients more services at lower costs by combining the research, media, and creative resources of several agencies into one. Some have combined media research and buying divisions from several owned agencies and spun them off into separate entities; for example, WPP Group combined the media departments from Ogilvy & Mather and J. Walter Thompson to form Mindshare. Although certain functions of the advertising agency can be consolidated in the conglomerate, many of these functions are considered backroom functions such as accounting and finance. Frontline services directly responsible for individual client services are kept entirely separate because one of the goals of consolidation is to allow competition among clients within the same corporate framework while ensuring that the accounts have separation and integrity. A client's business and trade information must be kept confidential from competitors. The separate agency structure within the corporate conglomerate is designed to do just that.

Theoretically, consolidation and vertical integration, on both the sell- and buy-side of the media market, should benefit both sides. Consolidated media should be able to offer package deals to advertisers. Consolidated advertising agencies should be able to offer more and better marketing, media, and creative services to clients and use their buying clout to obtain better media deals. Evidence is not available yet on whether these structural changes will benefit one side or the other, or both. One media buying agreement between Procter & Gamble and Viacom Plus may signal a wave of the future. In this deal, P&G agreed to advertise on twelve Viacom properties, including CBS, MTV, UPN, Nickelodeon, and others, presumably realizing a cost savings. A decade ago, P&G would have had to deal with each television network and cable channel individually, negotiating media costs and placement schedules.

Consolidation is likely to continue for some time. At this writing, the courts have asked the FCC to further explore a relaxation of rules that currently prevent any one company from owning stations that reach more than 35 perc7ent of the television audience. Ad agencies continue to consolidate, merge, and acquire each other, and major accounts move about from one agency to another, often winding up with the same major holding company. Young people entering the field during the next decade will work in an industry that is constantly reinventing itself and should be prepared for a "wild ride."

Technology

While some technology represents a threat to commercial television, other technology presents opportunity. Earlier in this chapter, we discussed the advent of PVR technology and the threat it poses to commercial advertising. Digital technology will soon change television and its advertising in many ways—some known and others that we can only guess about. Besides the marked improvements in image and sound quality, and in production processes, that digital technology has already brought to programs and commercials, this technology makes a kind of marriage between computer and television possible.

With digital technology, broadcasters will have flexibility in how they use their allotted spectrum. They could, if they choose, divide their spectrum into several signals and broadcast standard television—a digital picture the same size as the current NTSC television picture—on as many as four different channels. One possible use of this division of spectrum would be to broadcast a sporting event, for example, and allow the viewer to switch channels between different camera views. Or, the station could broadcast a single high-definition signal. Or, the station could broadcast four different shows. No one knows where the audience will gravitate—to HDTV or to standard television signals that offer viewing options. Advertisers will follow the audience, and one benefit of digital technology may be that it will be easier to know where the audience is because of interactivity.

From the point of view of the audience experience, the most intriguing possibility is interactivity. We already have interactive channel guides, video on-demand, and other new services. But if computerlike capabilities can be incorporated into television programming, including commercials, it will be possible for entirely new genres of entertainment to be created, and for the television commercial to become only the beginning of what could become a commercial *transaction*. It was the promise of the technology talked about in this chapter's opening anecdote, so far unrealized, but nevertheless very exciting to advertisers.

A benefit less obvious to the audience, but possibly even more exciting to advertisers, will be the ability for advertisers to learn much more about their audience. Broadcasting (and cable and satellite television) has always been one-way—the program is sent from the source (a broadcast tower or a cable head-end) to consumers but nothing comes back. Digital technology, and in particular interactivity, can open a *back channel*—a means for a message of some kind to be sent from the consumer to the source. In a marketer's dream-come-true, that message could contain information about individual consumers, their program preferences, their buying habits, and much more. This information could, in turn, be used by the advertiser to target customized commercial messages on an individual basis to consumers.

This view of the possibilities—all of which have already been attempted in various pilot projects—raises questions about privacy and other ethical issues, as well as production and talent issues. These questions and issues are beyond the scope of this book, but they need to be addressed as television and the advertising industry march on.

Two other phenomena, which pose interesting challenges for future television commercial designers and producers, are occurring simultaneously. The first is the growth of media options for consumers causing audience fragmentation. The other is the growth of the global economy—the opening of markets outside the United States for television advertising produced here and the opening of the U.S. marketplace for advertising produced elsewhere.

Audience Fragmentation

Not only is the television landscape becoming littered with viewing options (hundreds of cable and satellite channels) and new viewing experiences (interactive programming), but viewers are also finding other forms of information and entertainment to fill time they once devoted to television. Not only has the Internet pulled people away from a strictly television experience in the family room, but all forms of home technology are diverting audiences away from televisions. A study by Knowledge Networks/SRI examined the proliferation of home technology—digital cable, DVD players, home theaters, caller ID, wireless Internet, personal digital assistants (PDAs), digital cameras, video gaming systems, broadband, and numerous PCs. They correlated a family's propensity to own these things with what their favorite channels are from among thirty-one major networks. HBO, Showtime, MTV, The Disney Channel, and VH1 had the highest index of home technology among the cable channels and WB and UPN the highest among broadcasters. These are channels specifically programmed to attract the 18 to 49-year-old market—the target group most desirable to advertisers.

The growth of entertainment options has caused a serious erosion and fragmentation of the television audience, once nearly monopolized by the networks, although the lowest-rated network shows still compare favorably to the highest-rated cable programs. Television viewers now have far more choices than they once had, which has both helped and hindered advertisers. On one hand, it is difficult to find a mass audience in any one place at any one time; the one exception is the opening ceremonies for the Olympic Games, which have been known to draw a worldwide audience of more than a billion. The Super Bowl,

The World Series, the Oscars, Election Night, and presidential debates are other events that draw well.

On the other hand, it is now possible for advertisers to reach a very targeted audience. Cable television has spurred the creation of niche channels devoted to sports, news, home improvement, food, movies, and music; even special-interest channels devoted to golf, car racing, and the Catholic Church. The niche audience has created a dilemma for advertisers. While the audience reach (size) on a niche channel is not as great as that the original national networks provided, the audience is easily identifiable—the audience for MTV is quite distinguishable from the audience for HGTV.

Creating a message that resonates with a niche audience is a bit more straightforward than creating one that resonates with the mass audience; however, the audience is still discerning, so the commercial must be of high quality. There is now a need to produce commercials that have the same high production values, and attendant costs, as network commercials even though the audience is much smaller. This creates a cost–benefit quandary for the advertiser as it struggles to justify the expense of a commercial that reaches a smaller, more targeted audience. There is also a challenge to create advertising that reaches the audience wherever it is and to develop creative and intriguing cross-platform commercials; for example, commercials that work on television, the Internet, and wireless devices like cell phones.

A Global Economy

Although the audience is fragmented, it is in fact growing. Political, economic, cultural, and social changes around the globe have broken down barriers that once isolated both products and the media that promoted them within national boundaries. French (Vivendi), German (Bertelsmann), and Japanese (Sony) companies now control American media companies, for example. It is now unusual to buy a product in the United States that does not have instructions for use in several languages because products are distributed internationally, including everything from small appliances to skin care products, disposable diapers to home improvement products—major advertisers' products. Universal packaging and branding is followed closely by international promotion and advertising. IBM used this strategy with great success while reinventing itself under CEO Lou Gerstner during the 1990s (see chapter 4 for an example of this).

The globalization of the television commercial will make media research and buying more challenging (many countries do not have ratings services), design and production more complicated (creatives need to contend with language and cultural differences), and effectiveness more difficult to measure. Television commercial globalization will create new opportunities for students who understand the advertising business, international relations, and cultural differences; who know a foreign language or two; and who enjoy travel.

SUMMARY

The television commercial is at the epicenter of a business model that supports a more than $45 billion industry in which advertisers, ad agencies, broadcasters, production companies, and consumers benefit. This business model was adopted by the television industry because it worked so well for the radio industry that preceded it. Many of the networks, programs, stars, advertisers, and ad agencies that dominated radio simply moved right into the television business in 1950, bringing their show-sponsorship model with them.

The introduction of videotape and the demise of live broadcasts, replaced with filmed and prerecorded programming and commercials, brought about the decline of show sponsorship and the growth of the television commercial as we know it today. Television commercials with high production values were soon produced; they were similar to those used in Hollywood films and television programs and were carefully placed on programs watched by the mass audience.

It became important for advertisers to know what television programs were being watched by the audience they wanted to reach, which gave birth to the audience measurement business currently dominated by Nielsen. Four times a year during sweeps weeks, Nielsen gathers viewing data about every program for virtually every major market in the country. This data is trusted by the entire industry and is used not only to select which shows to advertise on, but what the price of the commercial timeslot should be. Many other firms conduct similar forms of research to assist advertisers to understand the psychographics and demographics of target audiences, which helps them with creative development of commercials.

The advent of cable television, satellite service, and the Internet has fragmented the audience from mass to niche. This has caused a dilemma for broadcasters who have seen their ratings decline and also for advertisers who now must make multiple media buys to reach a mass audience.

Advertisers must adhere to certain rules; regulations; and ethical, if not legal, restrictions while formulating commercial messages. The FCC, FTC, U.S. Justice Department, and various industry and consumer groups keep a watchful eye out for fraudulent or misleading commercials. Among other things, advertisers must provide affidavits and substantiations that claims made in their commercials are true.

The future will present interesting challenges and opportunities for advertising in general and for the television commercial in particular.

DISCUSSION QUESTIONS

1. Would television broadcasting have grown at the rate it has if people had to pay for programming? What were they accustomed to?

2. Why are consumers willing to pay for cable service and watch commercials, too?

3. What are some of the differences between watching television and using a computer? Think of the differences in terms of where these activities take place, whether you are alone or with others, and whether you are an actively engaged or a passive viewer. Given these differences, can Internet advertising ever be as pervasive as television commercials? Why?

4. What do you think the future for television is, and for television commercials?

5. Will the audience experience with television become more interactive? What do you imagine an interactive commercial would be like? Will consumers respond positively to these kinds of changes?

RECOMMENDED READINGS AND WEB SITES

Dominick, Joseph R., Barry L. Sherman, and Gary A. Copeland. *Broadcasting/Cable: An Introduction to Modern Electronic Media.* New York: McGraw-Hill, 1996.

Head, Sydney W., Thomas Spann, and Michael A. McGregor. *Broadcasting in America.* 9th ed. New York: Houghton Mifflin Company, 2001.

Walker, James, and Douglas Ferguson. *The Broadcast Television Industry.* Needham Heights, MA: Allyn and Bacon, 1998

Zeigler, Sherilyn, and Herbert H. Howard. *Broadcast Advertising.* Ames, IA: Iowa State University Press, 1991.

Advertising Age—http://www.adage.com/

A popular trade magazine; an excellent source for the latest news and information, trends, account movements, and more.

Advertiser and Agency Red Books Online—http://www.redbooks.com/

The Advertiser Red Books deliver the quality and depth of information necessary for thorough research on agencies and advertisers worldwide.

Adweek—http://www.adweek.com/

One of the most widely read weekly trade magazines of the advertising industry.

American Advertising Federation (AAF)—http://www.aaf.org/

One of several organizations representing the interests of ad agencies. This group holds the ADDY awards competition and has excellent college outreach and internship opportunities.

American Association of Advertising Agencies (AAAA)—http://www.aaaa.org/

The national trade association that represents the advertising agency business in the United States.

Clio Awards—http://www.clioawards.com/

Web site for one of the most prestigious awards for advertising excellence.

FCC—http://ftp.fcc.gov/cgb/consumerfacts/advertising.html

This site, maintained by the Federal Communications Commission, discusses offensive advertising and what the FCC can, and does, do about it.

Nielsen Media Research: Unlock the Power of Media—http://www.nielsenmedia.com/

Web site for the company whose research is depended on by all segments of the broadcast industry.

NOTES

1. Levy, Jonathan, Marcelino Ford-Livene, and Anne Levine. *Broadcast Television: Survivor in a Sea of Competition* (OPP Working Paper No. 37), p 98. Washington, DC: Federal Communications Commission, September 2002.

2. Remarks by Jamie Kellner, Chairman, Turner Broadcasting. *Comm. Daily,* 22(135): July 15, 2002.

3. Consumers eventually pay the price, of course, because the cost of advertising is included in the price consumers pay for the products and services they purchase.

4. AdAge.com, August 15, 2002—http://www.adage.com/page.cms?pageId=919.

5. Zeigler, p. 5.

6. Ibid., p. 7.
7. Dominick, p. 53.
8. Walker and Ferguson, p. 24.
9. Information from the *I Love Lucy* display at Universal Studios, Hollywood.
10. Walker and Ferguson, p. 25.
11. Head, Spann, and McGregor, p. 304.

CHAPTER THREE

ADVERTISING RESEARCH AND STRATEGY

AMY P. FALKNER

Mike Sweeney could have been the proverbial fish out of water. As he sat in a bar in Wahoo, Nebraska, killing time watching football and drinking 75-cent drafts, the New York City ad man was wondering how to find the insight he needed to help the Dirty Water ad agency woo a potential new client, Pegasus Communications/DirecTV. Pegasus states that its mission is to bring advanced digital services to America's rural and underserved communities; however it didn't told the ad agency it understand its customer the way it should.

So Sweeney's boss sent him out with this charge: go find out about rural America, and fast. Sweeney, the director of customer insight at the time, contacted an acquaintance in Wahoo and arranged to meet her the next day. He'd caught an early flight and had four hours to kill before meeting her and her family. So he left his room in the town's one hotel, which cost only forty bucks a night, and went to the one bar in town. In walked farmer Roy Akerson.

"I met him and found out he didn't live in that town of 3,000," said Sweeney. "He considered that a big city. He lived in a town of 125 people. And that's where I went." Sweeney continued, "Spent an hour talking to him and his wife and they invited me over for breakfast the next morning, and that's where it started. Four and a half days, basically seventeen hours a day, in this town of 125 people."[1]

Sweeney decided he needed to learn as much about these people's lives as possible before asking about their television viewing habits. Every night he would send an e-mail to the agency describing what he had learned about rural America. After the third day there, he wrote that he hadn't asked any satellite questions yet, but he would the next day. That did not make his bosses very happy. They sent a rather terse e-mail back, edited here for family reading; basically, it said "you're a researcher, ask the questions, pay them the money, and get us the information." Sweeney had other ideas.

> I wrote them back saying, I will not do that. In fact, how about I just leave now and you take my place. And you know what, why don't you bring some Prada or Gucci gift certificates

from Fifth Avenue in New York, and hand them out to the farmers and you ask the questions yourself. And we always laugh about that because I knew I had started to understand what these folks are like. And the more I got to know them, the more they appreciated the questions I asked about understanding rural life. In turn, they asked me questions about what New York City was like. It was a real sharing; we had started to build a relationship and if you think about it, that's what good brands do. They build relationships. It wasn't until my fourth day that I started asking satellite and TV questions and they happily answered every one because they knew me and they felt more comfortable then.

Dirty Water won the pitch based on the strength of that research. They were the only agency that did not present any creative storyboards, saying they felt they knew one town well and had gained some insights but wanted to do more. Sweeney slogged 7,000 miles through seven rural states, spending time on farms, in living rooms, and at local diners. He harvested maple syrup in the snow with a Vermonter, rode a corn combine with a Nebraska farmer, and hiked through Montana's Big Sky country to find out about rural America and the role television and entertainment played in their lives. Sweeney continued:

> From that we gained a lot of context. The more we understood them, the easier and clearer it became to us how to sell the product. It all fueled the strategy. We knew what sort of product benefits we could tout in the strategy—that was easy. It was more about the tone and the manner and our approach, and that all came through the context research. That really helped the creative at the end. It worked really well because we were talking to folks as opposed to just shouting out deals and specials. We knew what made them tick.

Sweeney believes the team would not have been successful if they had relied on surveys or traditional focus groups. "The point is to get away from the desk and get a fresh perspective because often it's natural for us as people to have stereotypes about other targets and how other people are living." He paused and then went on:

> I will fully admit that before I did the DirecTV project, I thought the people—I actually said out in the middle of nowhere, and I found out they hate that phrase—I thought as far as technology and communications and things like that, they would at least be five years behind us. That they would not be in touch, that they would not be connected, that they'd be backwards, all that kind of stuff. And when I went out there, I learned a lot. I learned a lot because I actually spent time out there. I didn't read a magazine article; I didn't do a Lexis-Nexis search and get a thousand articles about rural America. I went out there and experienced it.

For more about what Sweeney learned, see the case study "There's More to Farmers Than Corn."

This is the big buzz of advertising research—get as close to the customer as possible through an ethnography, basically spending a day in the life of your target audience or, in Sweeney's case, several days. This is part of what is called primary research, which is primary data gathered through original research, usually by or at the request of the advertiser, including focus groups and surveys. Secondary data is existing information, such as those magazine articles Sweeney referred to, company reports, sales-volume statistics, and audience measurement studies like Nielsen ratings. When an advertising researcher systematically studies preexisting data, he is performing secondary research.

In this chapter, we talk more about both kinds of research, and how they are used to develop an advertising strategy, which eventually leads to the design and production of a television commercial. Other research is used to "place" the commercial on the television show that best reaches the target audience.

In this chapter, you will learn the following:

- The difference between marketing research and advertising research
- What primary and secondary research are and how to conduct both
- The definition of strategic advertising research and evaluative advertising research
- How ad agencies use all of this research to make creative and media placement decisions
- How ad agencies are structured and the roles and responsibilities of each key department
- What a creative brief is, and how creatives use it to design the commercial

■ ■ ■ ■ ■

CASE STUDY
THERE'S MORE TO FARMERS THAN CORN

City boy Mike Sweeney (right) with his new friend Roy Akerson, a retired farmer in Colon, Nebraska. Sweeney's research on behalf of his client took him all over the rural United States.

Mike Sweeney's experience in Colon, Nebraska, and other far-flung towns led to several insights. Here's what he found out in his words:

Stereotypical "rural" communication was never going to cut it. Talking *to* rural people would never cut it. It was crucial that our communication began a conversation (a relationship) with rural Americans. If we tried *to be like* them we would fail.

Key Findings

- Geographic isolation brings people together, thereby strengthening connections between people, actively and emotionally.

CONTINUED

- People prefer to deal with companies that possess the same values as they do: reliability, honesty, tenacious work ethic, live up to what you say, and so on; little-known companies have to "earn their local badge."
- Consumers told us that the post-purchase relationship is just as (or more) important as the initial store purchase. Within this consumer television market, no advertisers were providing anything beyond hardware (dishes and receivers) and pictures on the screen. In the customers' minds, no one was committed to them and their needs.

Pegasus changed all this by saying (in advertising) that they were "working harder" to meet customers' needs. To come out and suddenly say they were the "premier satellite television provider" would not have been believed, mainly because rural consumers only believe something when they see extra effort being put into it, especially after being let down by other companies so many times in the past.

In this sense, "working harder" demonstrated an intimate understanding of the local mind-set. Strategically, "working harder" took a leadership position in the category.

The Result

A campaign that drove a new "service message" based on consumer-driven insights. Sweeney said that sales records were attributed to the campaign and that salesforce strategies were overhauled based on this new consumer understanding.

Sweeney has since left Dirty Water to form his own research company called Frontal Lobe, which specializes in ethnographic, qualitative consumer research. In one of his latest projects for Warner Brothers, he scoured the globe searching for kids and parents who are Harry Potter *fans.*

The field of advertising research is much larger and the issues more complex than can be covered in a single chapter, so the goal here is to give you a good overview. We recommend several books in the bibliography, and there are journals, trade magazines, and Web sites that report on the most current research trends and practices if you want to learn more. We don't expect you to be a polished focus group moderator by the time you finish this chapter, but you should have a sense of what research is germane to commercial design and production, who conducts this research, which research methods are available, and how to use research results. In the latter half of the chapter, we detail some secondary sources and research methods you can apply to your own assignments.

MARKETING RESEARCH AND ADVERTISING RESEARCH

Sounds like these should be the same thing, but they're not. *Marketing research* is a broad term that refers to the acquisition, development, and analysis of new information used for marketing, advertising, or marketing communications decisions.[2] This research can be totally or partially completed before the advertising planning process begins. Marketing research includes everything from product development to distribution. Strategic and evaluative advertising research is a subset of this. *Strategic* advertising research is done to help plan, develop, and place ads. *Evaluative* advertising research monitors the effectiveness of ads. In their book, *Advertising Principles,* Bruce Vanden Bergh and Helen Katz explain this planning process, which is illustrated in Figure 3.1.

Let's walk through an example using a product line that is currently in its introduction stage. In September 2002, Frito-Lay announced that it was rolling out several new, lower-fat products endorsed by Dr. Kenneth Cooper, the father of aerobics.[3] This was in response to the heat that fast-food and fatty snack manufacturers have taken over their role in the increase in obesity of American consumers. In fact, one consumer had filed a lawsuit accusing McDonald's, Burger King, KFC, and Wendy's of contributing to his obesity and ensuing health problems. In response, Frito-Lay and others in the food industry began to actively market and advertise their own health-oriented programs. For Frito-Lay, these better-for-you brands include Baked Doritos, Rold Gold Braided Twists, and recently launched Tostitos Organic and Lay's Natural. The theory is that making these products with healthier oils and less salt means lower calories and less fat per serving without sacrificing taste. Ultimately, of course, the consumer will be the judge.

Marketing and Advertising Planning Process

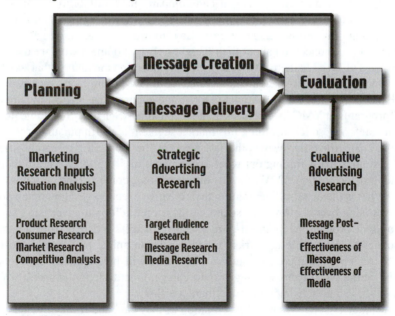

FIGURE 3.1

Source: Adapted from Vanden Bergh, Katz, and Katz, *Advertising Principals* (Chicago: NTC Publishing Group, 1999), p. 219.

Marketing Research

So how does Frito-Lay fit into this marketing and advertising planning process? Let's look at marketing research first. This starts the process and is usually done by the client's own marketing department with the help of independent research firms, and sometimes the agency.

Frito-Lay must do what is called a *situation analysis,* which is broken up into four parts—product research, consumer research, market research, and competitive analysis (see Figure 3.1). The goal is to analyze the current market situation and where these new products will fit in. *Product research* tries to find answers to questions about the product relative to the target such as: How does the taste of Tostitos Organic compare to regular Tostitos? Which do consumers favor? How important is a low saturated fat level to consumers? In September 2002, this product was four months into a two-market test to find answers to these questions.

Consumer research tries to get into the minds of individuals in the target audience: What motivations or attitudes do they have toward the product, or the category as a whole? Are consumers willing to sacrifice good taste for healthier snacks? Would they pay more for a healthier snack option? Are the chips still "fun" if that feeling of guilty indulgence is taken away? This kind of research often leads to a repositioning of a product based on consumer usage patterns and attitudes.

Market research—as distinct from market*ing* research—studies individuals as a purchasing group or market segment; it can compare the profitability of market segments. Market research analyzes the total market based on known segments and attempts to find new segments in the market: Does Frito-Lay go after young, single, 18- to 24-year-old women who are concerned about their weight or baby boomers who are trying to hold off the ravages of time? Is there a way for Frito-Lay to define the market that would give them an advantage over other snack manufacturers with low-fat products, such as Pringles? Is it worth pursuing the age 12 to 17 teen market, or even preteens? Frito-Lay already supports kids' programs at YMCAs and has sent a video called "Sensible Snacking" to directors of school cafeterias, so it must think this market segment is worth pursuing.[4]

A *competitive analysis* is the last piece of the marketing research puzzle; it's just what it sounds like—finding out what the competition is up to: What are their marketing and advertising strategies? What kinds of promotions, contests, and coupons are they running? What is the main selling point in their creative executions? How much do they spend on advertising overall? Are they spending more on traditional advertising such as television or trade promotions (point-of-purchase advertising)? Where do they advertise? Which magazines? Which cable networks? Do they have an online presence? Frito-Lay is planning to set up store merchandising displays that will house all its products under one theme—at the time of this writing, "Smart choice, great taste, good snack." What will the competitor, Pringles, have in the supermarket aisle?

Marketers collect as much information as they can, and if they decide to bring in an advertising agency, the agency can expand on that knowledgebase. Agencies generally subscribe to a number of syndicated research studies, such as the Simmons Study of Media and Markets and Mediamark Research, which help analyze target audiences in terms of demographics, product usage, and media habits. CMR, a Taylor Nelson Sofres company, breaks down advertisers' media spending by brand, medium, and geography, and the previously mentioned Nielsen Television Index helps determine who is watching which show. We'll go into more detail about some of these later in the chapter. For now, let's assume Frito-Lay is ready to move on to the next stage.

Strategic Advertising Research

Target audience research identifies the target audience, describes its characteristics, and examines product usage and media habits using some of the sources listed previously. A new product, such as Lay's Natural, won't be analyzed in Simmons or MRI just yet; however, profiling current users of Baked Lay's potato chips, which are lower in calories and fat, will give the researcher a good picture of the potential target audience. Demographically, clients want to know the basics: age, gender, income, education, occupation, race, geographic region, marital status, and presence of children (see Figure 3.2).

Frito-Lay and its agency will also be interested in this target audience's *psychographics*—values, attitudes, personalities, and lifestyles of individuals most likely to purchase the product: Are they outdoorsy types or are they couch potatoes? Do they spend time with their family on the weekend or will they head into work for a few hours on a Saturday? Do they value their health, their looks? Do they go to the gym? Psychographic research firms, such as SRI International and Yankelovich, do research on these kinds of questions. In 1978, SRI developed a questionnaire called Values and Lifestyles (VALS) and later revised it to the VALS Typology[5] (see Figure 3.3).

This system shows eight types of consumers, grouped on the basis of resources (the vertical dimension) and primary motivation (the horizontal dimension):

1. *Innovators* have abundant resources and high self-esteem. They are change leaders, interested in technology. They are very active consumers and their purchases reflect cultivated tastes for upscale, niche products and services.
2. *Thinkers* are mature, satisfied, well-educated people. They value order, knowledge, and responsibility. Thinkers look for durability, functionality, and value in the products they buy.
3. *Achievers* are status- and career-oriented. Family is also important to them. They are successful and respectful of authority. Achievers favor established, prestige products that have demonstrated success to their peers.
4. *Experiencers* are young, impulsive, live-for-the-moment types. They like the offbeat. Experiencers are avid consumers whose purchases reflect the emphasis they place on looking good and having "cool" stuff.
5. *Believers* are conservative, conventional people with modest incomes who favor proven, American brands. Family, church, community, and country are important to them.
6. *Strivers* emulate those who have money, but they don't have enough of their own. They are trendy, fun-loving, and impulsive shoppers. Strivers favor stylish products because they are concerned about the approval of others.

Women Who Are Users of Baked Lays

	Percent of Users Who Have Characteristic	Index to Population
Education		
Graduated college	25.5	122
Attended college	28.3	106
Graduated high school	34.4	98
Did not graduate high school	11.9	69
Age		
18-24	11.0	122
25-34	18.7	95
35-44	25.5	110
45-54	18.4	103
55-64	11.5	97
65+	15.0	81
Household Income		
$75,000+	25.9	132
$60,000-$74,999	12.5	127
$50,000-$59,999	8.2	95
$40,000-$49,999	11.0	104
$30,000-$39,999	11.3	93
$20,000-$29,999	13.2	98
$10,000-$19,999	11.5	77
Less than $10,000	6.5	61
Marital Status		
Single	14.7	90
Married	64.0	111
Other	21.3	83
Parents	43.6	108
Working Parents	32.8	118

Simmons and MRI send questionnaires to a nationally representative sample, who record the products they use, what TV shows, magazines, newspapers and radio formats they listen to, and their demographic characteristics. This information is crosstabbed and compared to the general population.

This is a portion of MRI data. The "Index" column on the right compares the demographics of women who buy Baked Lays to those of "Total Women" in the U.S. Any time the index is over 100, that means the women who use Baked Lays are more likely to have this characteristic than women in general. When the number is less than 100, they're less likely. In the "Percent of Users" column, look for the biggest numbers for profiling (i.e.) 25.9% of women who use Baked Lays have household incomes of $75,000+.

At a glance, the 18-24 age group has the highest index, but the 35-44 group is more than twice as large. Which has the most sales potential?

FIGURE 3.2

Source: Mediamark Research, Inc., Spring 1999.

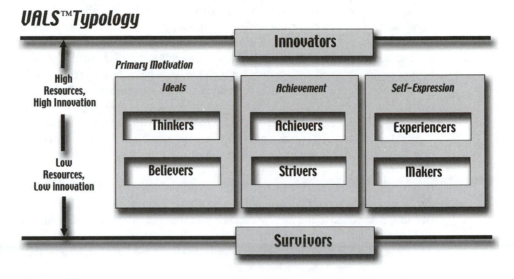

FIGURE 3.3

Source: http://www.sric-bi.com/VALS.shtml.

7. *Makers* are self-sufficient and suspicious of new ideas. They are unimpressed by material possessions other than those with a practical purpose. Makers would rather fix their own car or house, and they buy basic products.

8. *Survivors* are poor, without much education or many skills. They are primarily concerned with safety and security and are loyal to favorite brands, especially if they can purchase them at a discount.

As you might imagine, survivors and makers are of the least interest to advertisers. These profiles help the agency form a clear picture of the target and which advertising techniques and messages can be used to persuade them to buy a particular product. Take the survey yourself at www.sric-bi.com/VALS/presurvey.shtml to find out your VALS profile.

In addition to demographics and psychographics, understanding the target audience requires an assessment of its knowledge about the product category: Are consumers even aware of low-fat and no-fat versions of snack foods? Were they turned on or off by Lay's WOW! Chips—a previously introduced no-fat potato chip cooked in olestra oil? How do they find out about healthy innovations in food products? Is their purchase decision made in the grocery aisle, sitting at home with Sunday newspaper coupons, or succumbing to a request from their fifteen-year-old daughter to try something new?

Message research studies the characteristics of the advertising message and its impact on target audience members before it runs in the media. Also called *pretesting,* it includes (a) concept testing and (b) copy testing. Concept testing often happens in a focus group, where members of the target audience are exposed to different ad concepts and asked for their opinions. The session is often videotaped. Sometimes more formal survey questionnaires are used. Today, these services can be done online. For instance, Frito-Lay would want to know which main idea to emphasize: fat reduction in the cooking process, same good taste, or a doctor's health endorsement. Copy testing, which evaluates the verbal and visual elements of an ad, happens after the best concepts are turned into ads and before they are run on any media. What works better: showing a close-up of the product or showing people having fun with the product? Which message helps brand recall? At the time of this writing, health guru Dr. Cooper is separating snack foods into three classifications based on calories and fat levels. Frito-Lay is testing how consumers respond to Dr. Cooper's endorsement in advertising and whether it's likely to make any difference at the cash register.

Media research seeks a match between target audience characteristics and the profile of a particular media audience: How much of the Frito-Lay target audience is included in the readership of *Cosmo* magazine or the audience of *Friends*? Will running ads in these two media vehicles reach an even larger portion of the target audience or is there a lot of duplication—do some *Cosmo* readers also watch *Friends*? What happens if Fox's *American Idol* gets added to the mix? Audience measurement is the key element here since it establishes the advertising rates for a particular show or magazine.

The more people who watch commercials or read ads, the more the medium can charge advertisers. This is where Nielsen ratings and shares come into play. NBC charges advertisers approximately $456,000 for *each* :30 spot on *Friends*—a perennial Top 5 show (though in its last season as this book was written).[6] *Friends* was ranked third by the end of the 2001–2002 television season with an average 12.5 rating and a 21 share; it started the 2002 TV season ranked number one with a 19 rating and a 30 share. That translates into 29 million viewers each week, which is why NBC thinks it's worth the nearly half million dollars per spot.[7] Conversely, a show that has fewer viewers on a smaller network, such as *Buffy the Vampire Slayer* on UPN, gets about $59,000 for a :30 spot. Rates for television commercials are negotiated, but there always is a starting point. *Advertising Age* conducts a survey of media buyers and network executives each year and estimates the primetime going rates as shown in Table 3.1.[8]

What we know from Nielsen is only how many viewers tuned into a particular show, not how many people actually saw any particular commercial. Nielsen measures only that

TABLE 3.1   Fall 2002 Estimated Rates for :30 TV Spot

RANK	TELEVISION SHOW	NETWORK	RATE/:30
1	*Friends*	NBC	$455,700
2	*ER*	NBC	$438,514
3	*Survivor*	CBS	$418,750
4	*Will & Grace*	NBC	$376,617
5	*Everybody Loves Raymond*	CBS	$301,640
6	*Monday Night Football*	ABC	$298,000
7	*Scrubs*	NBC	$294,667
8	*West Wing*	NBC	$282,248
9	*CSI*	CBS	$280,043
10	*Good Morning Miami*	NBC	$279,813
	Average for a primetime :30 spot	**—**	**$115,799**

there was the *opportunity to see* the commercial, meaning the television was tuned to NBC during the *Friends'* timeslot. The research method doesn't record if viewers took a bathroom break or made a snack during the break for commercials. New research measurement tools for determining actual viewers of commercials are still in the development stage.

Evaluative Advertising Research

Frito-Lay will no doubt run some television spots for its new, low-fat snack foods and then its agency, with the help of outside research firms, will run some tests to see if the commercial and/or the campaign accomplished what it set out to do. *Evaluative research* tests the effectiveness of a campaign's specific messages and their media placement. *Message post-testing* occurs after the target audience has seen the ad and usually measures its impact by evaluating recall or recognition of that ad. *Message effectiveness* evaluates the effect of the communication on the target: What should the target audience know and feel about the new Frito-Lay product after seeing the message? What does Frito-Lay want them to do as a result of seeing the ad? Try the product? Ask for more information? Tell others about it? Finally, *media effectiveness* compares the actual media placement to the original media plan, looking to see if audience levels guaranteed by the media are met or to see, for example, if the *Friends'* spot was more successful at persuading the target than the *American Idol* one.

WHO PLAYS THE AD GAME?

Now that you know what strategic and evaluative advertising research is, it's important to understand the different parts of an advertising agency so that you can see who the players are and how they interact with the client and the consumer. Most national advertisers and large retailers use outside agencies, as opposed to in-house agencies. Organizational structures vary, but generally someone from the client's marketing department is the liaison to the ad agency.

Companies that market several brands, especially those in the packaged-goods category, often use a *category management approach*—an individual or a small team is in charge of all marketing for a single product or brand in that company's portfolio. For example, for a leading national advertiser, such as Procter & Gamble, a product category manager oversees all hair care products and individual brand managers are then assigned to Pantene, Pert, Physique, and Herbal Essence. The brand managers are involved day-to-day with agency personnel. However, many local retailers do not use outside advertising agencies at all. Small- to mid-size retailers rely on media salespeople for counsel and to design ads using the media organization's creative services unit. While the advertising agency world has undergone some dramatic changes in the last few years because of consolidation and the emergence of both specialty creative and media buying shops, the full-service agency traditionally handles the following four areas: creative, research, media, and account management.

The creation and execution of ads is the job of the creative services department. An art director–copywriter team develops the creative idea and various television and print production people help it come to life. The roles are discussed in greater detail in the next chapter. The research department helps different departments with any research needs. The media department plans the media strategy and executes it by buying specific vehicles. Finally, the account management group is the primary client contact and coordinates all of the agency's activities into a cohesive plan for the advertiser. In addition, an office management function does a number of things, including hiring and firing personnel, paying bills, and keeping records of expenses and revenues. Figure 3.4 shows a typical full-service advertising agency's organizational chart by functions.

A new player—the account planner—has changed the dynamics of American agencies during the past twenty years. Started in England in the 1960s, this concept made its

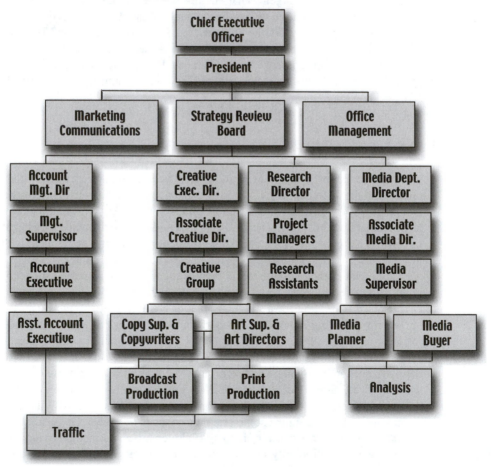

FIGURE 3.4

Source: From Bendinger, *Advertising & the Business of Brands* (The Copy Workshop, Chicago, 1999), p. 255.

way to the United States in 1982 at Chiat/Day and has taken on increasing importance since. An account planner's job is to be the voice of the consumer in the advertising planning process. Planners are researchers, skilled at interpersonal communications, whose job function is somewhat of a hybrid. They work closely with account managers and creative teams, advising both on consumers' perspectives and buying behavior. Some planners are part of the research department and some research departments have new names, such as Strategic Services, to accommodate planners. Regardless of the structure or title, the goal for the account planner is to unearth some key consumer insight that will help develop better advertising. Mike Sweeney's work at the beginning of this chapter is a good example of what an account planner looks for.

After much time is spent researching the consumer and the brand, this insight is used to develop an advertising strategy, which the account executives and planners present to the creative team. Typically a one-page document, a strategy is usually written by the account executive with help from a planner, although in some agencies, planners write what is called a *creative brief.* On occasion, creatives with a lot of knowledge about a particular brand are invited to kick around strategy ideas with the account team. Media is also consulted to make sure it's known what the preferred ad mediums are and that budget constraints are identified.

Strategy formats vary from agency to agency, but basically a strategy, or brief, is a statement that explains how to sell the product. It identifies the target consumer and the consumer mind-set. The strategy explains why we might expect the consumer to purchase the product in preference to the competition's: What is the basic benefit the product offers? Is there a problem the product solves for the consumer? A strategy doesn't include specific copy suggestions or images—those are left up to the creative team.

The strategy is intended to give the creative team some direction and inspiration. That's where insight comes into play. A good strategy is not just a laundry list of data: What is it about this particular target audience, as it relates to the brand? This intersection of consumer, brand, and opportunity is usually where the "big idea" comes from. That elusive nugget of information is often the key to developing great advertising.

Strategy Statement

Here's an outline of a strategy statement, which is based on a model McCann-Erickson uses and authors Jerry Jewler and Bonnie Drewniany illustrate in their book, *Creative Strategy in Advertising.*[9] The goal is to keep a strategy short and sweet. Unless otherwise noted, a few sentences under each question are fine.

1. *Who is our target?* Try to give a rich description of the target audience. Don't rely solely on demographic information, but use as a starting point. Add personality and lifestyle information. Identify whether you are targeting current users, nonusers, or users of competitive brands.
2. *Where are we now in the mind of this person?* Explain what the target consumer thinks of your product (i.e., they don't know us, they think we are too expensive, they know us but don't use us, they don't understand what we can do).

3. *Where is our competition in the mind of this person?* Same as 2, but focus on the competition.
4. *Where would we like to be in the mind of this person?* This is where you position the product: Product is the best choice because...
5. *What is the promise for the consumer, the "big idea"?* This is the toughest sentence of any strategy to write, and you should try to say it in *one sentence,* if possible. It's also called the *selling proposition:* the point of the campaign—the best argument your brand can offer. It's not a slogan, but it sums up what the campaign is trying to prove.
6. *What is the supporting evidence?* Presumably, you have identified some consumer benefit in 5. What is the reason why you provide this benefit? Sometimes these are simply product facts or product benefits (see "Going up the Ladder" sidebar for more details).
7. *What is the tone of voice for the advertising?* Tone is a guide for how to talk to your target. Describe the appropriate tone—serious, funny, warm and fuzzy, startling, mild guilt, and others.

■ ■ ■ ■ ■ ▬▬

GOING UP THE LADDER

Strategic discussions focus on the benefit a product offers the target. In his book, *The Copy Workshop Workbook,* Bruce Bendinger explains that sequencing these factors is called *laddering.* Listed from "bottom to top," the following are his definitions.[10]

- **Product attribute:** Characteristic of the product, usually inherent or natural. *Each jar of Jif contains 1,218 peanuts, more than any other brand.*
- **Product feature:** Aspect of the product, usually based on some manufactured or designed aspect. *These hot roasted peanuts are sealed warm.*
- **Product benefit:** A benefit to the consumer, usually based on a product feature or attribute. *Jif peanut butter has a creamier, smoother, fresh-roasted flavor.*
- **Consumer benefit:** A benefit to the consumer, usually based on how the product benefit delivers a positive result to the consumer. *My children get extra flavor, which tastes good so they'll eat it.*
- **Value:** Related to internal needs and self-image. *I'm a good mother because I serve Jif.*

To move up the ladder, ask people *why* that feature or benefit is important. The issue is where to focus. Carried to extremes, every food product reinforces nurturing values, every business product allows you to "be your best." Generally, farther down the ladder you are more product-specific. Higher up, you are dealing with the consumer's life and less with differentiating your specific product.

REAL-LIFE EXAMPLE

Crystal Anderson is a brand planner for DDB in New York. Her background is in child psychology, so naturally she got assigned to the Hasbro toy account. She says a lot of clients want to make the selling proposition—that key sentence in the strategy—very product-based, and it requires going up the ladder to find the consumer benefit. Says Anderson:

The proposition is always the hardest line to write, and it's where the creatives focus most of their efforts. It's one line: What is it that this commercial is promising, the main idea of the entire spot? It's hard to get it down to one sentence and have it be single-minded. There are so many things—"it does this, and this is cool, and we know they are going to like this." But you have to figure out the *one* thing. With Hasbro, it's "two-year-olds will particularly like this toy because of the flashing lights and moving balls." We ask why do they like the flashing lights and the moving balls? What is it about this? We try to take it from a product-based benefit to an emotional benefit. That's what really works, to kind of hit a nerve.

We talked about independent play, that because of the lights and the moving balls that kids are very engaged. So they are playing on their own, and they are learning how to be an independent person. They don't need somebody to play with. To a mom, the proposition would be keep your child busy for a long time, but we always try to word it from a kid point of view. The reason it gives independent play or a sense of independence to the child—and this is the "why is this true" part—is because it has flashing lights and moving balls.[11]

Gaining That Elusive Insight

Let's take a look at what some real-life planners and account execs do to gain consumer insight and how you might be able to use some of these techniques to start developing strategies. Earlier we discussed primary and secondary research. While certainly beneficial, primary research is expensive to conduct; therefore, secondary research always comes first. That means you should be on a fact-finding mission; gather all the secondary data you can about your target audience, the product category, the brand, and the main competition.

Keep in mind that there are different types of data—*quantitative* and *qualitative*. Quantitative data comes from research that grew out of the natural sciences, where observations could be made of regularly occurring natural phenomena and conclusions and predictions could be made. As the name implies, quantitative research involves the gathering, processing, and interpretation of *numerical data.* The most common example is a survey in which representative groups of people are asked questions, and their answers are used as representational of a larger population. Nielsen Media Research collects quantitative data.

Qualitative research is used to collect and evaluate data about social and cultural phenomena, and it recognizes that the subjects of the study are always people. Qualitative research is typically conducted in a relatively short period of time among relatively small, nonrandom samples. Qualitative methods include the use of focus groups, observations, and interviews and reveal the beliefs and motives of people in the target audience to the researcher. People can *tell* you what they like, don't like, want, need, and aspire to have. It is also up to the researcher to sort through what people think she wants to hear and to discover their real motivation.

Starting Your Research

Ideally, you can start research with your own clients. Often, they have primary consumer or marketplace research to share with you—for example, national and regional sales figures, seasonality trends in sales, and figures on best-selling varieties. They may have their own database gathered from product warranty cards or online registrations. Sometimes they have information they don't even know might be useful to an agency, so don't be afraid to ask. For example, Anderson also works on the PSAs for the National Highway Traffic and Safety Administration (Friends Don't Let Friends Drive Drunk Campaign). The NHTSA has volumes of research, Anderson explained, because it's a government agency that often has to justify its funding to legislators, but it did not really realize how valuable some of that information would be to the ad agency. Anderson wanted to know why people are repeat offenders, and shortly after posing the question to the client, a box was delivered to her desk with piles and piles of research. "They never thought this was relevant to their communications," she said. "Once you explain it to them, they are like 'oh yes, you probably do want to understand the target.' It saved the client a lot of money, too, to use that secondary research."

Secondary Sources

Without client help, you can still read company reports and press releases, of course, with some caution due to the optimistic slant most often given to both. If you call up a company and ask for information, sometimes letters from satisfied customers are included in packets and these can give some insight. A pit stop at your university's library reference desk will tell you whether you have access to market guides and statistical information that many agencies subscribe to and have in house. This includes sources such as Simmons and MRI, which, as we discussed earlier, give a demographic profile by product usage and have information on media habits. You may still find older versions of these two sources in a series of bound books, but more recent versions are on CD-ROM; this allows you to configure data any way you like to find answers using specific cross-tabs.

Other useful market guides include the following:

- *Lifestyle Market Analyst*—great for lifestyle information on Americans; interests, hobbies, and activities are broken down both by demographic group and metropolitan area.
- *Editor & Publisher Market Guide*—market information on U.S. and Canadian cities in which a daily newspaper is published; includes data on population, number of households, disposable personal income, and retail sales.
- *Survey of Buying Power*—a guide to consumer purchasing trends that ranks markets by population, effective buying income, retail sales, and buying power index; includes five-year spending forecasts for every U.S. metro and media market.
- *Demographics USA Zip Edition*—1,500 pages of demographic, economic, and commercial/industrial estimates by zip code.

While you are at the library, there are more than 300 business periodicals, which are great resources. Some of these are also available online; however, some are by subscription only. The major ones are: *Advertising Age, Adweek, American Demographics, Brandweek, Businessweek, Forbes, Fortune, Mediaweek,* and newspapers with a business bent—the *Wall Street Journal* and the *New York Times.* Academic publications, such as the *Journal of Advertising Research,* can also be helpful.

Industry trade publications related to your product are very specific and are excellent research sources. There are literally thousands of these publications, such as *Automotive*

News, Chain Store Age, and *American Banker,* that can give you insight into a particular category. Trade associations keep track of industry data too. Some associations are rather well known—think American Dairy Association—but there are hundreds of obscure associations like the Soap and Detergent Association. The *Encyclopedia of Associations,* available at most libraries, is a reference guide to what thousands of associations do and how to get in touch with them.

Psychographically, questionnaires such as VALS that was described earlier, and public opinion surveys conducted by companies, such as Roper, Gallup, and Yankelovich, can give you insight into your target's attitudes and opinions. The polls and surveys sponsored by these three companies often get press coverage in major newspapers and publications such as *American Demographics.* This publication also does a lot of trend analysis by various demographic groups or product categories, which can give further insight into your target. Professional trend watchers, such as Faith Popcorn, often issue annual trend reports that delve into the American psyche; her Web site at www.faithpopcorn.com/trends/ trends.htm details some of her thoughts.

Further, the U.S. Government Printing Office publishes thousands of books and pamphlets. A quick way to find some of these 15,000 publications is through the *Subject Bibliography Index.* The granddaddy of all statistical sources is the U.S. Census—its data was updated in 2000 and is available online at *www.census.gov. A word of warning:* This Web site has so much data it can be overwhelming; start with the American Factfinder link and you will find it easier to navigate.

It's beyond the scope of this chapter to go into detail about all the possible secondary sources, or how to analyze them, but this is a good start. That is what secondary research is—a good start. These kinds of studies are a way for you to get up to speed on a product quickly and to zero in on a potential target, but they are often not specific enough to reveal the true motivations of a consumer or any emotional connection to the brand. That's where the "big idea" comes from. For that, you need to conduct some primary research, so let's move on.

Primary Research

Primary research methods are both quantitative and qualitative. Quantitative data is gathered through surveys and experiments. Researchers cannot make direct observations of every individual in the population they are studying. Instead, they collect data from a subset of individuals called a *sample,* and then use those observations to make inferences about the entire population. Ideally, the characteristic(s) of interest of the sample corresponds to the larger population. In that case, the researcher's conclusions from the sample are most likely applicable to the entire population.[12] If the goal is projectability to the entire population, the sample must be randomly recruited. Random sampling ensures that each member of a population has a known chance of being selected for inclusion in the sample and that no bias is employed in choosing who will be interviewed or measured.[13]

Not all surveys are random samples. Most people have been asked to complete a survey while shopping in a mall. While this is still useful information, you cannot project this to the general population because the subjects were selected on the basis of their availability (i.e., they walked by in the mall). The consequence is that an unknown portion of the population is excluded (i.e., those who did not go shopping). The sample could also have a disproportionate number of teens and/or the elderly since those groups frequent malls.

Experiments are designed to discover the difference between cause and effect; that is, does spending twice as much on advertising result in twice the gross sales revenue? This kind of research is very expensive to conduct but very valuable to the client. Qualitative research, like that conducted by Mike Sweeney at the beginning of this chapter, also costs money but not as much. Some great information can be gained for as little as it costs to drive to the local grocery store. The following sections describe some qualitative methods employed by folks in the business, some of which you can do yourself. You'll see that these methods often lead to the breakthrough moment that inspires the campaign.

Firsthand Experience.   The first, and most obvious thing, is to try the product yourself. When an art director dumped a box of cereal on his kitchen table and counted all the raisins, it inspired the line "Two scoops of raisins in every box of Kellogg's Raisin Bran." So try your product, and the competition's while you're at it. Analyze their strengths and weaknesses: Why would you choose one over the other?

However, don't assume everyone thinks like you. First of all, you have been sensitized to advertising just by reading this chapter. In addition, you may not even be part of the target audience, so your analysis is less valuable. Putting yourself in place of the target audience is easier said than done. At some point, you may work on a campaign that is intended for the gender opposite of yours, or a totally different age group: What is the experience like from that perspective? Some agencies go to great lengths to find out.

Spencer Baim, at the time an account planner at Mad Dogs and Englishmen in New York City and now with Fallon in Minneapolis, went with a fellow agency employee to a Staten Island bank. The pair wanted to see if they could get a loan and open a checking account.[14] Maybe it was the way he and his colleague looked at each other, or maybe it was when he told the bank that the two men wanted a joint account. In any case, the bank officer got very nervous—that moment of apprehension turned into a campaign for gfn.com, a gay-oriented financial Web site.

Baim's team posed as gay and lesbian couples at banks and other businesses to try to gauge the reaction of heterosexual employees when they realized a customer was gay and to find out what it felt like from the gay person's perspective. One of the creative people on the team went so far as to "come out" to her parents just to see what the response would be. "Nothing beats the experience of seeing what it's like firsthand, to actually see and feel and hear things," Baim said. "We got 'inside' the gay community."

In addition, gfn.com got a campaign that, close to its breezy, tongue-in-cheek personality, tweaked the straight business community for its "homo-ignorance." "It's not quite as bad as outright homophobia but very subtly different," said GFN founder Walter Shubert, "and it can still make gay consumers uncomfortable." "The ads focused on this two-way discomfort," Baim said, "but in every other way, the ads were very similar in factual content to everyday bank or financial institution ads." If his team hadn't detected this subtle difference, they would have ended up with more stereotypical ads. "A lot of stuff we were coming back with was sort of flamboyant and over the top," Baim said. "It was almost too gay, which tends to happen with a lot of advertising targeted at the homosexual community. The community wouldn't have welcomed it, and we also wanted ads that would be embraced by everybody."

Focus Groups. Focus groups remain one of the most commonly used qualitative research methods. A group can vary in size from six to a dozen people and should be made up of people in the target audience. A moderator encourages everyone to speak and tries to keep the conversation on track. The goal is to record the group's feelings and opinions about your brand, the competition, and the product category. These sessions are often conducted in research facilities where interview rooms can be viewed by client or agency personnel through a one-way mirror.

The big idea for the "Got Milk?" campaign for the California Milk Processors Board came from a focus group. The agency knew that 90 percent of milk consumption was in the home, so they asked participants to stop using milk for a week and to keep a diary of everything they ate and drank. At the end of the research, people said they did not realize how much they missed having milk to complement foods they typically enjoyed with milk. The ensuing print and television spots reminded people to keep milk in the house and offered lots of appealing must-have-milk situations, resulting in an increase in milk consumption.[15]

Focus groups are often asked to try out a product as well. Cindy Tsai, an assistant account executive at Foote, Cone & Belding in Chicago, has witnessed numerous focus groups. Her accounts for SC Johnson include Shout, which recently introduced the Color Catcher—a washcloth designed to work like a sponge to absorb and trap loose dyes in the wash so that they can't be redeposited on other clothes. "Loose dyes are always present in the wash," Tsai explained, "and they either redeposit or wash away. This doesn't mean your blue shirt dye will turn your yellow shirt green if you happen to mix them up in the wash, but that your shirts will just fade and look a little weary over time." The Color Catcher is designed to keep colors vibrant and whites bright. The problem, quickly identified in the first set of focus groups, was that consumers didn't think it was a problem in the first place. Said Tsai:

> You have these stay-at-home moms and they were like, "oh, well, I sort *very* well. I don't need this product. It might be for my boy who is just starting college, but I don't need it." We realized it was an educational issue. You have to tell people, no matter how well you sort, the loose dyes come in the water, they redeposit, etc. But we know they are not going to want to hear that they need it because they say they are great sorters. So it became: "no matter how well you sort…you still need it." This insight came out of the focus group.[16]

The group was sent to test the product and came back believers. "They needed to try it, take the sheet out of the washer and see that it was not the color that it went in as," Tsai said. "The whole idea is, the proof is on the sheet. No one would believe it." Apparently it was so unbelievable that when the storyboard concepts were tested in more focus groups, to Tsai's surprise, the testimonial version topped the demonstration one. "We had great demos, but I guess it is just so unbelievable to the typical stay-at-home mom. They were like, 'hmmm, you are just making it look like that,' but when they heard a real woman say it, they were like, 'oh, okay, it must really work.'"

Observations.   It's one thing to talk to people about a product; it's another to watch them use it in their daily lives. Anderson, the planner from DDB, does this for Hasbro. They pay moms an incentive and follow them throughout the day, from the time the kids wake up through pick up at day care. Afterwards, it's a trip to the toy store. "Then we could see really who had the pull, how the purchase decision was made, what were the toys the child went to right off the bat," Anderson said. "That's really where you get your richest research because when you are in a focus group room, it's very clinical. Everybody knows that there are people on the other side of the mirror."

Interviews.   Sweeney, the ad man on the corn combine, agrees, which is why he prefers focus groups for pretesting of ads. Otherwise he would rather interview people where they are most comfortable—in their home, their car, their local diner. He simply tells people he works for an ad agency and it's his job, as the insight guy, to understand people. He doesn't start the conversation by firing questions about his product.

For a project he did for Jiffy Lube, the oil change company, he went to a house in southern New Jersey and interviewed a woman and four of her friends. Said Sweeney:

> When I do in-home discussions, I will spend two hours talking to them about stuff and I may spend the first forty-five minutes to an hour about whatever they want to talk about, not about the product, because I want to find out, again, context. What are their lives like? What's important to them? What's not important to them? What pisses them off? What makes them happy? And from there, by asking the right questions, or provocative questions, I can get them talking about a specific category without them really knowing that I'm doing that. And then they start talking about that category, but because they feel like they're leading the discussion, it's much more natural.

So Sweeney first learned a lot about these women's lives, kids, and homes, and eventually he asked them what was valuable in their life at that moment. One woman said it was her new house, another said a piece of art that was a gift, and a third mentioned jewelry passed down from her great-grandmother. Finally, the last person, while qualifying it wasn't as important as the other items mentioned, said her car was in the shop that day and she realized just how valuable it was.

"Bam. For the next hour and forty-five minutes we are talking about cars. We talked about tune-ups, brake fluid, transmission fluid, mechanics, everything," Sweeney said. When the homeowner said she checked her own fluids, Sweeney didn't believe it, and said so. After all of them marched into her garage, it turned out she knew every dipstick and every level. When they got back upstairs, Sweeney thanked them for their time, but the women were shocked and apologetic, feeling like they had just gabbed away the afternoon and not talked about anything useful to Sweeney, which was the opposite case.

Projective Techniques.   Using projective techniques, researchers ask respondents to draw, tell stories, finish sentences, make collages, play word-association games; or compare companies with animals, colors, cities, or other descriptors. When a direct line of questioning comes to a standstill, these techniques can help consumers articulate how they feel. Through six months of interviews, which included some projective techniques, Anderson was able to glean some insights for the New York Lottery.

The eventual Lotto campaign included regular New Yorkers in different occupations attempting to sing "If I Had a Million Dollars," a song by the Barenaked Ladies. It's humorous and folksy, because most people in the spots cannot sing particularly well, but they appear to have a great time trying. During the research, DDB was trying to distinguish between Lotto, the in-state jackpot game that has had jackpots as high as $90 million, and a newer game called Mega Millions—a multi-state game with the potential to reach jackpots of $500 million or higher. Would people play both or switch to the higher-paying jackpot? Anderson asked people how they would spend $10 million, and invariably, the answers came back the same: pay off debts, save for the kids' education, buy a house and a boat. And that was it. "It was easy for people to spend, especially when everybody knows that half of it goes to taxes," Anderson said. "So Lotto became very much about real people and real dreams, which is why you see average-looking people singing that song. It's just kind of down-home New York."

When asked about Mega Millions, people would start with the same list and then stop. They couldn't think of anything else. Then they were asked, "If Lotto were a car what would it be?" The answer: a limousine or a Lexus. For Mega Millions?: "People would come up with these exotic cars, like a Bentley. I mean how many Bentleys do you see? You can see a Lexus. They drive around. It was definitely this insight that people felt like it was something kind of unattainable, so rare, and so kind of out there."

The campaign theme based on that research became Dream Bigger. "We really thought it was fun to think that if these people are getting stuck, what if we challenged them to take their dreams to the next level?" Anderson explained:

> While you're sitting here thinking about all these things you would have, it's not about having a house in France, it's about *owning* the south of France. It was a really interesting insight just to see that people couldn't spend that amount of money; it almost stumped people, it was an astronomical amount.

Dig Down

Sometimes there is an "aha" moment in advertising research; sometimes there isn't. All the ad professionals interviewed for this chapter said it's a process of revisiting the secondary data and replaying the videotapes and transcripts of the primary research to gather that insight. Cautions Anderson:

> There's always something under what people are saying. There's a difference between an observation and an insight. So when we go and watch people, the insight isn't that teen girls like to buy makeup, it's that teen girls are especially self-conscious at that age and so they feel they have to buy makeup in order to either look older, or fit in, or be prettier. There's always a psychological thing behind every doing.

It's up to the planner or account exec to synthesize that moment to make the selling proposition in the strategy truly inspirational. Anderson said:

> Most people can't verbalize what's going to be that proposition on your piece of paper. Every once in a while, you'll be in a focus group and somebody will say something so brilliant and you'll be so excited because that was it. That doesn't happen very often at all. It's really a lot of analysis and looking back at the secondary data and the research of talking to people, and kind of digging and finding it yourself.

SUMMARY

Marketing research starts with a situation analysis. Marketers conduct research on their own product, consumers' attitudes about the product, the potential market segment, and the primary competition. This information and analysis foundation is used to guide further advertising-specific research. Advertising research is a subset of marketing research and is broken into two parts: strategic advertising research and evaluative advertising research.

Strategic advertising research is done before the ads run, during the planning and development stage. It focuses on clearly defining the target audience and identifying the best message to reach that audience. It also involves matching target audience characteristics to the appropriate media type and media vehicle that will reach the target in a cost-effective manner.

Evaluative advertising research monitors the effectiveness of the ads after they have run. It tests recognition and recall of the brand and whether the campaign has inspired the target audience to do whatever the objective was: become aware of the product, try it, buy it more frequently, seek more information, and so on. Evaluative research also includes an assessment of the effectiveness of the media plan.

Once a marketer decides to use an advertising agency, the agency can help with all areas of research. At a full-service agency, there are typically four main areas: creative, research, media, and account management, plus an office management/human resources function. An account planner, a relatively new position, is often part of the research team and is charged with finding the consumer insight that fuels the advertising strategy.

The strategy explains the target audience and identifies the "big idea"—the best way to sell the product. This one-page document, written by either an account manager or a planner, is given to a copywriter–art director team who in turn comes up with the ideas and executions to turn into a campaign. The media planners and buyers develop the media plan and place the ads. The account manager is the primary client contact and makes sure all agency team members are on the same page, meet deadlines, and make budget.

To find the big idea requires insight into the consumer. This means understanding the context of consumers' lives, not simply stating that heavy users of mayonnaise are women, age 25 to 44 who have 2.5 children. Both quantitative and qualitative research is used to identify the target audience and to gain some insight into their lives. Quantitative research involves the gathering, processing, and interpretation of numerical data, ideally projectible to the general population from a random sample. Qualitative research is typically conducted in a relatively short period of time among relatively small, nonrandom samples.

A sweep of secondary sources is the best way to start gathering insight. Secondary research is research based on other resources; primary research is where you generate your own results. For advertising purposes, secondary sources include Simmons and MRI, VALS, market guides, business and consumer periodicals, trade publications, and government sources. Primary research, while expensive, often leads to that elusive nugget of information needed to develop great advertising. Primary methods of research include quantitative measures, such as surveys and experiments, as well as qualitative methods such as personal experience, focus groups, observations, interviews, and projective techniques.

DISCUSSION QUESTIONS

Lisa Fortini-Campbell wrote an excellent book, *Hitting the Sweet Spot: How Consumer Insights Can Inspire Better Marketing and Advertising.* In it she details lots of hands-on ways to become a "good consumer detective." We adapted some of her exercises here.

1. Go to a large grocery store and buy something inexpensive such as a candy bar, a bag of chips, a bottle of shampoo or deodorant, or a box of cereal. Notice everything you can about your purchasing process, the grocery aisle, and the variety of brands. Why did you pick the brand you eventually chose? Go home and use the product...slowly. Pay attention to what you are doing every second, how you're feeling, and what you're thinking as you use it. Everyone knows the best way to eat an Oreo cookie is inside out, and Nabisco's ad agency reminds us constantly! What small details do you notice as you use your product? Was there some part of the process that really captured the feeling of the whole experience?

2. Use your hometown's zip code and then pick a zip code for a city in another part of the country; if you're stuck, go to *www.usps.com/ncsc/lookups/lookup_ctystzip.html* and look up the zip code for a city you're interested in. Using secondary sources, find out the basic demographics of both zip codes. What's different? What's similar? What can you find out about the lifestyles of each geographic area?

3. Collect a few ads for a single product or service. Is the target audience evident based on these ads? (Don't base this solely on the ad placement; a flawed media plan can result in faulty logic.) Can you figure out what the intended strategy is? Is a problem demonstrated in the ad, and is a solution shown? Can you identify the product's features and benefits? Go "up the ladder" and figure out the consumer benefit: At what point on the ladder does the ad focus?

4. Pick a product and find a member of the target audience. (You may need to consult Simmons or MRI if you're not sure.) Now ask the person in the target audience if you can observe him using the product. For instance, watch a mom feed baby food to her child or give her a bath. Watch a man shave. Watch someone clean the kitty litter; okay, that's a little gross...how about watch someone feed the dog?

5. Spend time with a latchkey kid when he gets home from school: What does he eat? How much? What gets turned on first—the computer, the TV, the Xbox? What do you notice? Did anything surprise you? If you were to write a strategy about a product he had used, is there an insight you can use to help fuel the strategy? Can you boil it down to one sentence?

RECOMMENDED READINGS

Abrams, Bill. *Observational Research Handbook: Understanding How Consumers Live with Your Product.* New York: McGraw Hill/NTC Books, 2000.

Bendinger, Bruce. *The Copy Workshop Workbook.* Chicago: The Copy Workshop, 1993.

Fortini-Campbell, Lisa. *Hitting the Sweet Spot: How Consumer Insights Can Inspire Better Marketing and Advertising.* Chicago: The Copy Workshop, 1992.

Goebert, Bonnie, and Herma Rosenthal. *Beyond Listening: Learning the Secret Language of Focus Groups.* New York: John Wiley & Sons, 2001.

Haley, Eric, Margaret A. Morrison, Kim Sheehan, and Ronald E. Taylor. *Using Qualitative Research in Advertising: Strategies, Techniques and Applications.* Newbury Park, CA: Sage Publications, 2002.

Jewler, Jerry, and Bonnie Drewniany. *Creative Strategy in Advertising.* Belmont, CA: Wadsworth, 2001.

Morgan, Adam. *Eating the Big Fish: How Challenger Brands Can Compete Against Brand Leaders.* New York: John Wiley & Sons, 1999.

Ogilvy, David. *Ogilvy on Advertising.* New York: Vintage Books, 1985.

Steel, Jon. *Truth, Lies and Advertising: The Art of Account Planning.* New York: John Wiley & Sons, 1998.

Sullivan, Luke. *Hey Whipple, Squeeze This: A Guide to Creating Great Ads.* New York: John Wiley & Sons, 1998.

Sutherland, Max, and Alice K. Sylvester. *Advertising and the Mind of the Consumer.* Crows Nest, Australia: Allen & Unwin, 2000.

NOTES

1. Phone interview with Mike Sweeney conducted by the authors, August 29, 2002.

2. Vanden Bergh, Bruce G. Katz, and Helen Katz. *Advertising Principles,* p. 218. Chicago: NTC Publishing Group, 1999.

3. Example information gathered from: Thompson, Stephanie. "As Fat Fight Rages, Frito Battles Back." *Advertising Age* (September 2, 2002), p. 1.

4. MacArthur, Kate. "Food Makers Weigh in with Ads," *Advertising Age* (September 2, 2002), p. 27.

5. "The VALS™ Segments," available at *http://www.sric-bi.com/VALS/types.shtml* (accessed October 26, 2002).

6. Goetzl, David, and Wayne Friedman. "*Friends* Tops Ad Price List," *Advertising Age* (September 30, 2002), p. 1.

7. "Top 20 Primetime Series by Households," available at *http://tv.zap2it.com/news/ratings/season/020922season.html* and *http://tv.zap2it.com/news/ratings/season/021006season.html* (accessed September 30, 2002).

8. Goetzl and Friedman, p. 58.

9. Jewler and Drewniany, p. 80.

10. Bendinger, p. 116.

11. Phone interview with Crystal Anderson conducted by authors, September 4, 2002.

12. Herek, Gregory M. "A Brief Introduction to Sampling," available at *http://psychology.ucdavis.edu/rainbow/html/fact_sample.html* (accessed September 5, 2002).

13. Bendinger, p. 539.

14. Example information taken from "GFN.com Wins with Gay Consumers," *Thompson Financial Media* (April 10, 2001), available at *http://www.gaywired.com/index.cfm?linkPage=/storydetail.cfm&Section=13&ID=4457* (accessed September 1, 2002).

15. Vanden Bergh, Katz, and Katz, p. 39.

16. Phone interview with Cindy Tsai conducted by authors, August 23, 2002.

CHAPTER FOUR

CREATIVE DEVELOPMENT

Long before Ogilvy & Mather, IBM's new (in 1994) agency, came up with what became known as the Subtitles campaign and was preparing to pitch the concept and its director choice to the client, the IBM marketing team knew what it wanted. They just hadn't seen it yet. Roy Schecter, an advertising brand producer at IBM headquarters in Armonk, New York, had been part of the client team that had defined the message IBM wanted—no, *needed*—to get out there.

The company had hit hard times. Young competitors in Silicon Valley were outperforming IBM in markets the company had dominated for more than thirty years. Some analysts thought it was time for IBM to break itself up—sell unprofitable parts and focus on a few core enterprises. But that's not what Lou Gerstner, IBM's new CEO,[1] had in mind. "Gerstner saw that IBM's *strength* was in the diversity of its product lines and its global reach. As a former IBM customer at American Express, he knew that what consumers really wanted was somebody who could put together the whole package for them," said IBM's Schecter. Far from breaking the company up, Gerstner wanted the company reunited under one, strong brand: "He told us to put IBM back on the map."

One of the first things they did was unify the advertising under one roof. IBM fired more than forty agencies that had been working for various units all over the world to create advertising for individual products or services with almost no central theme. The cacophony of voices and advertising messages had created confusion about the brand. Ogilvy & Mather, which had developed a strong relationship with Gerstner while he was at American Express, got the IBM account. "With the new agency, we did all kinds of focus groups with consumers to find out what they thought of IBM. We found that we were becoming irrelevant to them. The word 'dinosaur' kept coming up," Schecter said. People not only thought IBM was big and slow, but that it was also bureaucratic, arrogant, antiquated, and out of touch.

Schecter and his colleagues worked on the strategy; their research showed that the strength of the brand was in the company's size and scope, and in its depth and breadth of offerings. They also had to dispel the belief among consumers that IBM was cold and corporate and out of touch with ordinary people. Ogilvy & Mather had to show the global reach of IBM, while at the same time humanize the company. "The big assignment for us was to create a brand campaign for IBM that could be used around the world," said Schecter. "It had to work everywhere. That was the brief we gave to the agency."

The Ogilvy team came back with three concepts; one of them stood out from the others—Subtitles. It featured people in foreign countries, who, by virtue of how they looked

FIGURES 4.1 AND FIGURE 4.2 The "French Guys" and "Italian Farmer" spots were part of a pool of commercials directed by Leslie Dektor for Ogilvy & Mather and its client, IBM. These spots helped to warm up the IBM brand after consumer research told the company that people thought it was cold and out of touch.

Courtesy of IBM, Inc., and Ogilvy & Mather. Reprinted with permission.

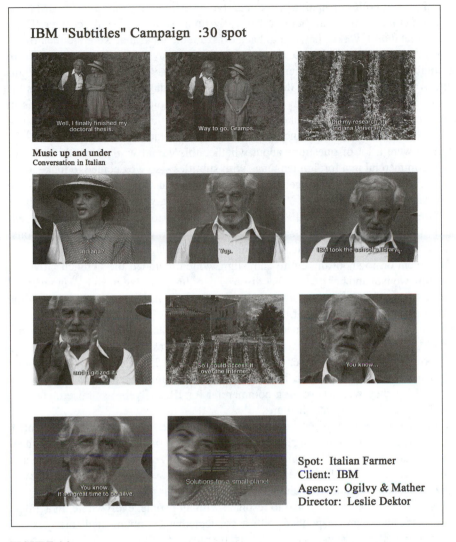

IBM "Subtitles" Campaign :30 spot

Well, I finally finished my doctoral thesis.

Way to go, Gramps.

Did my research at Indiana University.

Music up and under
Conversation in Italian

Indiana?

Yup.

IBM took the school's library,

and digitized it.

So I could access it over the Internet.

You know...

You know... It's a great time to be alive.

Solutions for a small planet

Spot: Italian Farmer
Client: IBM
Agency: Ogilvy & Mather
Director: Leslie Dektor

FIGURE 4.2

and where they lived or worked, were unlikely users of information technology. Surprisingly, though, they looked to IBM for solutions to their problems. "We tested the scripts with consumers in focus groups," said Schecter, "and that's where the tag line came from. Somebody in one of the focus groups came up with it."—"Solutions for a small planet."

The focus groups helped the agency zero in on specific scripts and story ideas that would get the message across—a company with global reach, but with a human touch. Establishing the right tone was crucial. One of the original scripts featured trapeze artists swinging through the air while discussing an IBM product whenever they sort of passed by in mid-air. While humorous, focus groups thought it came across like burlesque. It crossed over the line between the unlikely and the absurd. "No one claimed or thought that the situations [in the Subtitles campaign] were *real,* but our target audience allows IBM to be witty and sometimes whimsical, but never broadly funny or goofy," said Schecter. There were others that didn't work. They had to back off from the ideas that were too theatrical.

The first script they decided to do was the "French Guys" spot (see Figure 4.1). In this commercial, two older Frenchmen, who look like they may have been resistance fighters during World War II, walk along the Seine on a quiet Sunday morning, and one tells the other about a new IBM storage drive that uses laser technology. Their discussion is in French, with English subtitles that take liberties with the translation. When the Frenchman, amazed by IBM technology, says "Incroyable," the subtitle reads "Cool!"

"There were a lot of questions about whether this would work. Nobody had ever done it—a commercial in a foreign language with subtitles—so we decided to make a test commercial," said Schecter. The agency hired a small production company and shot the spot in Bryant Park, near the New York City public library, with two actors who spoke French. "We shot it, and it worked! The agency showed it to people and they laughed! They said, 'Oh, this is delightful!'" said Schecter. "And there was actually some nervousness that when we shot the real thing, it wouldn't be as good!"

They went on to shoot the entire campaign, which included the "French Guys" in Paris, a young woman and her grandfather discussing online learning in an Italian vineyard (see Figure 4.2), and a group of nuns talking about IBM's new operating system while walking to mass in a Prague convent.

The commercials were very successful, in the United States as well as in other parts of the world where the spots ran. At one point, Schecter was with the film company in Thailand preparing to shoot another Subtitles commercial. He was sitting in the hotel lounge when a tourist nearby asked him what he and the filmmakers were doing there. Schecter told her they were shooting a commercial for IBM. Eyebrows raised, she told him, "You'll never do better than the nuns."

Some time between writing the brief describing what IBM needed to accomplish with its advertising and focus-testing a number of potential scripts, something almost magical happened at the agency. The commercial concept was *created.* The creative director, writer, and art director at Ogilvy & Mather had a brief to start with—IBM needed to leverage its size and scope, and breadth and depth, while portraying itself as warm and *human* to the consumer. The concept also had to resonate with all people, everywhere, in a global market. The creative team responded with a concept that communicated this message almost perfectly with words and visuals. This is, literally, a textbook example of creativity in the service of solving a specific communication problem.

This chapter describes creative development at the agency, where, in case after case, day after day, this magic moment occurs. We cover the people involved in the creative process, and the methods they use to arrive at concepts and themes that carry the client's message.

In this chapter, you will learn the following:

- Who is on the creative team at the agency and what their roles and responsibilities are
- The importance of understanding the client's product and brand, marketing goals, target market, and the marketing message the commercial must deliver
- How the creatives use advertising research and add their own inspiration, intuition, and an innate talent for communicating it

- How to arrive at the creative concept and theme and the ways of expressing it with copy, art, storyboards, and animatics
- Focus group testing the concept and then modifying it based on input from focus groups
- The client pitch meeting, in which the concept is "sold" to the client

THE CREATIVE TEAM

At advertising agencies, the creative team's task is to take the basic message that the client's marketing strategy defines for the brand and develop an advertising concept and theme to carry the message to the target audience. Their job is to come up with the big idea—the basic creative approach—that serves the client's need, or, more accurately, *solves the client's problem.* This is a very important notion—perhaps, the most important thing to understand about advertising and creativity. Jeremy Bullmore, long-time advertising creative executive, goes so far as to say:

> The word creative is a dodgy one. It deflects the mind dangerously towards the fine arts—and advertising has nothing to do with the fine arts.... In the creation of a work of art, there is no problem to be solved, even though creation may be inspired by the existence of a problem. In scientific thought, and in the creation of advertising, there always is—either a problem to be solved or a task to be undertaken.[2]

Creatives may bristle at this, but he's not saying there's no art in advertising. Bullmore suggests there's more *directive* in its making and it must have measurable results.

At every agency, big and small, there is at least one creative person tasked with creating the concept for the client. In small local agencies, the owner may be the producer, media buyer, creative director, writer, and art director all rolled into one. But at most medium-size to large agencies, there is a team of creative people who work on a brand or product together, each bringing to the effort his special talent or gift. Typically, the creative team is headed by the creative director, who is joined by a writer and an art director.

Remember that the typical creative team develops advertising concepts for all media—print, transit, outdoor, Internet, as well as broadcast. Some teams (or team members) specialize in certain media. This chapter focuses on the team as it develops broadcast spots. Working alongside the creative team is the account executive who represents the interests of the client within the agency, the account planner, as discussed in the previous chapter, and the broadcast producer who will manage the production later. The account executive knows the client and its product inside out and helps to keep the creative team focused. The account executive, the account planner, and the producer often play the role of sounding boards for the ideas that originate with the creative team.

The Creative Director

The creative director is usually the senior member of the team, if not in age and experience at least in terms of her ability to motivate and to steer the team in the direction it should be

February 1, 2001

LUBRIDERM
TV :30
"WORKOUT"
VISUAL TREATMENT

We open on a workout club; spacious upscale, high key in color palate.
Soft tones with lots of light streaming in. The spot should indicate morning light.

Equipment will be state of the art, shiny metallic or white. We see attractive
women approximately 30 years of age, in good shape wearing aerobic outfits,
doing arm lifts, and getting a massage. Other women are in the background doing
various exercises. We reveal the gator in each scene doing the same exercise as
the women. (ie., getting a massage, doing arm lifts, using a treadmill.) The gator
is in on the joke. As camera pans the massage area, she could wink to camera or
roll her eyes in gator ecstasy.

A series of product shots and application shots follow. The areas to be covered in
application are the backs of arms, (triceps area), hips and upper thigh. Supers will
also occur in this sequence.

We finally cut back to gator on a treadmill as we iris out to white and bring up the
label.

The tone of this commercial should be smart with a light smile. It is not a comedy
but we should not take ourselves too seriously.

The music should be fun, contemporary and in style, but different and introductory.

FIGURE 4.3   At an early stage in creative development, a treatment, or story, for the
commercial is written. This text is for the Lubriderm "Treadmill" commercial created by
J. Walter Thompson for its client, Pfizer, Inc.

Courtesy of Pfizer, Inc., permission granted by J. Walter Thompson U.S.A., as agent of Pfizer.

headed and to recognize and to amplify ideas that show promise. The creative director is often multitalented—she can write, draw, articulate, and communicate. The creative director typically pitches the concept to the client after the team creates the presentation materials—script, storyboard, and perhaps an animatic.

The Writer

The writer is very often, in fact most of the time, the person who comes up with the idea in the first place. At the earliest stage, what the writer writes is the *concept,* which suggests a thematic approach (slice-of-life or testimonial, for example) but doesn't yet have specifics—actors, settings, dialogue. When the concept is more fully polished, it consists of what the audience will see and what it will hear; the writer puts this in the form of a *treatment* (see Figure 4.3)—a story that describes the spot as a viewer will see it. Later, she may structure it into a two-column script, which has the visual ideas on the left and the audio script on the right.

The Art Director

The art director has drawing and illustration skills and can visualize what the writer has come up with. When there is only a rough concept, she may make some quick concept sketches that bring the idea to life, making it possible to "socialize" the concept with other members of the team, the account executive, and the brand manager. As the concept becomes a story, the art director draws the *storyboard*—a series of drawings (perhaps photographs) that suggest the action and flow of shots and scenes for the commercial. Eventually, the storyboard will be pitched to the client and used to get bids from production companies and other contractors.

Are there always these roles, and does the writer always come up with the idea? No. Creative teams come in all shapes and sizes, and there is quite a bit of crossover on roles. Many creative directors are writers or artists, or both. Sometimes, that's why they *are* the creative directors. Sometimes it's the art director who just holds up a drawing or sketch and says, "How about this?" Sometimes the creative idea comes from somebody's spouse over dinner.

Creative teams work in a myriad of ways. Sometimes they have brainstorming sessions in which all ideas are brought up, tossed around, discarded, or embellished. At other times, the writer comes into a meeting with three or four specific ideas and the team spends time evaluating each one, narrowing the choices down to one or two. There are times when the creative team has complete freedom to come up with a brand new concept, and other times when there are strict parameters. The client may have a long-term arrangement with a particular celebrity, or a cross-promotional deal with another company, or a mascot that must be used in commercials. Far from feeling as though their hands are tied, most advertising people see creative challenges in working within these kinds of constraints and rise to the occasion.

■ ■ ■ ■ ■ ▬▬▬▬

PROFILE OF A WRITER: DANIELLE TESCHNER

Danielle Teschner started her advertising career in 2001 as a creative assistant at D'Arcy in New York. This is a fairly common career path for large agencies' creatives who typically spend about a year as an assistant before moving up to a copywriter position. Dani was promoted after nine months and soon thereafter got her first television assignment. Her description of the process, from strategy to production, follows.

In April 2002, after nine months of being a creative assistant, I was promoted to junior copywriter. My new art director and I started working together, and we got along great; lucky for us, there was a ridiculous amount of work to be done. So much work, that our creative directors passed one of their assignments on to us.

It was for television. My partner and I couldn't wait. We had to create a :30 spot for a cough medicine. Hardly a glamorous assignment, but we knew we had some room to play with—in the past, the brand's ads have always been funny.

We met with the account team for a briefing. They explained the brand character, target audience, product benefits, and reasons to believe why the product works. But what we really took away from the meeting was to tell moms, ages 25 to 54, to buy our cough medicine instead of the competition because ours lasts twice as long.

This was by far the most grueling part. The "big idea" came pretty easily—a cough is intrusive to you and the people around you. Executions were another story. My partner and I presented scenario after scenario to our creative directors—anywhere from 10 to 15 executions at a time. They liked pieces of some. Hated others. Then, they sent us back to think of more. That cycle went on for more than three weeks. We had ideas with nuns, astronauts, sleeping bags, and Amish people. All to sell cough medicine to moms. But that's what it took to get down to the few ideas we'd eventually present.

We finally fleshed out three scripts to show the account team. They checked to see that the creative idea communicated the strategy, that the benefit to the consumer was obvious. And, that all the mandatory elements of the brief were there—for example, the competitive comparison, the product benefits, and so on. Then, it was time to present the work to the client.

All three executions went to the meeting. Each spot was laid out in storyboard format—a series of basic drawings lined up with the respective parts of the script. One execution took place on a boat, one in an RV, and the third on a waterbed. We knew the first two were "leaps" for the client, but we also knew they pushed the brand to a fresh, new place. The waterbed spot was funny and believable, but closer to the work done for the brand in the past.

The clients bought the work they felt was safe. And we sold our first commercial.

After a few rounds of storyboard revisions, we started preproduction. My agency has an internal production department, so my partner and I were paired up with a producer. She showed us directors' reels and helped us narrow our list down to two. We met with both directors to talk through our boards. One director wanted to dramatize the effect of the cough. The other wanted to keep it realistic. One wrote copy to add to the spot, the other presented a storyboard with camera angles we'd never imagined. I was completely impressed by what they brought to the spots. It wasn't an easy decision, but we finally chose one director and awarded him the job.

Then, the meetings began. Constant meetings to discuss progress, details, and when to have more meetings. The one I remember most was the pre-bid. It's the last meeting before the shoot that involves the client, director, creatives, and account people. It's one of the few opportunities for everyone to get together and voice opinions, concerns, and expectations about all aspects of the commercial. We discussed the overall look of the spot, the kind of people we want to cast, music, location (Los Angeles!), wardrobe, set design—all of the details. But the most important reason to have the meeting was to prevent confusion and misunderstandings when on location.

Casting began immediately after the pre-bid. Talent agencies out West called in hundreds of hopefuls. Auditions were recorded and shipped to us in New York every day, for four days straight. We spent two hours a day watching tapes. A few auditions stuck out. Most didn't. We chose our favorites, got approvals, and packed our bags. It was June. And it was time to shoot.

A total of five spots were being shot. My partner and I had one, our creative directors, the other four. We flew out a week later than everyone else, landed at LAX, checked into our Santa Monica hotel, and drove to Universal Studios for the pre-light. Our passes waited for us at the gate.

What was more amazing than my pass into Universal Studios was seeing our set for the first time. In person. It wasn't a marker drawing on an 8-½ by 11 sheet of paper anymore. It was real. And I was in LA, standing in front of it.

The next morning, we got to the set at 7 A.M. The crew had been there for an hour, setting up. Our talent was ready. The director knew it was our first shoot, and invited us to sit with him, right in front. On my lap was the three-page storyboard we'd created in the office. In front of me, it was all coming to life.

We were on the set for fourteen hours that day. I was in awe the whole time. It was the most amazing thing to watch: twenty-five crew members clutching lights, microphones, and cameras to capture everything on the set. Everyone there was contributing to the little idea we brought with us from New York. And we could tell from the constant laughs that everyone was having a great time.

At the end of the day, one of our creative directors told us, "It's gonna be a great spot." Then he laughed, "Just don't fuck it up in editing."

Hopefully, we didn't. After countless cab rides to the editor, presentations to the client, and a few weeks of extremely successful testing, my partner and I finished our first :30 spot. And, we're both really proud of our 30-second reel.

CREATIVE CONCEPT STARTING POINTS

This section elaborates on those things that guide the creative team as it solves the client's problem. You could think of these as the raw materials from which a creative concept is fashioned. The creative team cannot even think of getting started unless and until it understands the client, as well as its marketing goals and objectives and its marketing strategy. The marketing strategy defines the key message that the commercial must deliver, and the creative team must know what that is. It must become familiar with the brand and product, and the target market. Only then can the creative team begin the process of developing the creative concept, the theme, and a specific story for the commercial.

Class Exercise: Stop and Think

There is a danger in mistaking advertising for entertainment. It can be entertaining and, often, is quite enthralling, but entertainment should be an outcome, not a goal, of creating the commercial concept. During a course one of the authors cotaught called "Designing and Producing the Television Commercial," a group of film students tasked with coming up with a creative concept for a PSA to promote voting presented their idea. They chose as their target audience youth aged 18 to 24. They suggested that the spots run on FOX, MTV, VH1, and other youth-oriented cable channels. Their concept, which they storyboarded and presented to the rest of the class, was to portray a number of "typical voters" in very unflattering ways—doddering old people, bikers, gap-toothed hillbillies, skin heads. They were to be shown clumsily filling out ballots, mindlessly delighted with their choices. The tag line at the end was something like, "Do you really want these people running the country? Get out and vote." The professors raised various objections to this idea, as did many in the class, but the students presenting it protested saying, "But it's *funny.*"

Take a moment to think about this concept. What kind of research would it be appropriate to do about voting? About voters? About the target audience? Is the word *funny* an apt description of the concept? If the goal is to encourage voting, would this concept be effective?

Understanding the Client

In the class exercise here, we described a creative concept arrived at by students who clearly did not understand their clients—democracy, popular rule, and the right to vote. One of the most treasured and solemn rituals in our country, one for which people willingly gave their lives, is teased as something only boobs and bozos do. Not only does this concept insult those who do vote, but it also strips the act of voting of the seriousness with which it must be taken and of the dignity that it provides to avid voters. Even if, by some miracle, it managed to raise the voting numbers among 18- to 24-year-olds from the rock-bottom percentage of 27 percent of eligible voters in that age group, it will have tarnished the whole concept of voting and the spirit of national respect and unity it traditionally promotes. Is the client served by this?

In chapter one, we said that there is a difference between selling ads and image ads, but here we will amend that notion slightly to say that all advertising affects the image of the client. Therefore, creatives must be sensitive to the image that the client lays claim to, or wishes to establish for itself, in the market. Just like an individual, every client—even a huge corporation like IBM—has a personality and self-image that greatly affects how it wants to be portrayed through its promotion. On the local level, a self-made man who owns and operates a men's clothing establishment that has become an institution in the community has an image to maintain. The new health food store around the corner, run by the hip young couple who hope to lure those with similar lifestyles, has an image to create. Agency creatives cannot possibly get started with concept development until they understand the client in terms of its image—the lasting impression the audience will have of the advertiser whatever else the commercial does.

The Client's Brief

As described in chapter 3, and as you saw in the example at the beginning of this chapter, the client develops a marketing strategy for the brand, which includes the basic message it wants to communicate to the consumer through all of its promotional efforts. When this message is given to the agency to work from, it is called the *brief*. The brief is based on a thorough evaluation of the client's studies, analysis, reports, and market research. It states a *communication problem* the advertising must solve to achieve the client's marketing objectives.

A brief usually has at least the following parts, sometimes more, depending on what the agency needs to work with:

- The rationale for advertising—What is the communication problem we need to solve?
- Who is the target audience—Whom do we need to reach with this message?
- The knowledge gap the advertising must close—What does the audience know? What would we like them to know?
- What is the single most important message—What is the focus for the advertising?
- What will make them believe this message—What can we do to be convincing, believable? What do we have in the way of proof?
- What are the creative guidelines?—What are the parameters for the creative approach?

As the name implies, the creative brief is actually "brief." Plenty of additional information is available to the creative team if they need it, including all the backup research and data that led to the brief in the first place.

The Product and Brand

The client provides the agency with its marketing study, which is full of data and analyses of the product and the brand, and an articulation of the marketing and promotion strategy. We covered much of this in chapters 1 and 3. While conceptualizing the commercial, creatives look carefully at these reports, and generally zero in on the following aspects of the product and the brand:

- *The product's attributes.* Obviously, creatives must start here. What is it about this product that makes it the best choice for the consumer? Is it cheaper? Does it last longer? Is it environmentally friendly? Is it union made? Does it have safety features the others don't? What are its strengths? What are its weaknesses? In the example at the beginning of this chapter, IBM made Ogilvy & Mather aware of what its research said was its brand strength, its size and scope, and its weakness, its coldness. The agency creatives developed a concept that tackled both simultaneously.

- *The competition.* You must know not only your own product, but what it's up against in the struggle for marketshare. What are the strengths and weaknesses of the competition in relation to your product? When trying to get this information from a client, you will never be told that the competition's soft drink tastes better, or that its furniture really does last longer. Typically, you'll hear that consumer *perception* is that the competition is better. Is this an important distinction? Yes. As an agency creative person, there is nothing you can do about competitive reality. Perception is the only thing you can attempt to modify.

- *The brand's history.* Creatives must know where the brand is in its life cycle: how long it has been around, what its marketshare is now, and what the trend seems to show. Is it growing or fading? Why? The creatives may want to leverage a strong brand or, as in the case of IBM, try to reinvent it.

- *The brand's promotional history.* What has been done for this brand in the past, and how well did that creative approach work? What do evaluations of past campaigns say about why the creative was effective, or not? Are there aspects of it that the marketing promotion strategy wants to build on, or do we start with a clean slate?

- *The competitors' promotion.* Creatives must be aware of what key competitors are doing with their advertising, and how well *that* is working. What does their advertising tell you about what their strategy is? Are they trying to position their brand similarly, or are they staking out different "turf"?

The Target Audience

There's a terrific scene in the film *What Women Want,* starring Mel Gibson, in which he plays an advertising executive who must come up with a concept for a new client that sells women's sporting goods. To get into the target market's frame of mind, he takes home some women's products and, in a hilarious routine in his penthouse apartment, he shaves his legs and tries on nylons. His daughter comes home with a friend and isn't at all surprised to see him that way. He's a creative guy, for heaven's sake.

Most creative people at agencies don't go that far, but they do, quite often, become customers of the products they create for, and they do rely on focus tests and other research (see chapter 3) to help them get into the head of the typical prospect. How does the creative use this information? Somewhere in the pile of data about the prospects—the demographic, psychographic, and ethnographic information—is a piece of *knowledge* about what kind of message they would listen to. Or, more accurately, how the message would have to be presented so that they notice it, listen to it, understand it, and remember it. It is the *how* of the message that creatives search for.

Creatives sort through all of this material, and usually see two sets of useful information. The first is the *demographic* of consumers of this particular product—basically, who they are—and the second is all about the relationship consumers have or could have with this product *because* of who they are. In other words, from a creative standpoint, it is insufficient to know that the consumer is of a certain age, sex, income level, educational level, and with or without children. It is much more instructive to know how they see themselves, how they see themselves in relation to others, what their aspirations are, and what role the product could have in support of this sense of self. This is known as the *psychographic* of the consumer.

In actual fact, the first set of data (demographics) may be only tangentially connected to the second (psychographics). For example, there are corporate executives—the target market for retirement plans, vacation homes, a Lexus—who cannot wait for the chance to retire and work for social justice causes. They may still be in the market for golf clubs, but a Craftsman toolbelt for their Saturday morning work project with Habitat for Humanity may also be on their minds, perhaps, even foremost.

There are four things about the target audience that creative people get the most "juice" from—what the consumer *thinks,* how the consumer *feels,* how the consumer *behaves,* and what *motivates* the consumer. Let's study all of these in relation to the product or brand.

What the Consumer Thinks.   Here, you are trying to define the *rational* thoughts the consumer may have toward the brand. Rational thoughts have to do, usually, with actual product features, and how those features meet an actual need. There is logic behind it. The consumer arrives at what he thinks about a product by evaluation, comparison, perhaps his own research—price shopping, Internet searching, word of mouth, reading *Consumer Reports.*

It is important to know what both users and nonusers think of the brand. Interestingly, both groups could think about the brand identically, and use it or not use it for nearly the same reasons. SUVs are a product category that has strong support from one market segment, and strong disapproval from another. Advocates think the SUV is large and roomy, luxurious, full of safety features, and a status symbol. Nonusers think the SUV is large and roomy, luxurious, full of safety features, a status symbol *for others,* has very poor fuel economy, and is hazardous to smaller cars that get in its way.

How the Consumer Feels.   There are a number of parts to this. One thing you're going for here is how does the consumer perceive the brand? Roy Schecter wanted to know what people thought of IBM, and he got an earful about arrogant, out of touch, and irrelevant. Consumers did not necessarily arrive at this by carefully evaluating IBM products, or from actually dealing with the company. The perception came from innumerable messages that left people with a negative *sense* of IBM. Where those messages came from is anybody's guess, but the perception wasn't arrived at *logically,* or necessarily by having firsthand experience with IBM and its products. The perception was an emotional response. The whole marketing strategy was based on turning this perception around. The creatives at Ogilvy & Mather used this information to arrive at a concept that portrayed IBM as homey, connected to average people, and sensitive to the consumers' particular problems.

What are the consumers' perceptions about the actual users of the brand? If the product has a reputation that associates it with a certain demographic, does this turn off certain other segments of the market? Is this perception of the users a detriment to attracting new customers? This is an important issue for certain product categories such as automobiles, cosmetics, and fashions. Oldsmobile had a very difficult time attracting new, young buyers because the brand had become too closely associated with the "older" generation. GM even ran ads with the slogan, "This is not your father's Oldsmobile." For the most part, this didn't work; saying it doesn't make it so. Bombardier, maker of four-wheelers used by outdoorsmen to tool around in the woods, runs ads showing helmeted hunters and fishermen plowing through the forest. In one shot, the rider crashes through some underbrush. One segment of the audience is impressed, another aghast—some Sierra Club members would like to see that guy bounce off a redwood.

The second thing you want to know is how do consumers feel about themselves? What is their self-impression? What is their fantasy? How can the product serve them? In a local commercial for Boom Babies, a retail store that sells vintage clothing and gowns targeted at the young female prom-goer, writer/director A. J. Schultz shot beautiful teens stepping out of a limousine in front of a fancy hotel—all lit up under a bright marquee. Handsome young men escort them into the affair while flashbulbs pop. This is every young girl's fantasy prom. Suddenly, one girl shows up with a horrible dress and poorly chosen shoes and accessories. The photographers look the other way. She's humiliated. This is every young woman's worst nightmare.

Flash backward to the same young woman shopping at Boom Babies, where the helpful staff set her up with the perfect look. Flash forward to prom night. This time she steps out of the limo and she's not only acceptable, she's the *star* (see Figure 4.4). The Boom Babies spot is an excellent example of a commercial that states a problem, then the solution, in a personal situation that the target audience *feels* deeply about.

How the Consumer Behaves.   If the product has been on the market for some time, consumers have already developed some habits about using it. What are those practices? Here, you would want to know about heavy buyers versus occasional buyers, and for what purposes they purchase the product. The main difference between heavy and occasional buyers of a product may be in their behavior—how they use it—rather than in what they think of the product or how they feel about it. You would like to get the occasionals to become heavies.

Is the product an impulse buy, or do people buy it only after careful consideration? Do people buy it for special occasions or for all occasions? You may have a food product that could be eaten every day, but people buy it only for dinner parties. Duck, for example, rarely shows up on family dinner tables except on Christmas. Cranberries and pumpkins are purchased seasonally, though available all year long. What, if anything, can be done about these behaviors?

Do people wait for opportune times because of price or quantity? Do they buy at full price, or wait for discounts? Do they buy in bulk? What are their buying habits? If you can determine what the behavioral differences are between heavy users, occasional users, and nonusers, you often can throw a spotlight on something to spark your creativity.

What Motivates the Consumer?   The key word for creatives while pondering the target market is *motivation*—a driving force that comes from deep within the human psyche. Before you can arrive at a concept to motivate the consumer to buy the product, you may have to know "What motivates the target market to do *anything*?": Is the target market motivated to buy products that make life easier? That make them healthier? Are they concerned with appearances? Hip? Cultured? Intelligent? Rich? Conscientious?

Psychology and the social sciences have produced reams of studies on what motivates people; however, the various theories and conditions are way beyond the scope of this book. But there is at least one important concept for creatives to hang onto: People are

Boom Babies :30 "That Girl"

Techno music up: cut on beat

Quick cuts on attractive teens...

Tilt up on dresses

Red dress

Blue Dress

Green dress

Our girl appears - puffy sleaves, no style.   Music: off tempo

Narr: Don't be *that* girl...

Come to Boom Babies and choose from thousands of gowns in stock..

With sizes from 2 to 24 you can choose the unique style you want...

with the fit you need. With our register and personal brand of

service, you'll be treated

Client: Boom Babies
Writer/Director: A.J. Schultz

like a star.

Boom Babies. Open weekdays 11 to 8 and weekends 12 to 5.

FIGURE 4.4   In this commercial for Boom Babies, a vintage clothing store, writer/director A. J. Schultz captured the fantasy of being a "star" at the prom that many teenage girls have.

Courtesy of Lorraine Koury, Boom Babies, Syracuse, New York. Reprinted with permission.

motivated to buy products to satisfy needs, some of which (as we alluded to earlier) are rational needs, while others are emotional. We all have both real and imagined needs. We have real needs to eat; sleep; go places; and/or have shelter, clothing, and companionship. Our imagined needs define for us what we eat, where we sleep, where we go and how we get there, what kind of house we have, what we wear and how it makes us appear or feel, and who we associate with. Does anybody have a *real* need for a Rolls Royce? A 25,000-

square-foot house? Corinthian leather? The forces of nature motivate us to look after our real needs, while our imagination motivates us to discriminate between various products to satisfy those needs. The most effective advertising speaks to the consumer about satisfying *both* needs.

THE CREATIVE CONCEPT

Now we are at the magic moment when the creative team, armed with all of the material, data, and information about the client, message, brand, and target market, creates a commercial concept. What might the concept look like? In its earliest stage, the creative concept can be just a random thought, which then takes on a life of its own as it "catches fire" with the team and goes through further development.

We weren't there when a creative team member at Ogilvy & Mather came up with the concept that led to the Subtitles campaign, and chances are, those who were would not remember the initial idea. But it's possible it was something like "Ordinary people doing extraordinary things!" That premise, which is the basis for almost every character-driven narrative film, aptly describes what the commercials eventually portrayed. The premise for some celebrity commercials, by the way, is "Extraordinary people doing ordinary things." Of course, there are a number of themes that can be used to get across the idea of ordinary people doing extraordinary things, and we talk about that in the next section. Let's focus here on the premise—the "big idea."

Coming up with the big idea is often a series of mental states that begin with hard work (almost drudgery) and moves on through inspiration, and then intuition. The Sufis, a religious sect long thought to be the mystical branch of Islam, believe that we think and act based on an impetus that comes from our mind, our heart, and our gut. Likewise, the three states of creativity can be thought to take place in these spaces inside of us. We cover these states of creativity next. Remember, the creative concept is the big idea—a very high-level notion of what the commercials could say. The concept gradually gets refined into actual copy and art—specificity in the form of scripts and storyboards—a little later.

The Hard Work of the Mind

Every creative task should probably start here, and many end here. The *hard work* is mentally processing and fully understanding all those things covered in the previous section. Thoroughly knowing your client and its marketing needs, the central message of the marketing communication, the brand and product, the competition, and the target market can be hard, logical, and almost computational in nature. Using this material to create the concept is safe, mitigates risk, and provides creatives with the rationale they will need to sell their concept back to the client. It may not *feel* like creative work to some people. But some creatives need this, and only this, to arrive at a good, workable advertisement for the client—one that serves its needs, solves its problem. Commercials that just lay out the facts (i.e., the rational reasons why you should buy this product instead of the other) often pop out of this stage.

At the very least, the hard-work stage will prevent you from totally missing the mark. It eliminates certain creative concepts and helps creative people focus on those that seem to have some promise. The downside of leaning too heavily on hard work is that it relies too much on an intellectual rather than an emotional exercise. Steven Novick, the vice chairman and chief creative officer at Grey Global Group articulated the downside of relying too much on logic and data during the creative process in an *AdWeek* comment.

■ ■ ■ ■ ■ ▬▬▬

HANDS OFF: HOW NOT TO DRAIN THE LIFE OUT OF YOUR COMMERCIAL

From *AdWeek,* March 11, 2002, p. 12.

by Steve Novick, Vice Chairman/Chief Creative Officer, Grey Global Group

I recently spent several hours in a meeting where we dissected the objective of every frame of a proposed commercial. We identified the angle of every shot, analyzed the import of every word and gesture. By the time we were done, nothing was left to the imagination. And that was exactly the problem.

All the life had been drained out of what might have been a wonderful spot because nothing had been left to chance. And leaving nothing to chance means there will be no spontaneity, no serendipity, no unexpected moment that might lead to an unscripted bit of magic.

I'm concerned that this is becoming a trend. Clients are nervous—and justifiably so—about the economy. They are fearful that their money isn't working hard enough. And to combat anxiety, they are trying to avoid surprises. The popular solution is, "More is more." More discussion, more words, more explanations, more meetings—more control.

But controlling creativity can be counterproductive. Managing, predicting and contriving every image and phrase leaves no room for nuance. I'm not suggesting we go into productions unprepared. But there is a big difference between being prepared and being programmed.

Let's get back to what we're all trying to do in advertising: connect with people. People who have to be persuaded not to tune out when they know a commercial is coming. People who see hundreds of spots a month and thousands a year and are still expected to remember some minute but meaningful detail that will lead them to prefer your product.

But here's the catch: Preference doesn't happen on the left side of the brain—it's based on feeling, not logic. Beating commercials to death with logic won't help them connect.

What creates a connection? It's the little moment that is difficult—no, not just difficult—impossible to script in advance. The lift in a phrase, the pause between words, the moment of suspense before a punch line. It's timing and delivery, it's shades and gradations, it's subtlety. It's the value of what is left unsaid. The pause may speak louder than the words themselves. We'd be smart to take a lesson from the great movie directors who allow the actors time to act.

Not everything can be communicated in words. It's why artists don't talk about painting, they just paint. It's why great singers don't talk about singing, they sing. It's why Tony Bennett, at seventy-five, is a superstar among people who are twenty-five. He has perfected the art of the nuance. Once he's recorded a song, it's hard for anyone else to perform it. Why? The answer is not an explanation: It's an experience.

Advertising must rise to this level if we're going to capture people's hearts and minds. Deconstructing scene objectives and analyzing key visuals may offer direction, but we will

CONTINUED

never enthrall the consumer unless we leave the time and space for the talent to do its magic. That's what infuses a spot with feeling. It's the difference between charm and predictability, between poetry and text. The deft nuance is a bridge to a feeling we cannot plan. And it happens when we leave a few things unsaid.

Inspiration from the Heart

What Novick really writes about is *inspiration,* that voice that rises up from deep within you at the oddest time with the solution to your problem. It comes in the form of a mental image—a picture perhaps—or a deftly turned phrase that becomes the tag line. You must know that inspiration does not spontaneously generate in your mind (or heart), out of thin air. Inspiration, which is a new thought, always originates with old experiences. Novick does not discount the usefulness of research, and data, and hard knowledge about clients, consumers, and brands. What he laments is when all of those foundational elements *become* the creation. He notes that in stressful times we sometimes do not allow the old experiences, the data, to flower into the new idea. We sometimes stop because where we are is so safe.

When we create something new—a recipe, a drawing, an architectural plan, a piece of music, a poem, or a commercial—whether we know it or not or like it or not, we are always building the new thing out of memories. The new creation is always a metaphor—a representation of something we are already familiar with—and what makes it inspirational is when it looks like a metaphor to everybody else, as well. Inspired work is a new construction of old ideas or, as the late Robert Abel, one of the most creative minds in advertising design, used to say: "It reminds people of something they never saw before."

The perfect creative concept—one that solves a client's problem—can happen when creatives fill their minds with the memories that hard work provides, and then allow those memories to "flower" into an inspired idea (see Figure 4.5 for an example of a creative's brainstorming activities). As Leo Burnett said: "Creativity is the art of establishing new and meaningful relationships between previously unrelated things…which somehow present the product in a fresh new light."[4]

Intuition—the Gut Feeling

Intuition usually kicks in when the creative has an inspired thought, verbalizes it (or draws it), and something inside says "Yes, that'll work." If hard work provides the foundational material, and inspiration emerges from that, intuition *confirms* the idea. Whereas inspiration results from cognitive activity that is intensely reflective—the churning and consideration of ideas and concepts—intuition is largely experiential. Intuition is an expert response, usually based on an amalgam of experiences over a fairly long period of time, that requires very little conscious thought, and manifests itself as something we call a *feeling.* For example, one might say, "I had a feeling he would call," or "I had a feeling we'd like this restaurant." We *sense* that it's the right concept. Intuition is every bit as valid as any other stage in the creative process, but it's almost impossible to document and rationalize. No less an authority on

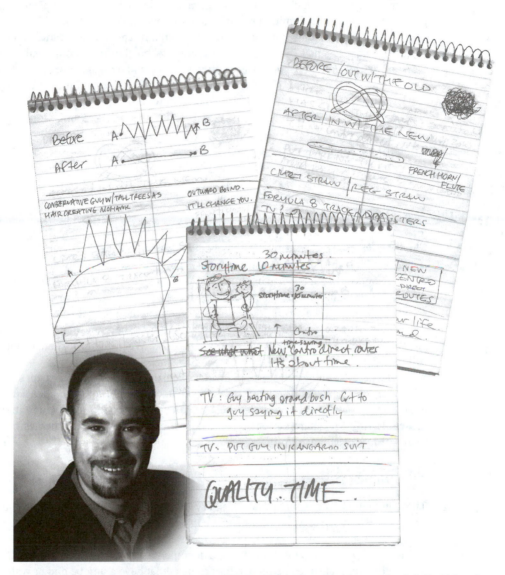

FIGURE 4.5 Creative director/writer Pete VonDerLinn came up with a notebook full of ideas for spots based on the creative brief that Centro was introducing new, direct routes. The creative process often begins with a flurry of ideas, one or two of which often "pop out."

Courtesy of Central New York Regional Transportation Authority and Eric Mower & Associates. Reprinted with permission.

creativity than Albert Einstein said: "The supreme task of the physicist is to arrive at those universal laws from which the cosmos can be built by pure deduction. There is no logical path to these laws; only intuition resting on experience can reach them."[5]

Robert Saxon, long-time agency creative director and later a commercial director, remembers many agency brainstorming sessions when the team could only say, "That's bullshit," in reference to a client's marketing strategy and message, even though it was supported with data and analysis. They would come up with something Saxon describes as "totally off the wall," but what intuition told them was the right approach. There are countless conflicts about creative concepts that arise when *hard work* tells you to go one way with an idea and intuition tells you that's wrong, or vice versa. The best results sometimes come from a synthesis of the two opposing views. Other times, it only has the effect of watering-down a concept or, worse yet, making it incomprehensible.

THE THEME

The creative concept, however it is generated, must take further shape—it must have a *theme,* which is the story of the commercial. That is, the way the concept is to be presented to the audience. In the advertising business, you may hear the word *format* used instead of theme, but format is also used as a "handle" for other things (tape format, file format, etc.), so we prefer to use the word *theme.* In some themes, the product is first and foremost; in others, the people who use it are the most important. There are many, many themes and variations of each, and combinations of two or more. We present the main categories in the following sections.

If a creative at Ogilvy & Mather had in fact suggested that the concept should be "ordinary people doing extraordinary things," consider the myriad of themes such a concept could have shown. Remember, the brief was that IBM needed to leverage its worldwide presence, while humanizing its appearance. All of the commercial themes here have, as their setting, a foreign country.

The Product Demonstration

The commercial could feature an ordinary person in Nairobi, perhaps a small business owner, skillfully using what most people consider a complex software program on an IBM computer system, explaining the system right to the camera. He shows how easy it is to do an inventory; perhaps, it even looks like a documentary film crew is capturing it. The product demonstration theme is effective for products that have a unique and provable attribute, and most of the time the product is the star, not the person using it. You've seen spots for tires, braking systems, Super Glue, vacuum cleaners, and other products or product features—in many of them, you don't even see the talent.

The Product Comparison

An ordinary person in Brazil visits with a friend, who is having a hell of a time getting all of the various parts of her computer system to communicate. Her computer is from Compaq, her printer from Hewlett-Packard, her Zip drive from Iomega, her modem from still another company. She keeps getting "Device not found" messages on her monitor. Her friend says his system is from IBM and that everything is compatible right out of the box.

The comparison theme should only be used when everything shown is provable, including the incompatibility of the other system. In general, it is a lot easier to compare quantifiable features and price than it is to compare performance. "Oh, your computer has only a 10-gigabyte hard drive and you had to pay extra for the monitor?" Here again, the focus is on the product, away from the talent—product features take center stage.

Testimonials

Find real, genuine, ordinary people, and get them to tell their stories to the camera—how IBM saved their hide by getting their computer system for a research project shipped halfway across Finland during a blizzard—and IBM was so nice about it! Testimonials can be very effective, especially when the audience can identify with the talent and the problem. Chapter 3 has a good example of this—the color saver product for which concept testing showed people identified with the user first, not the product. With testimonials and some of the other themes described next, the focus shifts to the talent whose credibility and audience appeal is the primary selling force.

The Presenter

Establish a spokeswoman who talks about the IBM brand, and how its products are being used in a German school to teach immigrant children from North Africa how to speak German. She goes on, one country after another in subsequent commercials, explaining how ordinary people can do extraordinary things with IBM products. The stand-up presenter is one of the earliest, if not *the* earliest commercial theme. During the days of live television, you were pretty much limited to what you could say and do in a small corner of the studio. Today, many products become associated with the presenter, and many presenters actually become minor stars if the commercials "pull" well and are aired for a long period of time. There is, at this writing, a character named "Steven," loosely based on Eddie Haskell of *Leave It to Beaver* fame, who pitches Dell computers. Does he sound familiar to you?

The Celebrity Presenter

The same details apply as in the previous section, but this time the presenter is Lance Armstrong—well known and admired around the world for his triumph over cancer and his victories in the Tour de France. We see him visit the school in Germany and admire young people who are overcoming a language problem by using IBM technology. As we discuss in later chapters, associating your product with a particular celebrity has both pros and cons.

Music Video

We find a current top hit that's also doing well in Europe and Asia, buy the rights, change the lyrics slightly, and produce a music video that shows delighted customers all over the world using our computer systems. In fact, they're *creating* the music video on their computers by shooting home videos and streaming the shots to each other over the

Internet! The music video theme is used more now than ever before because of its popularity with the young (and very desirable) 18 to 49 age group. Because the basic appeal of the music video is the poetry of synchronized music and imagery, it does more to create mood and emotion than it does to tout a product's specific attributes.

Slice-of-Life Spots

This is the theme Ogilvy & Mather eventually pitched for the IBM campaign. The creatives may have had a conversation like this:

> Let's just show people in other countries the way Americans usually think of them—you know, dancing at a wedding in the middle of some town square in Sicily. Then we get tight on a conversation in the corner, and two old guys are arguing about how many megabytes you need for this or that. It would be, you know, kind of a surprise to find these unlikely foreigners talking high tech.

This would have gotten the attention of the art director, who might have said, "We could do a whole bunch of these surprises—each one in a different exotic location. Barcelona would be great!" The creative director might say, "Not arguing, though, but sharing information. Word of mouth. Helping each other." And on it would go.

The slice-of-life approach—basically looking in on somebody who uses the product and showing how he uses it—is a common and subtle means to show both the product and the target prospect together in a believable situation. The twist that the creative team added for the IBM commercial is that the situations were a bit unbelievable, at least at first. Until the *viewers* had to admit to themselves that it is their own claustrophobic view of the world that made it surprising to see foreigners who have computing problems like their own. The commercials made the audience laugh at itself.

There is nothing intrinsically wrong with any of the other themes for the IBM commercial described before. With enough polish and further development, any one would have worked, but the Subtitles campaign was *inspired*.

THE STYLE

Every one of the preceding themes could be presented in any of a number of *styles,* meaning humorously, seriously, tastefully, elegantly, trendy, down-home. Again, many styles (too many to list), lots of wiggle room within each style, and various style combinations are available. Consider how many different ways there are to be humorous. On one end of the spectrum, there is a sophisticated brand of British wit and on the other the grossest form of scatological humor (think *South Park*). In between there is dark humor, parody, sarcasm, satire, puns, double entendres, sight gags, jokes, and delightful surprises. You have to decide how far you go, based on the client, the brand, the message, and the audience.

The style you choose determines the dialogue, the action, casting, costuming, locations, how people behave, the music, and so on. Everything that is seen or heard is based on the style. Once you get to this point, you can begin the writing and design phase.

Class Exercise

Choose a commercial and try to deconstruct the creative process that led to the concept, theme, and style you see in it. What is the central message that you are left with? What could have been the brief to the agency? Discuss how other themes and styles could have been used in answer to the concept. Keep the client, the brand, the message, and the audience in mind at all times. You could write the scripts for these new commercials.

WRITING AND DESIGN

Finally arriving at the concept, theme, and style of the commercial, the creative team is ready to put their ideas into words and pictures. In common use for presenting the commercial design are the two-column script and the storyboard. The writer writes the script, which includes dialogue or narration, action, and visuals, while the art director draws the *storyboard*—a series of pictures that depict the commercial's key shots or frames. The storyboard includes, under each picture, the script for the audio to be heard simultaneously.

The writer and art director usually work together, trading rough ideas until the final script and storyboard are locked together. The final script and storyboard have the following four main purposes:

- To test the concept with the target market. This is often done in focus groups where likely viewers are asked to react to the idea, after which modifications can be made
- To sell the concept to the client; that is, to convince the client to approve production. This is usually done at a formal presentation.
- To send out to production companies and other contractors to get bids for production; the next chapter covers this
- To guide the director and other contractors while they are producing the various elements for the commercial; chapters 8, 9, and 10 cover these

So the script and storyboard have to accurately and unambiguously show the commercial the way the agency wants to produce it, though it may go through some alterations as it gets tested and presented to the client. Roles may shift around depending on the people involved; agencies all have their own creative cultures, so don't consider the following to be cast in stone.

Scripts

The writer writes the commercial's script focusing on two things—what happens and what we hear: action and sound. Like the screenwriter, the writer has a knack for dialogue (writing believable conversation) and actions (of both the talent and the camera) that when combined tell the story. In print, the writer and art director work together very closely as the writer writes the copy and the art director works on the single visual piece. But in television, there are the added dimensions of motion and time—what happens and when it happens—which usually fall to the writer to create in the script.

Service Campaign "Boomer Direct Routes" :30 sec TV

Video	Audio
Open on Boomer at a downtown Centro bus shelter. As Centro riders are boarding the bus, he addresses the people walking behind the shelter with a bullhorn.	Whimsical music up: Boomer: ATTENTION PEDESTRIANS! WALKING IS OVERRATED. RIDE CENTRO'S NEW DIRECT ROUTES TO CAROUSEL MALL, S.U., SHOPPINGTOWN MALL AND OCC!
Freeze frame: Super CENTRO LOGO and BOOMER. Regional Transportation Authority next to him.	Music stops: V.O. Boomer: REGIONAL TRANSPORTATION AUTHORITY!
CUT TO: Rough, home-movie style camera work two guys in a car desperately looking for a parking space in Armory Square. they pull up to a spot to see Boomer hanging out in a La-Z-boy with his feet up, sipping a beverage.	Music up again: Boomer: STILL LOOKING FOR A SPOT? SORRY, IT'S A KANGAROO-ONLY ZONE.
CUT TO: Boomer riding on a Centro bus. He stands at the front, tour guide style. Addresses riders with bullhorn as bus approaches gas station.	IF YOU'LL LOOK TO THE RIGHT...
CUT TO: MCU young man filling his tank.	HE'S GETTING HOSED!!!
CUT TO: Centro riders laughing. Boomer addresses man through driver's open window with bullhorn.	SIR, CENTRO'S NEW DIRECT ROUTES SAVE YOU TIME AND MONEY. STEP AWAY FROM THE PUMP. I REPEAT...
CUT TO: Boomer next to portable backlit sign at used car lot. He's rearranged the letters to say "Boomer sez...Ride Centro's new direct routes. Owner comes into frame, Boomer runs away	VO Announcer: CENTRO. NOW MORE DIRECT TO PLACES YOU GO TO THE MOST.
SUPER: Centro Logo	Music up and out.

FIGURE 4.6 The two-column script is commonly written for television commercials, but many other formats are used (see Figure 1.6, for example).

Courtesy of Central New York Regional Transportation Authority and Eric Mower & Associates. Reprinted with permission.

The two-column script commonly written for television commercials has the video portion on the left side, the audio portion on the right. The action or visual that corresponds to the dialogue or narration is adjacent to the audio—they line up with each other on the page. A number of other formatting conventions is generally used; for example (see Figure 4.6):

- Dialogue or narration is capitalized and double-spaced to make it easier to read, especially in the sound booth where voiceover, narration, and ADR (automated dialogue replacement) take place[6]
- Shot calls, such as close-up or long shot, are included as the initials CU or LS
- Transitions are indicated between shots using words such as "Dissolve to" or "Cut to"
- Writers sometimes use a / (slash) instead of commas, and // (two slashes) instead of periods in dialogue so that voiceover talent can see pauses and full stops long before they get there[7]

There are many other ways to present a script. Desktop publishing makes it possible to write the dialogue and, instead of writing the action, simply place a scanned storyboard panel right on the page (see Figure 4.7). Television is a visual medium, and what better way to explain a commercial?

Still another script format is the single-column script used by Ogilvy & Mather to present the Subtitles campaign to IBM and its focus groups. This format is similar to the format used for stage plays (see Figure 4.8).

Art Direction

The art director creates the look and feel of the commercial, visualizing practical things such as locations, sets, set dressings, props, wardrobe, talent (perhaps), and so forth. She also envisions more subtle artistic issues like the color palette, textures, line, and other stylistic elements. The art director brings the spot a sense of taste and style, which is based on the concept, theme, and attitude. Art directors have not only a sense of the history of art and culture, but also keep current with fashion trends and popular culture in general. Art directors can draw, sketch, and illustrate. Art director Kevin Tripodi even designed the Boomer cartoon character, who eventually became an actor in a kangaroo costume, used in the Centro commercials discussed throughout the book.

Storyboards

The art director draws the storyboard, shot by shot. Initially, the art director draws the board according to the visuals written by the writer. Then there may be some additional drawings and camera direction as the art director and writer begin to see how the commercial will play out. They may add a shot or a camera move, a close-up here, a reaction shot there (see Figure 4.9).

When the storyboard and the script are finalized and locked together, they are reviewed by the creative director, account executive, producer, brand manager, and others on the agency team. Each reviewer has the *big picture* in mind—the overall selling strategy as set forth by the client—but each also brings a personal agenda to the review process. The

Service Campaign "Boomer Direct Routes":30 sec TV

*SCRIPT AND SCENES SHOWN ARE CONCEPT ONLY. ACTUAL SCRIPT AND SCENES SUBJECT TO CHANGE AT TIME OF SHOOTING. (THIS SPOT WILL BE SHOT IN A 'REALITY TV' STYLE.)

WHIMSICAL MUSIC THROUGHOUT.

OPEN ON BOOMER AT A DOWNTOWN CENTRO BUS SHELTER. AS CENTRO RIDERS ARE BOARDING A BUS, HE ADDRESSES THE PEOPLE WALKING BEHIND THE SHELTER WITH A BULLHORN.

> **BOOMER: Attention pedestrians! Walking is overrated. Ride Centro's new direct routes to Carousel Mall, S.U., Shoppingtown Mall and OCC!**

MUSIC STOPS. FRAME FREEZES. SUPER OF CENTRO LOGO AND Boomer. Regional Transportation Authority. NEXT TO HIM.

> **VO: Boomer. Regional Transportation Authority!!!**

MUSIC AND FOOTAGE RESUME.

ROUGH, "HOME MOVIE" STYLE CUT TO TWO GUYS IN A CAR DESPERATELY LOOKING FOR A PARKING SPOT IN ARMORY SQUARE. THEY PULL UP TO AN OPEN SPOT TO SEE BOOMER HANGING OUT IN A LA -Z-BOY WITH HIS FEET UP, SIPPING A BEVERAGE.

> **BOOMER: Still looking for a spot? Sorry, it's a kangaroo-only zone.**

ROUGH, "HOME MOVIE" STYLE CUT TO BOOMER RIDING ON A CENTRO BUS. HE STANDS AT THE FRONT OF THE BUS, TOUR GUIDE STYLE, ADDRESSING RIDERS WITH HIS BULLHORN. THE BUS APPROACHES A GAS STATION.

> **BOOMER: If you'll look to the right ...**

ROUGH, "HOME MOVIE" STYLE CUT TO A YOUNG MAN FILLING UP HIS TANK.

> **BOOMER: He's getting hosed!!!**

CUT TO CENTRO RIDERS LAUGHING. BOOMER ADDRESSES MAN THROUGH THE OPEN DRIVER'S WINDOW WITH HIS BULLHORN.

> **BOOMER: Sir, Centro's new direct routes save you time and money. Step away from the pump. I repeat...**

ROUGH, "HOME MOVIE" STYLE CUT TO BOOMER STANDING NEXT TO A PORTABLE BACKLIT SIGN IN THE PARKING LOT OF USED-LOT ON ERIE BLVD. THE LETTERS ON THE SIGN HAVE BEEN RE-ARRANGED TO READ, 'BOOMER SEZ...RIDE CENTRO'S NEW DIRECT ROUTES'.

> **VO: Centro. Now more direct to places you go to the most .**

OWNER COMES INTO FRAME, OBVIOUSLY DISPLEASED THAT BOOMER HAS CHANGED HIS SIGN. BOOMER RUNS.

SUPER: CENTRO LOGO AND MAKING CNY WORK TAG.

FADE OUT.

FIGURE 4.7   It is so simple to include pictures in a document now, so many scripts include thumbnail sketches for illustration.

Courtesy of Central New York Regional Transportation Authority and Eric Mower & Associates. Reprinted with permission.

IBM Brand   **AS PRODUCED**
:45 TV   (English Subtitles)
"Italian Farmers/Digital Library" IMBR-5934
9/15/95

> *We're deep in the heart of the Apennine Mountains in Italy. It's dusk; the sun is setting over a farmhouse tucked away by itself at the end of a road. Behind the house there's a little olive tree grove. There we spy the farmer, a retired man in his late 60's, walking with his 25 year old granddaughter. In this particular corner of the world, it seems like things haven't changed that much in the last 100 years. We move in closer so we can eavesdrop on their Italian conversation.*

Grandfather:	Well, I finally finished my doctoral thesis.
Woman:	Way to go, Gramps. What was your topic?
Grandfather:	"Improvisation in the Music of J.S. Bach and Dizzy Gillespie."
	Did my research at Indiana University.
Woman:	Indiana?
Grandfather:	Yup. IBM took the school's library.... and digitized it.
Grandfather:	So, over the Internet.... I could access their scores and recordings.
Grandfather:	You know.... it's a great time to be alive.
Tag:	IBM. Solutions for a small planet.

FIGURE 4.8 This script for the IBM "Subtitles" campaign uses a format similar to the stage play format; although there are script conventions, there are no rules. In other words, do whatever you have to do to get your idea across.

Courtesy of IBM Inc. and Ogilvy & Mather. Reprinted with permission.

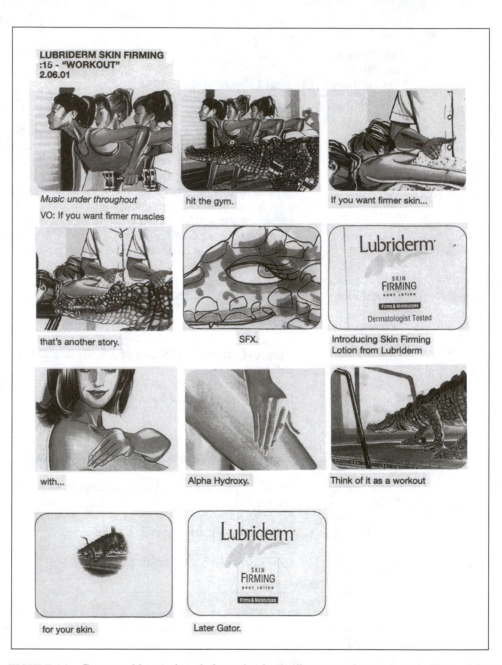

FIGURE 4.9 Compare this storyboard, drawn by the art director, to the treatment in Figure 4.2 for the same commercial. Concepts are generally tweaked and fine-tuned during the creative process until they reach this level of detail.

Courtesy of Pfizer, Inc., permission granted by J. Walter Thompson U.S.A., as agent of Pfizer, Inc.

account executive, for example, looks at the commercial from the point of view of the client, the marketing objective, and imagines whether he can sell the idea to the client. The producer tries to imagine what it will cost to produce and who might be the best choice to direct it. The creative director looks at it from the perspective of the whole campaign, including print, transit, and Internet ads. Reviewers raise questions, make suggestions, perhaps objections. All of the team members' input may lead to some revisions. When the agency, internally, is happy with the script and board but still has some questions, they may shoot an animatic—a very rough version of the spot.

Rough Track and Visual Animatics

An animatic is a rough version of the commercial made from the storyboards and other art (even photographs and miscellaneous footage), with a rough voice track, music track, and camera moves. The animatic is cut to length, meaning that it's 30-seconds long, and each shot within the spot is the intended length. To capture the visual components, an animatic can be shot quite easily with a video camera, or drawings can be scanned into a computer. Any number of graphics programs can be used to create camera motion, dissolves, and other effects to get an animatic to represent what the final commercial will be like as closely as possible. The producer records voices (most of the time, whoever is available) and uses music, maybe not the intended music but suggestive of it. What you get from an animatic is a good sense of the commercial and whether the boarded shots will really tell the intended story. An animatic may lead creatives to make more modifications to the commercial design—add or remove shots, change the transitions, and so forth.

At some point, when the agency thinks it has the spot idea it wants but before the commercial is shown to the client, the team tests it with the intended audience—a focus group. One of the first questions a client always asks when presented with an idea is, "How did it test?"

FOCUS GROUP

We discussed *message testing* in chapter 3, and you'll remember in the story at the beginning of this chapter that Roy Schecter and the agency tested the scripts for IBM's Subtitles campaign and that the focus group turned up some problems with certain concepts. This helped the agency whittle down the list of possible scenarios, and zero in on those the audience reacted to most favorably. The focus group also came up with the tag line—"Solutions for a small planet"—an unexpected bonus.

Nearly every media producer—ad agencies, television program producers, film producers, game producers, Web producers, magazine publishers—tests concepts. Even the publishers of this book sent early versions to reviewers who sent back valuable feedback on its content, features, accuracy, readability, and other things. Believe us when we tell you that this book is way better as a result of the focus group than it would have been if left entirely to us. So much is at stake when designing and producing a commercial, as we discussed in the preface of this book, that ad agencies cannot afford *not* to test the concept with the intended audience.

In major markets and for national commercials, agencies use outside, independent companies to test concepts. These companies not only keep the testing free of unintended "tainting" but also conduct the tests and present the results in a timely and professional manner.

They gather, sometimes right off the street, a group of people who match the profile of the intended audience. Agencies present animatics, test commercials, or just the scripts or storyboards in order to solicit comments from the group on a variety of issues important to them. What is needed varies widely depending on the brand, the intention of the commercial, the target audience, and so on. If the commercial is introducing a new product, for example, focus group members will be asked what they knew about the brand before the commercial, and what they knew afterwards. If the commercial is an image ad for a company or brand, the group will be asked what it thought about the brand before, and how it feels about the brand now.

All of the resulting data—some quantitative, other qualitative—is written up, as the example in Figure 4.10 shows, and given to the agency. Because some test results are quantitative, they can be graphed, or charted, and presented along with suggestions for how to proceed. Notice that the spot called Treadmill scored the highest, but it still needed some modifications to strengthen recall on certain product attributes, including "firming." Message testing helps the agency fine-tune the concept, as well as its actual intended execution.

CONCEPT MODIFICATION AND PITCH TO CLIENT

Two results from focus-testing are rare: (1) "The concept is horrible and should be abandoned" and (2) "The concept is perfect—go with it as is." If the concept was arrived at

FIGURE 4.10   Communication of Product Descriptor Ratings

ASI Market Research tested three different copy ideas for Lubriderm commercials for J. Walter Thompson and its client, Pfizer, Inc., and produced a report identifying strengths and weaknesses in the creative approach. Such focus group reports help the creative team modify copy and visuals as needed.

	JIGGLE	TREADMILL	MIRROR
Is a high-quality product	38	50	49
Makes skin feel soft	38	51	45
Absorbs quickly	34	43	31
Dermatologist tested	45	38	45
Recommended by dermatologists	43	38	41
Is an effective moisturizer	34	41	37
Contains AHA	33	28	37
Makes skin firm	22	19	23

Both Treadmill and Mirror helped drive strong product descriptor ratings; however, this was dominated by core Lubriderm equities, "high-quality product" and "dermatologists," while specific product attributes, "firming" and "AHA," were not as strongly communicated.

Courtesy of Pfizer, Inc., permission granted by J. Walter Thompson U.S.A., as agent of Pfizer, Inc.

using hard work, inspiration, and intuition as described earlier in this chapter, the most typ-ical result is "it needs tweaking"—modifications and fine-tuning. Before taking a concept to a client, the agency usually adjusts the concept to "honor" the test feedback; changes are made to copy or art direction and/or script or storyboard, and then the material is prepared for presentation to the client.

Next, the agency account executive sets up a formal meeting in which to present the creatives' approach to the client. The script, storyboard, animatic, focus-testing results, preliminary budget and production schedule, and other creative and production issues are on the agenda. Typically, the creative director presents the concept, showing visuals and describing the rationale for the approach. The producer then discusses production issues, including expected costs. The client is usually anxious to hear about the "message's" test results, which help to assuage any fears that the effort and cost will not have good results. When the client approves the creative concept, the agency has to take two additional steps before getting a firm and conclusive go-ahead on production. These are selecting the direc-tor and putting together a cost estimate for production for the client, which are covered in the next two chapters.

SUMMARY

The agency is tasked with coming up with a creative concept, theme, and style for a televi-sion commercial to solve a client's communication problem. It presents the concept in the form of scripts and storyboards and gets a sign-off from the client to produce it. There *is* a creative process even though every project seems to get done in a new and unique way. Typically, a team of people, each of whom has special skills, collaborates on creative development.

Every agency's creative effort has at least one, and usually three people, involved in creating the commercial. The creative director is the leader of the team, often because she has multiple skills—writing, drawing, and effectively communicating ideas to the client. The creative director usually has a good sense of what the client wants and needs and can keep the other team members focused on the task. The writer is often the one who comes up with the concept, then writes the copy, or story, for the commercial. The art director vi-sualizes the look of the commercial, draws sketches and storyboards, and later determines the overall appearance of everything in the spot.

The team begins the creative process by doing its homework—learning everything there is to know about the client, the brand, the marketing strategy, and the target audience. Much of this information comes from the client and from research conducted by the client, the agency, or third-party researchers. The client also provides the agency with what is called the brief—a statement of purpose (also called the message) that the commercial must get through to the consumer.

The team must learn about and process all of this background information and data because it forms the fertile ground from which creative ideas to solve the client's commu-nication problem can spring. Processing all of this information—basically getting very fa-miliar with the client's problem—is the hard work of the mind. Many commercial concepts can and do end right there, with a creative approach that is intellectually straightforward: "The product that you always thought was too expensive is now on sale for 60 percent off."

Inspiration is a magical moment during which the creative's mind seems to galvanize all of the new knowledge into a single premise, or concept, on which the message can ride. Inspired work is the product of past work; it is always founded on memories and it always reminds us of something we are already familiar with, even as it masquerades as something new. Intuition is a sense that what we have created is good, and right. Intuition is a gut feeling because it usually lacks a way to be verbalized or a rationale; however it can confirm to us that the inspired idea, which came from hard thinking, will work.

When the creative team has come up with a concept, it must now choose the theme and the style for the commercial. The theme is the presentation format for the concept; many themes have become standard in the industry, including demonstrations, stand-up presentations, slice-of-life vignettes, celebrity endorsements, and man-on-the-street testimonials. The style refers to the manner in which the theme is presented; for example, humorously, seriously, or seductively. The style determines the dialogue, action, casting, and other art direction elements.

The writer writes the script, the art director draws the storyboard, and the team works out details of both until the creative approach can be tested. Focus groups composed of typical consumers are asked to react to the scripts; storyboards; and, perhaps, test commercials called animatics. The groups' reactions are used to fine-tune the creative approach before it is presented to the client at a formal pitch meeting. If the client is pleased with the scripts and boards, the agency can begin to look for the right director for the project.

DISCUSSION QUESTIONS

1. This is an exercise in deconstruction. Look at commercials from a demo reel and try to determine what the brief would have been for the creative team to come up with the concept they did.

2. Describe your perception of consumers for these products: Harley-Davidson motorcycles, Saturn automobiles, Abercrombie & Fitch clothing, North Face coats and jackets, Pop-Tarts, Seven Up. Think of others too. Does your perception match that of others in your group? Is it negative? Would it prevent you from buying these or other products? Why? How would you solve this problem if you were tasked with creating an ad for these products?

3. Imagine what the IBM Subtitles commercials would have been like if the creative process had simply stopped before inspiration. What kind of mechanical, safe, and straightforward approach might the commercials have had?

4. The Centro commercials created by Eric Mower & Associates featured a character named Boomer who, as a kangaroo, symbolized getting around quickly. What creative approaches would you have used to solve Centro's communication problem if you did not have Boomer to use as spokesperson?

RECOMMENDED READINGS

Carter, David E., ed. *Creativity 30: Bright Ideas in Advertising and Design from 40 Countries around the World.* New York: HBI, 2001.

Cook, Albert C., and C. Dennis Schick. *Fundamentals of Copy and Layout.* Chicago: Crain Books, 1984.

Marra, James L. *Advertising Creativity: Techniques for Generating Ideas.* Englewood Cliffs, NJ: Prentice Hall, 1990.

Meeske, Milan D. *Copywriting for the Electronic Media: A Practical Guide,* 4th ed. Belmont, CA: Wadsworth, 2003.

NOTES

1. Gerstner retired in 2002 and was succeeded by Samuel J. Palmisano.
2. Bullmore, Jeremy. "The Advertising Creative Process." In Jones, ed., pp. 52–53.
3. Novick, Steve. *AdWeek,* March 11, 2002, p. 12.
4. Altman, Dennis. "Creativity communication." In Bendinger, ed., p. 405.
5. Ibid.
6. Interestingly, no two people (or books on the subject) agree about this particular convention, and many suggest capitalizing the video and using upper and lower case for the audio. It doesn't matter what you do, so long as the production people using the script know how to read it.
7. This particular convention dates back to when all television and radio was live and there was only one shot to get it right; this format is not common today.

CHAPTER FIVE

SELECTING THE DIRECTOR

When Foote, Cone & Belding began looking for a director for its Levi's 501 Blues commercials in 1984, they found a little-known documentary films director, Leslie Dektor, in South Africa. Here's the story:

> Mike Koelker, FCB's creative brand steward on Levi's until his untimely death in 1995, was interested in "showing kids as they really are," says Steve Neely, senior vice president/executive producer. To do so, the agency turned to Leslie Dektor, a director who had crossed over to advertising from documentary filmmaking. After seeing *Fat Cake,* a film he had made in his native South Africa about two musician friends, Koelker was convinced. "I don't know whether it was the attitude, the tone, the palette of the work, which was very cool and blue, or whether [Koelker] was attracted to the film's honesty and the people," says Dektor. "I hope it was a combination of the two."[1]

Dektor shot the Levi's spots, and scores of others, and went on to become one of the most sought-after commercial directors in the United States, winning the Directors Guild of America (DGA) award as the top director in 2001. He shot the IBM Subtitles campaign discussed in chapter 4.

The director is the person whose talent as a filmmaker —as a master of the techniques of the visual language—is highly regarded. The director interprets the concept and theme designed at the agency and shoots the live action (or directs the animation). He uses his expertise with camera angles, shot composition, lighting, directing actors or animals, directing the crew, pacing, editing, and sound to give the concept the best possible rendering on the screen and through the speakers. The decisions he makes result in the overall look and feel—the *gestalt*—of the final commercial and determine whether it reaches and resonates with the target audience on an aesthetic, ephemeral level. It is often said, and we repeat it here for absolute clarity, that the greatest director in the world can do little to improve a poor concept.

The previous chapter discussed the commercial being pitched, "sold," to the client. Now that the client has approved the creative concept, copy, storyboards, and other elements, production can begin. Or can it? At this point in time, a creative concept exists and only a rough cost and time target. Before production can begin, the agency must find and recommend the director it thinks is the best filmmaker to execute the concept.

Sean Baker directing Boomer, the mascot for Centro—the Syracuse transit system. He was hired because of his demonstrated knack for getting good performances from average people on the street when approached by actors in costumes like this one.

Courtesy of Central New York Regional Transportation Authority and Eric Mower and Associates. Reprinted with permission.

The agency narrows its potential choices for the project when it reviews demonstration reels of past work and gets a sense of directors' relative strengths. Agency people try to identify the director whose work most closely matches the genre of the commercial they envision; some directors are strong choreographers, others are skilled with special effects, and others shoot tabletop very well. The agency also considers a number of other factors during this selection process, including whether there is a pool, or campaign, of commercials to produce, as well as the budget and the time frame for the commercial's production. A selection ritual takes place almost every time a national or regional commercial concept is approved by a client, and the agency prepares to go into production on it.

In this chapter, you will learn the following:

- Steps the agency takes to find and recommend a director and production company to produce the commercial to the client
- Who directors are and why they are so important
- Roles and responsibilities of the director and the production company
- Role of the director's rep and how demo reels are used
- What the agency gives to production companies in the bid package
- How the director and the production company respond to the agency
- The difference between the firm-fixed bid and the cost-plus-fixed-fee arrangement

Thus you will understand what criteria to use when you are the agency producer who is to select the director for a commercial. If you are the director invited by an agency to bid on a commercial, you will learn how to respond to the invitation to bid, and how to leverage your skills and talents so that you will be awarded the job.

THE COMMERCIAL POOL

Occasionally, the client and the agency will decide that more than one commercial will be produced more or less simultaneously (or serially) to create a campaign. When these commercials are bid out and produced at the same time, they are called a *pool* of commercials. A campaign consists of some number of commercials that have the same general concept, or thematic approach, but differ in story or presentation. The IBM Subtitles commercials described in chapter 4 are a good example of this.

Thematically, pool commercials are similar, but each is quite unique in terms of characters, location, situation, even the product advertised. There are both efficiencies and downsides in contracting a single director to produce a pool of commercials like the IBM ones. The efficiencies come from saving preproduction and production costs, saving time, and possibly travel. Once a director leaves for Europe with her crew, she could stay there and shoot several commercials on location; however, the director and production company selected must be "right" for each commercial in the pool. If the commercials selected to be produced by the client are not similar enough to be directed by the same director, then pooling may not be an acceptable creative solution even if costs can be more easily controlled. No one wants to compromise the creative vision. In this chapter, and for the rest of the book, we discuss the successful production of a single commercial.

PRODUCTION COMPANIES AND DIRECTORS

Production companies are in business specifically to make commercials, although many also produce other short forms such as training films, documentaries, and music videos; some also do branch into feature films. These companies seek out directors who have either great potential, or a track record, and then they market them to ad agencies. Directors have various business relationships with the production companies they work with. Directors themselves may be the owners of production companies; may be under contract to the production company; or, in some cases, may be freelancers brought into the production company for specific projects. Production companies provide production support for jobs the director does, including office and sometimes production facilities and the producer who manages business and support tasks—secretarial, clerical, and payroll services, and so forth. This allows the director to concentrate on the creative tasks.

Rhythm & Hues is a large, full-service production company located in Playa Del Rey, California. The company provides live-action, animation, computer animation, and editorial services for commercials, feature films, and television programs. It has a large stage, where live-action commercials can be shot, and the latest computer graphics equipment and software. Two well-known live-action designer/directors—Randy Roberts and Michael Patterson—work out of their studio. Each has a *specialty*—a certain look that characterizes his or her work and attracts the interest of agencies in search of a visual "hook."

Patterson, for example, is famous for a music video, "Take on Me," which he shot for the band Aha in 1983. In it a lonely young woman is literally (visually) sucked into a comic strip and becomes an animated drawing in a love story. Patterson went on to direct videos for Sting, Donald Fagen, Suzanne Vega, Paula Abdul, and recently commercials for Intel, Hostess, Oscar Meyer, Nintendo, and *The Los Angeles Times*. His counterpart, Randy Roberts, has won ten Clio awards for his commercials, which have a different and unique look, often combining live-action with computer-generated effects.

Two other directors—Bill Kroyer and John-Mark Austin—whose expertise lies in computer graphics and traditional cel animation are also resident at Rhythm & Hues. Like Patterson and Roberts, each has a special skill or talent—an eye for a certain style with which they effectively direct their various projects. Rhythm & Hues provides all these directors with a base of operation, a support staff, and a vigorous marketing effort anchored by sales reps in the major markets and a well-maintained Web site.

■ ■ ■ ■ ■

COMPUTER GRAPHICS DIRECTOR BILL KROYER

Bill Kroyer, Director at Rhythm & Hues, Inc.

Bill Kroyer grew up in a working-class neighborhood in Chicago where nobody made a living as an artist. In fact, it was so inconceivable to his parents that *he* could that they wouldn't let him take art classes in high school. "They thought it would be a waste of time," he laughed. But he continued to draw on the sly. When it came time for college, he went to Northwestern on a journalism scholarship and learned to write, but he also spent four years as the cartoonist for the school paper. In fact, as time went on, he decided he wanted to become a political cartoonist.

While taking an advertising class, one of his assignments was to make a television commercial. "Everybody else shot live action," Kroyer said, "but I decided to do a little cartoon, because I liked to draw. So I went to the art store and got the Preston Blair book on animation and I read it. It's a very simple little book that explains the principles. How you draw a picture, change it a little bit, take a picture. And so on." He set up his drawing table, tripod, camera and cable release, and made a movie about a snake. "The minute I saw that film with that character moving, and coming alive and looking at the camera, I was so excited that I had given life to a drawing," Kroyer said. That one moment changed his life. "I decided that's what I want to do. I can do it, and I love doing it. And I never, from that day, ever thought of doing anything else."

And he hasn't. One week after graduation, Kroyer's career as an animator and director simply started and hasn't stopped. He set up a drawing table and supplies in his basement, and got to work. He didn't say, and this author didn't ask, what his parents thought about all this.

His first films were educational ones for the local food co-op, shot on super 8mm, and for a local college, shot on 16mm—films about co-ops, heart disease, and nutrition. For two years, he made a living making animated educational and industrial films, working as a completely self-taught animator with no real contact at all with any other animators in the world. "And then who comes to Chicago for a film festival but Chuck Jones, the famous Warner

(continued)

CONTINUED

Brothers animator," Kroyer said. "And I cornered him in a room and got him to look at one of my terrible educational films. And Chuck Jones, being a wonderful guy, watched the film and saw something. He turned to me and said, 'You should go to Los Angeles and learn animation.'"

Heeding the word from "the mountain," Kroyer loaded his van and headed west to knock on doors. He landed a job as an in-betweener even though he didn't know then what an in-betweener was. His first assignment: He in-betweened the "Mr. Clean" character for a commercial. He worked extremely hard, learned fast, and after a year was promoted to animator. After two years, Kroyer had about twenty commercials on his reel, and he applied for and got a job at Disney based on his work. "The nine old men from Walt's days were still there, and the new guys included Glenn Kean, John Musker, Henry Sellick, and Brad Byrd," Kroyer mused. "And I was surrounded with the greatest animators in the world learning the art form."

After working on a number of films at Disney and in outside studios, Kroyer became the computer image choreographer for the first computer animated film, *Tron.* He pioneered the combination of Disney-style animation aesthetics with the burgeoning technology of computer graphics—and stayed this path. His work and reputation in the combination of art and technology grew steadily, and he struck out on his own. Kroyer teamed with his wife, Sue Kroyer, to create a short film, *Technological Threat,* which won an Academy Award nomination. His Kroyer Films studio produced (and he directed) the feature film *FernGully: The Last Rainforest,* which was animated in the traditional Disney style but included many CGI effects. Work with Warner Brothers as a feature director followed, but the desire to get back to animation—in particular, computer animation—on a more personal, hands-on level drew him back to commercials. He joined Rhythm & Hues Studios as a director of CGI.

Kroyer is now one of the top CGI directors in the business. He spends almost as much time as an invited guest at animation and technology conferences in Europe and Asia as he does directing. He has become the go-to director for computer-generated character animation in feature films such as *Scooby Doo* and *Cats & Dogs.* He has directed spots for Novell, Coca-Cola, Cheez-Its, Kellogg, and Intel. Young aspiring animators now corner Kroyer at festivals and ask *him* to look at their reels. And the folks back home in that Chicago working-class neighborhood? They're probably pushing their kids into art classes.

While the production company brings all the support and logistics to a production project, the agency usually makes production decisions based solely on which director will shoot the commercial. The right director understands the creative and selling goals of the agency and can turn the concept into a blockbuster, Cannes Festival award-winning commercial. Because of the importance of the decision, director selection is taken very seriously at the agency and is one of the most involved and time-consuming tasks prior to actual production. Both the agency and the client are involved in the decision.

The key agency players in the selection process are the creative people who actually wrote, designed, and art directed the commercial; the creative director; the agency executive producer; and the agency producer. These people developed the commercial concept, sold it to their client, and have a clear idea of what they want. Now, they must match that vision with a person they can trust to bring it about.

Who Is the Director?

First of all, the director interprets and visualizes the creative concept provided by the agency. He can and should bring some of his own ideas and suggestions to the production and discuss them with the creative team so that they can all agree. But first and foremost, the director must demonstrate that he understands the basic concept developed at the agency, and that he knows what the agency wants and knows how to bring it about. The director communicates that he really understands the agency people's vision by writing a treatment to describe how he will interpret *their* concept (see example in Figure 5.1).

During the film shoot, the director determines the ultimate look of the commercial. He decides how the commercial will be lit, what camera angles will be used, how the image will be focused, what special effects will be used, what transitions will be used during editing, how the commercial will be paced, and so on. The director also will have input on casting. By carefully choosing the elements of the visual language, including sound, the director establishes the deeper message of the commercial, much of it reaching the audience on an emotional rather than a rational level. The real message is often below the surface and is interpreted by, and accepted by, the audience based on something other than logic. The agency looks for a director who has demonstrated from past projects that he has the sensibilities to create effective, likeable, persuasive messages.

Marketing the Director

To market or sell a director, all production companies provide demonstration reels of the director's work. These reels can be a general representation of the work or can be custom-made to show the agency why this director would be best for the current project. Years ago, demos were on 16mm film—just copies of what was supplied to television stations for airing. This is where the term demo *reel* originated. During the 1970s, the three-quarter-inch U-matic videocassette became available; it allowed much more flexibility in the preparation and distribution of reels because the tape made customization for specific presentations much easier. By mid-2002, DVD began to replace the videocassette; it provides superior quality, is much easier to handle, and playback equipment is less expensive than cassette machines. Many office computers now play the nonlinear DVD medium, enabling the viewer to skip around to see specific commercials or effects, to rewind instantly, to use freeze-frame easily, and to carefully study the director's work.

A key person in the selling of a production house and director to the agency is the production company representative, or rep. Usually, the rep is the liaison between the production company and the agency's creative personnel. She tries to maintain regular contact with the agency creatives both to keep the production company's capabilities fresh on the agency's mind and to find out what new projects the agency is developing. The rep screens reels to the agency on a continuing basis and makes a personal sales pitch on behalf of the

pre·duk'shen
PRODUCTION

J. Walter Thompson
Lubriderm Skin Firming
"Workout" - :30
Director's Treatment - 2/5/01
Director: Eric Heimbold

Open on

A brightly lit, upscale fitness complex - morning. The architecture is distinctive and the equipment and furnishings reflect a modern, artful sensibility. Morning light beams into the space through a large, dramatic window or skylight.

Music: Strongly rhythmic and upbeat.

VO: *"If you want firmer muscles... hit the gym."*

A number of well toned young women are working out in unison to the fast paced cadence of an insistent trainer. The camera dollies down a row of six women doing arm lifts, pumping their silver barbells in tight, synchronized movements. Judging from their perspiration and concentration, this is not an easy exercise. *"One-two... one-two... one-two..."*

As we reach the end of the row we discover a full-grown, realistic alligator pumping iron right in synch with the rest of the girls. Her endorphins racing, she's *working it* and from the expression on her face we can tell she's in her aerobic zone and proud of it.

Cut to - Fitness center - massage/spa area.

Music: Same upbeat track, new rhythm.

VO: *"If you want firmer skin... that's another story."*

The same group of women are all receiving massages on a row of tables in a tiled room -- an assortment of oversized bottles containing various colored, aromatic massage oils glow, translucently in the background. The masseuses, dressed in clinical white, are *chopping* in unison, *"chop-chop... chop-chop... chop-chop..."*

Last in line again is our gator. *"Chop-chop... chop-chop..."* She rolls her eyes and closes them as the corner of her mouth turns up in a blissful smile -- she releases a well deserved sigh of relief.

1040 n. las palmas • hollywood ca 90038 • 323.871.1362 f: 323 871.9119

FIGURE 5.1 The first page of a treatment by Eric Heimbold for the Lubriderm "Workout" commercial. He eventually directed the pool of commercials for J. Walter Thompson and its client, Pfizer.

Courtesy of Pfizer, Inc., permission granted by J. Walter Thompson U.S.A., as agent for Pfizer, Inc.

director. This contact and screening takes place not only when a new project is viable, but whenever the rep feels she has something that may be of interest to the creatives.

Class Exercise

To get a sense of what the agency must do to select the right commercial director, have your class ask for demo reels from a number of directors. You can find many of them at *ecreativesearch.com,* a Web site devoted to commercial directors and services. Study the demo reels to find the right director for the political ad you conceptualized while reading chapter 1.

What kind of director are you looking for? Dialogue? Action? You become the agency execs. You decide.

If an appropriate project materializes, the rep provides reels, confirms schedule availability, and gets involved in the bid process. She attempts to keep the production company informed about the agency's director preferences so that bids can be tailored accordingly and be as competitive as possible. A rep may be a production company employee, or she may be an independent contractor who represents several noncompetitive directors and possibly other production companies such as animation, music production, or postproduction studios. Reps usually work on a percentage basis just like talent agents; this means they get, perhaps, a fee of 10 percent of the total production cost. They generally have expense accounts for wining and dining, travel, and other costs related to sales.

Production companies usually have reps located in key advertising markets. In an example of one person wearing many hats, the production company's executive producer (not to be confused with the executive producer at the agency) may also function as a production company sales representative. Normally, the executive producer is the person at the production company who coordinates and prepares the company's bid documents.

Roles and Responsibilities

When the television commercial business started more than fifty years ago, the production company was responsible for nearly all elements of a finished commercial; today, the production company usually shoots only the live-action elements. During the shoot, the director, the agency producer and creatives, and sometimes the client and an account executive view the dailies and decide which takes should be used in the final edit. Major agencies now assume responsibility for, or contract directly for, the other production tasks that once were the responsibility of the production company. These include casting, special effects, animation, computer graphics, editorial and postproduction, recording of announcer tracks, final audio preparation, and recording and integration of music and sound-effect elements—this integration is known in the commercial and the feature film industry as *mixing.* While most or all of these will be handled by the agency, the director is often brought in to advise and sometimes even supervise. This happens quite a bit when two different visual elements, such as live-action film and computer-generated animation, have to be combined later.

Criteria Used to Select the Director

The agency and the client usually have lengthy discussions about directors that might be "right" for a particular job; numerous reels are screened. Creatives try to find a director who will understand the basic message of the commercial and the creative concept they have developed to carry that message. The first director Ogilvy & Mather suggested for the IBM Subtitles campaign (see chapter 4) was rejected by the client. "The agency looked at a lot of demo reels," said Roy Schecter, IBM brand producer. He continued:

> They didn't have anybody in mind when they started. The first guy they recommended was a kind of hot shot young guy, trendy, British, who did a lot of dark, slick stuff. We looked at his reel and said, "This is not what we want." We didn't see anything in his work that would help to warm-up our brand.

The creative director at the agency had worked with Leslie Dektor a lot, but he had not done anything like the Subtitles campaign either. The director told Schecter he thought Dektor could do it and brought in his reel. "His images were beautiful," said Schecter, "and I had some contacts in the industry and he came highly recommended. So we said, 'Well, Leslie could do the job.'" Dektor was brought to a meeting with the client, at which he pitched his Subtitles treatment for the campaign. He did something interesting for the meeting: Dektor brought in clips from old films to show the client how he would capture the story. It wasn't long before IBM told the agency to hire him.

Sometimes, an agency will strongly consider going back to a director it has worked with previously, especially to produce commercials that are a continuation of an existing campaign. The agency may feel comfortable with a director who delivered exactly what she promised, on time, and within budget for another project. At other times, even with a continuing campaign, the agency may want to get a fresh, or new look, for the work. If agency people see a commercial for another product on a reel, or on television, that excites or inspires them, they might consider this director for their current project. Generally, agencies are risk-averse and do not take chances with unproven directors, especially with important clients, unless there is something about director's demo reels or personal presence that persuades the agency that they are worth the risk.

Directors who have recently won awards and are considered "hot" in the industry are on every agency creative's "want to work with" list. Directors become known for being specialists in specific types of commercials, such as directing for automobiles, or commercials with dialogue, fashion and beauty, food photography, comedy, and so on. Directors develop reputations for executing a particular style of work—for example, an edgy or very contemporary versus conservative style.

Agency creatives are always looking for a director who will plus the commercial— bring that extra level of skill and effort that will add what is called *production value* to a commercial. Production value is a very difficult concept to describe, much less quantitatively measure, but it is the sum of the filmmaking efforts that make the spot watchable and memorable. As we have said elsewhere in this book, production value is not a function of the equipment or technology used, nor the set, set dressings, props, costumes, or other elements of the shoot that are based on the budget. Production value is added to the project by a skilled filmmaker who takes the time to carefully compose, frame, and light each shot and knows what shots are actually needed to tell the story.

Students who take film or video classes prove that this is true with every production assignment: A group of students takes off for the weekend with the same assignment and the same cameras, microphones, and lighting kits. On Monday they screen the final result of the assignment for the rest of the class. Some of them look astounding—there are establishing shots, close-ups, low-angle shots, clever and meaningful lighting, and decent acting. "A" work. Others look like they were thrown together at the last minute with no thought at all given to the meaning of every shot. "C" work. This happens in the real world, as well, and is the reason some are regarded as "A" directors but most are not.

Industry professionals do agree, however, that a great concept can be enhanced with good production, but good, or even spectacular, production really cannot benefit significantly from a weak idea or mediocre creative concept. This is why the creative concept developed at the agency is so important.

THE BIDDING PROCESS

When the agency has narrowed its list of directors down, it begins the bidding process. Normally, as a good business practice, three production companies are chosen to competitively bid. There are exceptions to this, but bidding to only one studio, known as sole-source bidding, should always be discussed with and agreed to by the client.

Prior to sending out a bid package to the selected production companies, there are preliminary discussions with them to see if there is an interest in the particular commercial and to determine if the director is available to shoot it on the agency's anticipated production schedule. The bid package's specification sheet—*spec sheet*—contains information about the commercials to be produced, including the following:

- Agency and client name
- Agency address and phone and fax numbers for a specific contact person
- Names of the agency producer, business manager, copywriter, art director, and executive producer
- Commercial code numbers
- Date the bid must be returned
- Itemized list of exactly what specific elements of the production will be supplied by the agency and client. The client often provides samples of the product—the automobile, the jeans to be worn by talent, the pizza with the gooey cheese. The agency generally provides the music, product graphics, voiceover narration.
- Details about what should be supplied by the production company or any third parties. The spec sheet may specify that the production company is to provide all costuming, sets, props, and of course all filming and film developing.

In addition to the spec sheet (see Figure 5.2), the bid package contains the storyboards that lay out the agency's visualization of the commercial and its scripts.

Production notes are also usually included. These notes are a narrative describing the general outline for the commercial—the tone, mood, and feel of the commercial; creative ideas about sets or locations, wardrobe, casting, and props; and other elements. Notes contain everything the creatives who conceived it believe is important for the production company/director to know when bidding the commercial. In addition to the creative notes, the producer includes notes describing specific elements and techniques that the agency has considered for the commercial's production and would like to convey to the production company. The package also includes any other available material that the agency believes will be beneficial information for the production company bidders, perhaps even an animatic.

Negotiations

Normally, there are numerous telephone conversations between the agency and production companies bidding on a commercial; these conversations are very important. Ideally, the director is available to talk with the agency during the bidding process. The director can get direct information from the creatives about how they visualize the commercial and what they expect from the finished production. The agency's creative team can get a good indication of the director's ideas about how he sees the commercial and how he would execute it. Many times, what the agency creatives hear from the director in these conversations sways their decision as to which director will be awarded the contract to produce the commercial.

The Bid

The production company producer prepares the bid for the commercial, usually after detailed discussions with the director who describes her ideas for how to shoot the spot. The bid to shoot the commercial to finished live-action elements ready for edit usually includes the following cost items:

- Preparation labor
- Travel and lodging
- Location expenses
- Props
- Wardrobe
- Stage rental
- Set design and construction
- Labor needed during the shoot, materials required to shoot the commercial, including cameras, lights, sound equipment, and other specialized equipment from cranes to helicopters
- recording storage material (film or tape)
- Director's fee
- Production company's overhead and profit—the production fee or markup

Leo Burnett

Leo Burnett USA, Inc.
35 W. WACKER DRIVE, CHICAGO, IL 60601
Ph (312)220-5959 Fax (312)220-3299

TELEVISION PRODUCTION DEPARTMENT
SPECIFICATION SHEET

PRODUCTION MANAGER:		DATE:	
BROADCAST MANAGER:		JOB NUMBER:	
AGENCY PRODUCER:		CLIENT:	
EXECUTIVE PRODUCER:		PRODUCT:	
SENIOR PRODUCER:		CATEGORY:	

STUDIO BID BASED ON:

___ COST PLUS FIXED FEE ___ COMPLETE JOB ___ 35MM ___ 16MM ___ VIDEOTAPE
___ FIRM BID ___ SHOOTING THRU DAILIES ___ SYNC ___ MOS ___ VIDEO DAILIES
___ DIRECTOR'S CUT

	TITLE	CODE NUMBER	LENGTH	ORIGINAL	IF NO, EXPLAIN
#1					
#2					
#3					
#4					
#5					
#6					

CASTING

CASTING DIRECTOR: TBD

TO BE PAID BY: ___ AGENCY ___ STUDIO

CASTING DAYS ___ PREP ___ CAST ___ CALLBACKS ___ POLAROIDS

VTR DAYS ___ EDIT ___ 3/4" DUBS SHIP TO: ___

COMMERCIAL WILL AIR: ___ NATIONAL ___ REGIONAL ___ WILD SPOT ___ TEST

AS APPLICABLE: UNLESS OTHERWISE INSTRUCTED, ALL TALENT TO BE EMPLOYED AT SCALE RATES. CASTING DIRECTOR IS RESPONSIBLE FOR CHECKING ALL TALENT MEMBERSHIP STATUS AND CLIENT PRODUCT CONFLICTS. PAYMENT QUESTIONS MUST BE DIRECTED TO AGENCY PRODUCER; DO NOT CONTACT SAG DIRECT.

TALENT INFORMATION

TALENT SESSION TO BE PAID BY: X AGENCY ___ PRODUCTION STUDIO

EXTRA TALENT SESSION TO BE PAID BY: ___ AGENCY ___ PRODUCTION STUDIO X OTHER: ENTERTAINMENT PARTNERS

COMMERCIAL	#1	#2	#3	#4	#5	#6	#7	#8
ON-CAMERA								
DOUBLE CAST								
VOICEOVER								
EXTRA								
HAND MODEL								
SPECIAL CONTRACT								

STUDIOS ARE RESPONSIBLE FOR COMPLETE AND ACCURATE PREPARATION OF ALL TALENT CONTRACTS AND TALENT REPORTS. POLAROIDS OF TALENT IN COSTUME MUST BE ATTACHED TO THE CONTRACT. TALENT REPORTS AND COMPLETED CONTRACTS MUST BE RETURNED TO THE LOCAL BURNETT PRODUCTION OFFICE IMMEDIATELY AFTER THE SHOOT.

FIGURE 5.2 A Leo Burnett USA, Inc. bid spec sheet, which ensures that all bidders get the same information about the commercial.

Courtesy of Leo Burnett Advertising. Reprinted with permission.

- Pension and welfare (P&W) benefits
- Insurance charges, if such coverage is not separately provided directly by the advertising agency with its own production insurance policy
- Any special requirements of the individual production job

In addition to the actual bid, a production company includes a director's treatment—a narrative of how the director visualizes this commercial and how she plans to shoot it. Often, this is the most important part of the bid. A low price alone will not necessarily win the job for a production company, and a high price will not disqualify a bid if it is accompanied by a great treatment. Elise Kleinman, who produces spots for Hasbro at Grey Worldwide, says: "I'll work with the producer from a production company who we want to work with if they come in with a high bid to help them get their costs down. We don't want to lose the right director."

Although bids today are normally for just through production of live elements, certain jobs are bid through to the finished commercial, including special effects, possibly animation, editing and finishing, and even sound work. The agency determines how the job will be structured and parceled out and exactly who will be responsible for each specific part of the production. These responsibilities are conveyed in the production bid package and in phone conversations with all bidders.

The Standard Bid Form

Bids for production are submitted on standardized bid forms so that it is easier for agency personnel to make comparisons between studios. The bid form is a format that was originally designed by the Association of Independent Commercial Producers (AICP) with advertising agency input and comments. Figure 5.3 shows a cover summary page to a multipage, detailed breakout of the bid. It should be noted that many times a bidder for a production company will add terms, caveats, and conditions to this cover page that may or may not be acceptable to the advertising agency. Negotiations of these terms and conditions as well as the bid price usually take place before a final acceptable bid is agreed on. From the agency's standpoint, it is very important to understand how a production company allocates charges within this format. Production companies use the format with slight variations. Making just category-by-category comparisons of competing bids can be misleading because what one company includes in one category another production company may include in a different category. To understand exactly what and how much is included in a production company's bid requires a very thorough analysis of the form. This is normally the responsibility of the agency producer and the agency business manager.

The Deal

Bids are nearly always submitted for one of two possible business deals, or payment agreements—the fixed-firm, or the cost-plus-fixed-fee bid. The agency will specify on the bid spec sheet how it wishes the bid to be submitted and how payments are to be made. Currently, the most common is a fixed-firm bid, which means that the production company's bid is firm based on the information supplied by the agency, and that it will produce the commercial elements as agreed to by this contract for the exact amount specified in the contract. Any additional payments to the production company would be made only for major changes in the job's specifications, subject to negotiation.

Less popular is the cost-plus-fixed-fee arrangement. When using this method of contract, all of the variable items in the bid are reasonable estimates of what the production

FILM PRODUCTION COST SUMMARY

[X] Firm Bid   [ ] Cost Plus   Bid Date: 2/21/02

			Job#:
	Job#:		
Production Contact:		Client/Product:	
Director:		Producer:	Tel:
Dir. of Photography:		Art Dir:	Tel:
Producer:		Writer:	Tel:
Editor:		Bus. Mgr:	Tel:
No. pre-pro days:		Commercial Title/Code/Length:	
No. pre-light days:		1.	
No. build/strike days:		2.	
No. studio shoot days:		3.	
No. location days:		4.	
Location sites:		5.	

SUMMARY OF ESTIMATED PRODUCTION COSTS		ESTIMATED	ACTUAL	
1. Pre-production and wrap costs	Total A & C			
2. Shooting crew labor	Total B			
3. Location and travel expenses	Total D			
4. Props / wardrobe and animals	Total E			
5. Studio & set construction costs	Total F/G/H			
6. Equipment costs	Total I			
7. Film stock develop & print	Total J			
8. Miscellaneous	Total K			
9. SUB-TOTAL	A thru K			
10. Director/Creative fees	Total L			
11. Insurance				
12. SUB-TOTAL	Direct Costs			
13. Production fee				
14. Talent costs and expenses	Total M & N			
15. Editorial and finishing	Totals O & P			
16.				
17. GRAND TOTAL	(Incl. Director's fee)			
18. Contingency				

Comments:

This bid is submitted under the stipulation of the adherence to the AICP Production Guidelines.

MediaBid(tm)

FIGURE 5.3   This is the first page of the AICP bid form. Commercial production companies complete this form and submit their bids, along with the directors' treatments, to agencies.

Courtesy of the Association of Independent Commercial Producers & Media Bid. Reprinted with permission.

company believes labor and materials will be. This estimated cost is then added to a fixed fee, which covers overhead and markup. At the end of production, the production company actualizes all of the costs and bills these costs plus the fixed fee. The complete cost-plus-fixed-fee method is quite complex and is based on very specific agency administrative rules, that are beyond the scope of this book; however, many in the commercial production business believe it gives the advertising agency and client greater control over costs. This method is not used often because of the high cost of administration and the need to divert key agency and production company personnel from their primary functions.

On some occasions, a firm bid cannot be accurately estimated at the time of bidding. In such cases, the agency and the production company may agree to make a reasonable estimate of this area and to allow adjustments in cost based on actual expenses, when they are known. Any up or down adjustments on this line item will cause the production fee to be adjusted as well. Examples of items that may require such adjustments are: film stock, especially for jobs that require high-speed shooting for a specific effect; the expense for a special working prop that must be designed and then custom built.

Bid Analysis

After the production companies submit their bids, the agency analyzes the bids, along with the treatments, and takes into account the telephone discussions with the director about his production ideas. Agency business managers, producers, and executive producers check the budget carefully. They ponder line items, unit costs, number of units, and all other elements included in the bid, plus they consider the cost assumptions submitted by the production company on the bid form or cover letter. Discussions and negotiations take place between the agency and the production companies to make any adjustments the agency believes are appropriate and the production companies agree to. Sometimes the client hires an independent contractor, known as a cost controller, to also review and comment on bids. Bids for shooting commercials in foreign countries are particularly difficult to analyze; the exchange rate alone can cause havoc.

Finally, a price is agreed on based on what the agency and the chosen production company agree will be required to do the job. While in a few cases a client has rules that a production job must go to the lowest bidder, this is not normally the case. Jobs are generally awarded to the production company and its director when the bid seems to be in sync with the agency's concept and the price is reasonable and justifiable for what is to be delivered. It is not unusual for the high bidder to get the production contract.

SUMMARY

National and regional commercials, which are most often designed by an agency and then shot by production companies, usually require the agency to hire a carefully selected film director to shoot the commercial. This process is not at all unlike the process that takes place in Hollywood when major film studios seek out and hire the best possible director for the style and genre of the film they want to produce.

A directors is often attached to a production company, which he may own or with which she may be under contract. The production company provides logistical and business support for the director, who concentrates more on the creative side of the production.

The job of the director is, first of all, to fully understand the creative concept the agency developed and sold to its client. This concept is part of an overarching creative approach that may also be executed in other media, such as print or outdoor. It is, therefore, not a stand-alone, isolated film project but part of a more complex advertising campaign. The concept was developed specifically to reach a targeted audience with a message, which was determined strategically at a much earlier stage. The director's job is to understand and to work within this reality.

The director must then interpret the concept in the film medium—he chooses the elements of the visual language that will be best to render the concept on film. What are these elements? The director chooses the setting (locations, for example) and the cast. He selects the crew, including the cinematographer. He chooses the camera equipment and lenses that he thinks about how these can be used to achieve the effect he wants. He chooses how the set should be lit and where the camera should be positioned and how it should be moved. The director frames and composes each shot, deciding on close-ups, medium shots, and long shots. The skill and time the director employs while directing all of these aspects of the shoot adds what is known as *production value* to the commercial.

An ad agency searches for the director who can understand its concept and then interpret it properly by studying demo reels of directors' past work. Directors are usually marketed by sales reps, who provide demo reels to agency producers and creatives and look for projects that are good matches for the agencies. The agency then invites several appropriate directors to bid on the commercial it has designed. The directors, through their respective production companies, submit bids that include all of the costs as well as a creative treatment—basically a narrative description of how the director would shoot the spot. Bids are submitted on standard forms called AICP bid forms. Because all production companies submit bids on the standard form, the agency can easily compare them.

Typically, the deal between the production company and the agency is called a firm-fixed bid, which means the cost of production quoted by the company is the price the agency will pay unless overages are approved later.

DISCUSSION QUESTIONS

1. Why would the agency wait until the client has approved the creative concept before looking for the director of the commercial? Why don't they do this first?

2. Why is the director so important, and why is so much time and effort devoted to finding the right one for a national or regional commercial?

3. Why would an agency choose a director and a production company that is not the lowest bidder for a commercial project?

4. What is the difference between the firm-fixed bid and the cost-plus-fixed fee deal that the production company and the agency may have? Why would some of the costs be too difficult to estimate? Can you think of some things a creative concept may call for that would be impossible to price-out ahead of time?

RECOMMENDED WEB SITES

Ad Age Magazine—www.AdAge.com

Ad Age is one of the premier magazines of the advertising industry, and its Web site provides daily access to the latest news and commentary affecting the industry. Annually, usually in May, it publishes the media expenditures for all advertising in the United States for the previous year.

Electronic Creative Search—www.eCreativeSearch.com

eCreativeSearch is a subscription-based Internet service for the commercial broadcast production industry. It provides access to a searchable and comprehensive database of directors, production companies, musicians and other talent, and support services, as well as sample commercials entirely online.

Association of Independent Commercial Producers—www.aicp.com

The AICP represents the interests of U.S. companies specializing in production of commercials on various media—film, video, computer—for advertisers and agencies. AICP members account for 85 percent of all domestic commercials aired nationally, whether produced for traditional broadcast channels or non-traditional use.

The Directors' Network—www.directors-network.com

A Web site of a talent agency for commercial directors and DPs. The site has a nice list of directors, along with a synopsis of their strengths (tabletop, dialogue, etc.); it includes directors' biographies and stories about how they got into the business. It's a good source of inspiration for the student filmmaker.

NOTE

1. See adweek.com. "Top Twenty Commercials of the Last Twenty Years," August 22, 2002.

CHAPTER SIX

THE CLIENT ESTIMATE

A commercial is a prototype. Al Lapides, then a production manager with Leo Burnett Advertising, made this point during a meeting with his client, General Motors, in the early 1970s. The client had asked the classic question, "Why do commercials cost so much?" Lapides had heard the question many times before, and answered in the form of an analogy that he thought would hit home with his client:

> I asked how much one of their current model cars cost to build when produced on their production line. (Bear in mind we are talking 1974 dollars!) The answer was $3,500. I then asked how much this car would cost if it was a new, never-produced model; all they had was an approved drawing but not an actual blueprint or clay model; they had to start the build at 7 AM and have it completed by 8 PM. They would have all the labor, equipment, and materials available that they could possibly need to build this car in one facility; [would] allow for design changes as it was being produced based on suggested improvements; and they had to have it ready for formal presentation to management the following morning at 9 AM.

Naturally, the questioner understood immediately that this accurately describes the production of a commercial. Every commercial is a one-off prototype based on an idea. It has to be transformed into a tangible piece of audio/video material and physically projected or transmitted in one or two days. During production, all labor, talent, materials, equipment, and support systems—everything from catering to electrical power—must be available and ready for use. Alternate lenses, additional wardrobe, a full complement of lighting and grip equipment must be on hand just in case. Many commercials require untested performances, rigs, and effects, and the filmmakers have to have backup plans in case things don't work as hoped. Strong egos must bend, or blend. There must be a marriage of art and commerce. Everything must come together in a very tight time frame so that when "wrap" is called at the end of the day, all of the live elements necessary to build the finished commercial are "in the can." All of this costs a great deal—sometimes close to $1,000,000.

In this chapter, we discuss an important step in getting a commercial's production off the ground—preparation of the client estimate and getting approval from the client to proceed. The *client estimate* is a breakdown of the costs to produce the commercial as it is conceived by the director, along with all of the other costs the agency will incur to produce other elements of the spot. It isn't possible to create an accurate client estimate until the director is selected, as you read in chapter 5, because her ideas about how to shoot the commercial affect its cost. The client estimate is so closely woven in with the creative and technical approach proposed by the director that the estimate and the approach are usually presented to the client during a formal meeting.

In the last chapter, you saw the agency find and recommend its preferred director and obtain a fixed budget from the director's company for his part of the work. Now the agency must find other contractors to take on other aspects of production, including music production, talent, animation, and special effects. Contracting for other production elements involves some complex negotiations with copyright holders for music, sound effects, and perhaps stock footage. There will be negotiations with agents for special talent; and discussions about adherence to union agreements (when a union has jurisdiction) regarding talent payments and reuse payments and to government regulations about using child talent. Most of these tasks are the responsibility of the agency producer, although she may delegate some of them to others.

At the agency, this is a time when the purely creative concepts come head-to-head with, and sometimes compromise, production realities. The agency production team becomes fully mobilized at this point; the various members assigned to work on the project evaluate the commercial concept from a production standpoint. Each member of the team brings a certain perspective and field of expertise, all of which are necessary for the successful completion of the commercial. While the agency production people may have been, in fact should have been, involved in the basic creative process that led up to the approvals by the client, they now become immersed in the project.

In this chapter, you will learn the following:

- Who the members of the agency's production team are
- What are the team's roles and responsibilities
- What costs go into the client estimate and how to get them
- What sources for music are available, and the differences in costs and getting rights
- What issues are important when casting talent, celebrities, and children
- How to get clearances from the network
- How to prepare the final client estimate

A considerable amount of work goes into the preparation of the client estimate, most of it by the agency production team in a relatively short period of time. The members make a lot of phone calls, send a lot of e-mails and faxes, gather costs and commitments from a number of vendors together, negotiate with talent, and check and double check the legality and tastefulness of the planned commercial. It is very important that the cost estimate, and the various production assumptions (and promises) made to the client be accurate. Trying to get more money, time, or a creative compromise from the client later can be extremely difficult (and embarrassing).

THE AGENCY PRODUCTION TEAM

At the agency, the production team usually consists of an executive producer, a producer, a production manager/business manager, and an associate production manager. The following job descriptions are used at Leo Burnett Advertising in Chicago, and probably at other agencies as well, perhaps with some differences to take advantage of the gifts and talents of specific individuals. At some agencies, particularly small agencies serving local or regional clients, some of the people will be *hyphenates*—they will perform more than one, perhaps all, of the functions described next. Small agencies that don't do a lot of television work often hire freelancers to handle some of these functions, or even turn over the tasks to the production company.

Executive Producer

The executive producer is a senior production person who is directly responsible for managing production activities for more than one client. He deals directly with clients on overall production issues, as opposed to production details, although the executive producer gets involved in solving specific problems when necessary. He reports to the head of the production department, with other lines of responsibility to the head creative person on the project—creative director, executive creative director, and so on. His role is to function as advisor to the creative group in areas of production. Because of his experience, the executive producer can look at a creative concept and make some judgments about costs, time frames, doability, and potential problems. He assists in selecting the production company/director.

The executive producer supervises producers who have more of the day-to-day management responsibilities for specific commercial productions. In some agencies, he has producers assigned to him, and in other agencies the executive producer may draw from a producer pool for personnel support. When this is the case, the executive producer tries to match the experience and strength of a producer to the needs of the commercial.

Ultimately, he is responsible to agency management and the head of the production department. He is responsible for approving production estimates prior to submission and may explain production estimates to the client. Because the executive producer is familiar with all production issues—what is possible, what things cost, how long things take to do—he often negotiates directly with production companies and other suppliers on specific issues and costs.

Producer

The producer has the "line function" responsibility; she is the primary agency representative who is responsible for all production suppliers on any production issue. The producer is present during every aspect of planning, shooting, and postproduction and is responsible for the myriad of small details that every commercial production entails. She acts as the liaison between creatives at the agency and production suppliers. Although largely a time-and-budget management position, the producer also can make creative suggestions. Because she is ultimately responsible for production budget management, she is directly involved in the selection of the director.

The following are some of the things the producer does during the cost-estimating process:

- Establishes the production calendar and delivery schedule. She plans the chronological sequence of events, who is involved, what they deliver or do, and how that leads into the next step. The producer must do this now so that, as she gets commitments from various other contractors and vendors, she can tell them when they are needed.

- Prepares production specification sheets. These need to be included in bid packages to other contractors and suppliers that may be needed.
- Reviews submitted bids. Bids (cost estimates) come in from the various other contractors and vendors; they need to be checked for accuracy and reviewed with the business manager/production manager and executive producer.
- Puts together the final client estimate and presents it to the client.

Once production begins, the agency producer will have a number of responsibilities, which we discuss in detail in the next several chapters. Briefly, they include the following:

- Review of all production invoicing.
- Attends all casting sessions, preproduction meetings, and shoots.
- Gives casting director go ahead to book talent.
- Participates in selection of voiceover and/or character voice casting.
- Attends all recording and music sessions.
- Signs and approves all talent contracts and prepares production reports.
- Ensures that all agency-supplied material, such as color-corrected art, packaging, stats, titles for postproduction, layouts for digital creation, get to where they are needed.
- Ensures that all necessary clearances are in place prior to production.
- Is responsible for getting all demonstration and testimonial affidavits, as well as any other releases and waivers needed during production.

We'd be getting ahead of ourselves if we went into detail here about what some of the terms and concepts are—we will cover them later. If you are anxious, go ahead and look in the glossary for definitions of the terms you are not familiar with—affidavits, clearances—and other important terms!

ELISE KLEINMAN, GREY WORLDWIDE ASSISTANT PRODUCER

Elise Kleinman is a twenty-five-year-old assistant producer at Grey Worldwide, one of the world's premier advertising agencies serving clients such as 3M, ConAgra Foods, Olive Garden, Glaxo-SmithKline, Hasbro, Kraft Foods, Slim•Fast Foods Company, and Procter & Gamble. Kleinman is based in New York and is responsible for commercial production on the Hasbro account.

In her wildest dreams, Kleinman did not know that she would wind up producing spots for a major client, managing schedules and budgets in the hundreds of thousands of dollars, and working with some of the top creative talent in the business. "I grew up in Cleveland and wanted to be an actor," she said. "I even studied theater at Indiana University." But after a year, she switched to telecommunications, believing it would provide her with a more steady career path. She took a particular interest in children's television, so she focused all of her classes and studies on it. Her thesis was on FCC guidelines for children's television and the criteria that would create the ideal kid's show.

Between semesters, Kleinman went to New York City in pursuit of an internship in children's television, "Without knowing a soul," as she put it. "I just knew I wanted to get a job in this field." She interned at Nickelodeon, and then at the International Radio TV Society, where she was placed in a production company doing sales and marketing. "This was *not* my cup of tea," she said, "but some of my fellow interns were at Grey Worldwide and they told me about the toy division, which interested me." She was extremely aggressive about applying for the job at Grey—focusing all of her energy at getting an assistant producer job on the Hasbro account. They liked her attitude and hired her.

Her job at the agency landed her in a "village." At Grey, everybody who works on an account is co-located in one area—near one another to foster communication and teamwork. Kleinman works in a group that calls itself BuzzGrey because, "We work on young, hip accounts, like Hasbro," she said. The group consists of creative people, producers, account people, and brand planners. Kleinman reports to the head producer of the group functionally and to the creative director administratively. Her main job is to produce commercials for Hasbro.

Each group is also a P&L (profit and loss) center—responsible for its bottom line. Not only does the group produce commercials for Hasbro, Mars, Smucker's, and Panasonic, but they also pitch new business. Whenever they identify a possible new client (maybe an advertiser is shopping for a new agency or coming out with a new brand), Kleinman produces videos for the pitch the creative people develop.

On all projects, Kleinman has certain responsibilities, certain authorities, and is held accountable for the bottom line and the final product. Her primary responsibility is to create and manage the budget for the spot. Her boss tells her the budget range, or the ceiling ("It cannot cost more than X"); it is her responsibility to figure out how to get everything done within that amount. Once things start, she coordinates everything—the creative team, the production company, the editorial company, the music company. "I have to make sure everybody is on the same schedule," she explains. It is Kleinman's responsibility to find the director, or at least to narrow down the selection and to present that short list to the creative director. "We have to bid three directors, so I start with maybe a hundred, winnow it down to maybe twenty, and then cut it down to three with the creative team."

At the end of the project, Kleinman is held accountable for the budget and the schedule and whether the commercial is any good. During the shoot, she can voice an opinion about how things look, but she must defer to the creative people who also observe and approve what the director does. "I always have an opinion, but the creative people have the last word. If they ask me, and I don't like what I see, they sometimes agree and say, 'Okay, go tell him.' But the creative team is really in charge, and if they like it, then it stays that way."

Kleinman has worked with companies in New York, Los Angeles, Seattle, and even London. "That was hard, because of the time difference," she said. "I'd be just getting to work and their day would be ending."

When asked what the most important attribute for a producer is, Kleinman didn't hesitate: "You have to be a really good people person. Producers come from a lot of backgrounds. Some of them used to be performers—from the creative side of things—and they have more respect for the director and the actors and the creative process. And then there are those who come from business, and are so concerned with the budget and that side of things. You have to be able to deal with a lot of personalities. And to be strong."

Business Manager/Production Manager

The production manager assists the producer in the preparation of bid packages, which include spec sheets, scripts, production notes, and storyboards, and is responsible for sending them to contractors for bidding. He maintains all the files related to production, creating what is known as the *paper trail*—a detailed record of every memo, letter, meeting, agreement, contract, invoice, and other documents mentioned before.

He prepares the production cost estimate based on input from the producer and various suppliers. The producer may delegate other tasks to the production manager, such as obtaining clearances, although this is sometimes handled by the client services department or by the agency's legal department. He works with the producer on the logistics of production and coordinates the delivery of agency- or client-supplied materials, products, or props.

During production, he maintains all the official records and files about the production and manages the job's overall budget by tracking all costs and doing continuous reconciliation—comparing what the costs were expected to be (the estimate) with what they actually turned out to be (the actuals)—with the estimate. The production manager revises the budget, as required, and notifies accounting to make sure people get paid in a timely manner. He books recording sessions according to the schedule, or as needed, and prepares and issues all purchase orders and production contracts, unless the agency's production department manager issues the contracts. He also provides input on policies to production management. Organizationally, the production manager may be part of the executive producer's group or he may report directly to the head of agency production.

Production Assistant

The production assistant assists the business manager/production manager or the producer. Many college students land here as interns, or as a first job after graduation. As an assistant, he may be the one who actually maintains the files. He takes minutes of all meetings and acts as the gofer, delivering paperwork, getting copies made, and assembling bid packages and preproduction notebooks. The production assistant may set up meetings, screen videos or DVDs for the producers and creative executives, send production-related communications, and perform other functions associated with production.

While job titles and job descriptions vary from one agency to another, all of the tasks performed by these individuals must be covered by someone from the agency. There are very talented people who can perform more than one job function, and some can double-up on the tasks—at small agencies, they have to. Others are so good at what they do that they have only one title and job, such as producer, but can work on more than one commercial at a time.

THE CLIENT ESTIMATE

The production team, using the agency's creative concept, the director's treatment, and the production company's bid price as starting points, pulls together all of the costs that will make up the client estimate. The estimate is a document submitted to the client by the agency; it itemizes all of the anticipated costs for producing the commercial. If the cost of the commercial agreed to with the production company, along with the costs for the other production elements (see next section), are acceptable, the client signs the estimate for the total production.

Class Exercise

Think it's easy to figure out what all the costs might be? It's pretty hard even when you're looking right at the finished product! Screen a commercial for the class and break down what the probable line items were. Start with location, sets, props, wardrobe, and other fixtures, then go on to talent and crew. What about film and development? Transportation? Copyright fees? You may have to finish reading this chapter to find out what some of the other cost items might be.

The estimate binds the client contractually to the commercial production and allows the agency to make contracts or issue purchase orders for all the items needed to produce it. The client often pays an agreed-on portion of the cost right away so that the agency has money to proceed with the work. Many agencies have prior agreements with production companies, postproduction companies, and music production companies with terms and conditions under which business can be done. Purchase orders for a work on a specific commercial will fall under the general terms of the existing agreement.

OTHER PRODUCTION COSTS

In the past, production companies shot, edited, and delivered a complete finished commercial. Over the years, however, the commercial production business has changed. A full-service production company with complete casting, animation, sound mixing, film compositing, studio, and editorial services is very rare. Rhythm & Hues, the production company profiled in the previous chapter, is one of those rare full service companies. Most production companies have become leaner.

Many production companies have a minimum staff to reduce overhead, and they hire all services on an as-needed basis. The services once found in talent under one roof at large companies have spun off and become independent contractors. In most cases, the agency contracts directly with others for services necessary for the production and completion of a commercial. For business reasons, occasionally the agency asks the production company to subcontract some of these services, but this would be the exception to normal commercial production practice today.

To assemble the client estimate, the agency production team has to find out what all of those other costs will be; to do this they must do the following:

- Get bids from other contractors who will create animation, graphics, or special effects
- Estimate how much postproduction will be needed and where it will be done

- Find out where to get the music for the commercial and what it will cost
- Determine the cost for special talent (celebrities, for example) to appear in the commercial
- Take into account the additional cost of having children appear in the commercial
- Factor in reuse payments and other ongoing costs of running the commercial

Bidding Other Contractors

Bidding for postproduction, animation, computer-generated animation, special effects, and music is handled in much the same way as bidding for live-action shots with a production company. This means that agencies have to review demo reels from many potential contractors; talk to many reps; and keep abreast of many small, niche companies. Bid packages are sent with specifications, notes, scripts, storyboards, and other appropriate materials. The agency spells out exactly which elements or services it wants the bid to be based on. Since so many new techniques have been incorporated into commercial production in the past several years, many more specialists are now contracted separately.

Postproduction

One of the most important of the subcontracted services is postproduction, where the final footage is usually transferred to tape or digitized into a computer system for editing, color-correcting, compositing different layers of images, adding special effects, adding graphics, adding computer animation, and syncing with sound effects and music. Postproduction is where all of the raw elements are creatively incorporated and timed out to get to the finished commercial. The agency contracts directly with postproduction houses, which usually have a rate card that states specifically what services they offer and at what cost. Most of the time, the agency pays by the hour to use the facility, but some facilities also give a flat rate for a spot. For the Centro commercial discussed in chapter 4, the post house Daily Post gave the agency, Eric Mower & Associates, a flat rate to edit one commercial. When the client and the agency decided to make five more commercials, Daily Post quoted them a new price. An agency often books time based on the availability of a particular editor or postproduction specialist.

Although major agencies use postproduction houses for work on commercials for major national advertisers, local advertisers have to keep costs down. Computer-based nonlinear editing systems, such as the Avid/DS HD Editor and Final Cut Pro (see Figure 6.1), are relatively inexpensive and have become commonplace at small local editing shops and television stations. In the hands of skillful editors, even locally produced commercials can have high production values.

Music Costs

Music is a key element in most commercials, providing mood, pacing, a sense of space, color, and emotion. It can be the mnemonic device that ties together the visual images even more effectively than the transitions, effects, and other visual elements. Over the years, certain advertisers have been able to use musical notation, just the notation, to create advertiser

FIGURE 6.1 The Final Cut Pro nonlinear editing system is affordable and very powerful; using it makes it possible to achieve a high-budget look even in small markets with low budgets.

recognition. More recently, with the advent of MTV, VH1, and the growth of the youth audience, music and musical talent have an even more heightened role in commercials.

From a producer's point of view, the two most important considerations, other than the creative decision about what the music should sound like, are the cost to acquire the music and the license to use it. Unlike film footage shot by the director, which becomes the property of the client immediately, several sources of music for a commercial remain the property of the composer, or another rights holder, and never become the property of the client. Instead, the client licenses the right to use the music in its commercial. The producer must have a working knowledge of copyright law to keep these ownership issues straight.

When music is to be used, creatives need to decide if music will be originally composed and arranged, or if it will be needle drop—it is already recorded and will be licensed for use in the commercial as is. A third possible source for music is known as public domain. A fourth option is library music, used almost all the time in local and low-budget spots. We describe each of these next.

Library Music. Let's talk about this last option first. Library music usually comes in the form of CD collections that represent a wide variety of styles and genres of musical pieces. Music production companies create these libraries specifically to be used by others for commercials, films, and television programs, and they license the entire library, royalty free, on very attractive terms. The Newhouse School at Syracuse University has agreements with several music libraries so that its students can have access to a wide variety of musical arrangements for their film and video projects (see Figure 6.2). The school also has licensed sound effects libraries.

Music libraries are also available over the Web. A simple Internet search will result in hundreds of hits if you use the term "music library" *and* "royalty free." InstantMusic Now.com, for example, offers music downloads, after you become a member, in MP3 format. Others offer CD libraries like those described before, but you can listen to samples online. There are two licensing arrangements for music libraries: (1) The licensee can pay a fee for the entire library and then pay the licenser an additional royalty fee, based on its length, every time a piece from the library is used; (2) the licensee can pay a higher fee for the library and then use it at any time, for any purpose.

Class Exercise

Remember that political ad from chapter 1? You discussed a possible creative concept for it in class, and chose a theme. What kind of music would be appropriate for it? Can you find the right music on the Web? Search for a music library and listen to samples. Choose appropriate music for the ad.

Original Music.   Creating original music for a commercial is sometimes the most expensive option, particularly if the music involves orchestras or large ensembles and singers. Not only will the client pay for the composition and the recording, but it may also want to acquire full ownership of the copyright to the music, which could involve still more costs. The client does not automatically own the copyright to original music even though it pays for composing and recording. According to copyright law, a copyright exists for a written score the moment it is fixed on paper—the publishing rights—and another copyright exists the moment the music is recorded—the mechanical rights.

FIGURE 6.2   A royalty-free music and sound effects library like this one at the Newhouse School at Syracuse University provides students with access to a wide range of music for their commercial production projects.

There are literally thousands of music arranger/composers/musicians who can be hired to write and record music for a commercial; they are located everywhere. Internet technology has made it possible for musicians to live wherever they please; to write and record music; and then to ship it to clients in MP3, Quicktime, or other standard digital formats via the Internet. When you use one of these composer/arrangers, it is a bit simpler to get the music you want and the rights to it because you can deal with a single individual for both the publishing and the mechanical rights. In either case, the copyright owner must *assign* the copyright to the client in a written agreement. Without a copyright for the music, the client can only license the right to use the music for its commercial and can not use it for any other purpose, including another commercial, without the permission of the copyright holder.

Needle Drop.   If previously composed and recorded music will be licensed for the commercial, it's called needle drop; the term *needle drop* dates from the days when music was stored on vinyl recordings and played on turntables. Audio technicians would literally lower the arm with the play needle over the cut on an album that the producer wanted to license, and the music would be copied onto the magnetic stripe on 35mm film. If the creative approach for the commercial calls for well-known and already popular music, it may be necessary to license a needle drop.

The rights issues can be quite complicated when prerecorded music is required. A composer may own the publishing rights, a musician may own the mechanical rights, and another party may own the television or movie rights. Because there can be so many rights holders in the music business, large agencies have a department devoted specifically to obtaining the rights for music; the producer just tells someone there what is needed and it is taken care of. Smaller agencies can hire independent rights clearance experts.

In a typical scenario, the agency producer (or the aforementioned department) negotiates a music license fee, along with other terms and conditions, with the music publisher who acts on behalf of the composer or rights holder. The fee is based on the commercial value of the composition, the intended use by the advertiser, and any potential future business that may be lost by licensing this music for this specific commercial project. A client may need to have a very long-term association with a piece of music; this must be given careful consideration by those charged with protecting a copyright.

There is evidence that the value and recognition of music is enhanced when it is used in a commercial; for example, the commercial value of *Rhapsody in Blue* by George Gershwin, has increased since it's been used by United Air Lines. It has used the piece for many years, which has actually raised public awareness of the song and the composer. This was true also when Marlboro cigarettes used music from *The Magnificent Seven*. What music are you hearing now in commercials, and does this make you more aware of it, the composer, and the artist?

On the other hand, music chosen for a commercial can become the signature of the product or service and become too closely identified with it. When this happens, the music copyright owner runs the risk of reducing its value for any other purpose. If the music becomes completely interwoven with the product or service, it may be difficult to license it for any other use. All of these are the concerns of both the rights holder and the agency when they negotiate a price and the terms of a licensing agreement.

Public Domain.   Public domain music is music in which no arranger/composer has any current legal right of ownership, usually because the copyright period has ended and was not renewed, or because it was never copyrighted. Such music can be used without a license agreement. However, even if music is in the public domain, a particular arrangement of it may have a current copyright. Marilyn Monroe's rendition of "Happy Birthday," which she sang to John F. Kennedy, is owned by her estate even though the music itself is in the public domain. In fact, the "Happy Birthday" lyrics are copyrighted, so *any* version of the song with the lyrics may not be used without separate licensing.

Other Cautions.   The agreement for licensing famous, recognizable songs should be worked out prior to the signing of the client estimate, as should the use of any special singers. Performers have rights to their performances; even if an advertiser obtains the rights to a song, the performance rights of the talent is nearly always a separate negotiation. There can be very serious problems if, while recording either licensed or original music, the style of a famous artist is infringed on. Use of "sound-alikes" for commercials is frowned on. It is a very bad idea to tell a music producer or a casting director that you are looking for someone *like* "so 'n so." Be careful not to mention specific talent or a specific song, or in fact anything you do not own or have a right to use in any script, board, or other agency communication. This can be used as proof of intent to imitate, which in today's world is legally actionable—they could sue you. Major clients with deep pockets are especially vulnerable. In all cases, it is best for a client to own a musical composition outright so that it can be used anytime, anywhere, and anyway the client desires.

Talent Costs

Although actual casting does not take place during the preparation of the client estimate, the producer must include a cost estimate for the talent. So, at this point in the process, the producer evaluates what kind of talent will be needed and what the costs, both short and long term, will be.

An audience identifies with people appearing in a commercial whose age, apparent lifestyle, and behaviors are most like its own; people also admire certain personalities, authority figures, and celebrities. This identification leads to positive and longer-lasting attention to the commercial and, ideally, to remembering the product. So casting ideas occur at the creative development stage when things, such as the demographics and psychographics of the intended audience, are carefully weighed. When making casting decisions, creatives also consider the genre of the commercial—comedic, romantic, action–adventure, or fantasy. When preparing the client estimate, casting ideas are explored from a practical point of view to arrive at possible costs.

The cast of the commercial may include actors (male and female, adults and children), nonactors who give testimonials, dancers, celebrities, announcers, and models. Models are also used for specific body parts such as eyes, feet, or hands. A hand model may be an expert at pouring a product or handling a package. Animals are often cast and hired as talent. Some talent will have featured speaking and/or visual parts—the principal actors—and others will be extras. There will be negotiations with celebrities—recognizable sports stars or politicians (Who can forget the Bob Dole Viagra commercial?); reviews of contractual obligations with the unions for payment, benefits, and reuse payments; and consideration of laws and regulations related to child actors and the use of nonactors who give testimonials.

Professional talents in the United States work under the jurisdiction of either the Screen Actors Guild (SAG) or the American Federation of Television and Radio Artists (AFTRA), both of which have contracts with commercial producers and agencies. These contracts are negotiated between talent unions and a Joint Policy Committee (JPC) made up of advertisers (ANA, Association of National Advertisers) and agencies (4As, American Association of Advertising Agencies). The contracts contain well over 100 pages that spell out in detail what the payment schedules are for scale talent. Even extras in many geographic areas work under the unions' jurisdictions; and, in some cases, union contracts must be honored even when producing outside of the United States.

The creative concept may call for regular scale talent,[1] or it may call for special talent—someone who has special appeal, name recognition, or endorsement value. The difference in cost can be considerable because union scale for SAG actors is currently $500.00 per eight-hour day, while a guest appearance by a luminary, such as Michael Jordan or Mariah Carey, could cost in the hundreds of thousands of dollars. Casting special "name" talent is risky, especially if the entire concept is premised on the talent. It requires careful negotiations and if those negotiations fail, the whole creative concept could be doomed.

If the commercial calls for children to perform, there are child labor laws and union rules that affect production scheduling, costs, and other logistics. It may be necessary for parents, tutors, or welfare workers to be present during the shoots. Agency producers must be knowledgeable about these requirements and account for the costs and tasks.

Certain situations call for using nonprofessional actors in commercials. An example is when the commercial includes testimonials from ordinary people. There are rules in the SAG and AFTRA contracts as to how this must be handled if the commercials are produced within these union jurisdictions. Nonunion actors/announcers can also be used in certain other situations. Sometimes, nonunion talent can be "bought out" for a period of time; this usually occurs in commercials for smaller, nonnational advertisers in nonmajor markets or when production takes place in other countries using foreign talent.

Besides the fees paid to talent for appearing in the commercial, the agency has to pay union talent for a call-back session during casting (usually two hours of work) and for holding fees and residuals when the commercial is run. *Holding fees* hold the talent to exclusive use in the product category. Residuals can really add up if the commercial runs for a period of time and/or runs in twenty or more markets. Every union actor in the cast will be paid on a sliding scale—it starts out high and drops down—for each showing of the commercial. During preparation of the client estimate, the producer must factor in all of these future costs.

Legal and Continuity Clearance

At this time, the producer must make sure that a commercial will meet all of the legal requirements, as well as the continuity acceptance requirements of the media. It would be pointless to get client budget approval for a commercial that cannot be used; needs significant reshooting or reediting; or, worse yet, exposes the client or the agency to legal actions.

Legal clearance usually involves the agency's client service staff, production business staff, legal staff or outside counsel, and the client's legal staff. They all study and evaluate the commercial copy and storyboard to look for potential legal hurdles. The following are some areas of concern:

- Factual accuracy—the truth of the statements made. Did the law firm really get every dime it could for its clients (see chapter 2)?
- Support of claims—If the announcer says the adhesive product will hold two tons of metal together, the client must have proof that it has done this.
- Substantiation of demonstrations—The agency must sign a document that says the demonstration of the adhesive product holding two one-ton I-beams together really happened, that it wasn't faked. Although this will be done at the time of the shoot, the producer must be sure it won't be faked.
- Adherence to all testimonial requirements—Michael Jordan really does wear Hanes underwear and is willing to sign an affidavit saying so.
- Proper releases—The owner of the home where the commercial will be shot signs a document giving permission to use his property.
- Avoidance of any infringement on some other person's and/or company's copyrighted trademark—The producer gets permission from the taxi company to use a "Checker" cab in the commercial for a florist.
- Committing an unlawful trade practice.

Continuity clearance is between the agency and the television networks. Each of the broadcast networks has standards and guidelines for what they will accept for broadcast commercials. Although these include the legal guidelines listed before, they also include standards for obscenity, lewdness, social behavior, and stringent standards to prevent possible exploitation of children. Among the major networks, there are more than 207 pages of published clearance standards and guidelines, which are similar to but not identical from one network to the next.

The original television networks—NBC, CBS and ABC—established commercial clearance from their roots in radio. The word continuity refers to the *copy,* or the original radio script for both program material and commercial material, which the continuity clearance departments cleared, approved. Of course, it was a natural progression for this function to move over to television. The area that we deal with here is *commercial* continuity clearance. The newer networks—Fox, UPN, WB, PAX—have also integrated commercial clearance into their operations.

Individual broadcast stations also clear commercials but, in practice, if a commercial is cleared by the network clearance departments, most stations, especially those that are owned and operated by the networks, will accept the commercials without hassles. Some stations have looser standards than the networks. Cable networks and local cable providers are not in the same regulatory situation as broadcast stations, so they have fewer restrictions on the material they can cablecast. The actual process of getting a commercial cleared is summarized next.

Clearance Mechanics

The agency producer or the agency clearance department, if it has one, submits a script and a storyboard to each network commercial clearance office as early as possible in the process. At the network, the clearance department uses specific guidelines and standards to evaluate the concept.

Some standards are set in stone while others are subject to negotiation or fine-tuning to gain network acceptance. Commercials for hard liquor or abortion services are not acceptable under any circumstance (although there seems to be some loosening of restrictions on alcoholic beverages). Rules as to how toys are portrayed in a commercial are subject to very specific guidelines, which are rarely bent. The networks have strict rules about what kind of language can be used in ads aimed at children; for example, an ad cannot urge a child to ask his mother to buy the product.

But the networks will negotiate on matters about many other issues. The networks may object to a few words of copy, a camera angle, or a costume. If something is in dispute, back-and-forth negotiations over an issue take place between the network and the agency. However, acceptance by one network does not ensure acceptance by another, and all acceptances are contingent on the final commercial. The networks may return material with comments, asking for substantiation of claims or changes based on their standards and practices; they may define specific problems or issues they have with the commercial. It is federal law (part of the Communications Act) that the sponsor of a broadcast advertisement be identified in the commercial. This identification can be in either the video, audio, or both. It seems that a well-known trademark such as the McDonald's arches or the Nike swoosh is considered an acceptable identification. Many creatives have tried to create "teaser" campaigns without an identification in the commercial. While this is an acceptable technique in most forms of media, it is not acceptable in broadcast. Normally, this is avoided by use of a small super. There are specific separate rules about sponsor identification in political advertising for broadcast.

Years ago, Leo Burnett executive Alan Lapides had to clear a commercial for a premium to be given in a store with the purchase of a client's clothing product. Here is his description of the event:

> It was a "rocket ring." In the commercial we showed kids in a backyard with a rocket ship. One network insisted that if we showed the "rocket" in the backyard it had to be built with materials readily available to kids and could be assembled by kids. We submitted the final commercial. The network representative told me that he agreed that this rocket could have been built by kids, provided the kids' father was head of the prop department of a major feature film studio. He threatened to reject it. But in the end he did allow the commercial to be aired. The final commercial was finished and submitted only a day or two prior to [its] first scheduled airing.

For years, advertisers have had issues with commercial clearances because there seems to be a double standard. What the networks disallow in commercials is routinely seen in both programming and network program promotions.

There is one type of commercial that the networks may not, by law, subject to clearance. The Federal Communications Act specifically prohibits any kind of censorship or preapproval of political ads. Numerous other parts of the law relate to political advertising, and these change from time to time. Visit the FCC and the Federal Election Commission Web sites to find the latest rulings.

PREPARATION AND DELIVERY OF THE CLIENT PRODUCTION ESTIMATE

The producer pulls together all of the costs and creates a formal cost estimate. The estimate consists of line-by-line costs for all of the elements needed to produce the commercial. It contains only those things that the agency and the client agreed can be billed to the client. Some items, such as secretarial and legal services, are not considered billable because the agency incurs these expenses in the normal course of doing business as an agency. The estimate includes an agency fee, which is either a commission—a percentage of the total amount—or a fixed amount that has been negotiated for production jobs as part of the client/agency agreement.

Although not all of the following items are a part of every job, and some jobs have specialized requirements, the ones here are typically included in the client estimate.

- *Production company costs*—The production company usually submits a firm-fixed bid for the commercial, so this amount is simply restated in the estimate.
- *Postproduction company/editorial*—Most postproduction work is bid on an hourly basis, so the producer must estimate how many hours the post sessions will take. A ten-hour postproduction session at $250 per hour, for example, will result in a $2,500 estimate for the postproduction, not including certain extra costs such as expendables.
- *Animation*—An animation company also submits a firm-fixed price for its work; this figure is included as a single amount in the estimate.
- *Computer-generated images*—If considerable computer work is needed, the agency will get a bid from a CGI company to create the animation or graphics and include the figure in the estimate. If there is only a little to do and if it's simple, the agency may have the CGI work done during postproduction, so will include the cost in the postproduction estimate.
- *Music*—The producer includes an estimate for the music based on whether it will be original, library, needle drop, or public domain. The estimate will also include future costs if the music is licensed and if there may be royalty payments later.
- *Voiceover recording*—This line item is for the recording session only, not for the talent. Typically, recording sessions are charged by the hour for use of a recording facility and engineers.
- *Casting*—This item covers the cost of using a casting agent and casting facilities.
- *Talent charges*—This is the estimate for paying talent for the shoot, for holding fees, and for residuals. The producer will have to estimate how many principal actors and how many extras there will be and make allowances for possible additional casting callbacks

- *Special talent charges*—Special talent, which includes celebrities as well as animals, introduce special costs. In addition to demanding higher performance fees, celebrities may require transportation, lodging, and meals that are out of the ordinary. Animals require handlers, cages or pens, special transportation, food, and so on.

- *Agency-produced/contracted art, including color-correction*—This may sound trivial, but some commercials require a great deal of special art, both of the product and logo, and for props, signage, and set dressings.

- *Track recording and mixing*—This work is usually done at a sound studio, or at the postproduction house, generally on an hourly basis. The producer must estimate how many hours this work will take.

- *Animatics and demo materials*—This needs to include the cost of creating the materials in the art department, recording voiceover, mixing music and sound effects, shooting the animatic, and making copies.

- *Storyboard production*—Necessary photostats are another art department charge.

- *Agency travel and per diem*—This can be a considerable expense if the commercial is shot out of state or out of the country. The producer has to anticipate when the travel will occur, who will go, how long they'll stay. Ground transportation, hotel accommodations, and even special dietary needs have to be considered.

- *Shipping*—This can include the cost of shipping an automobile or helicopter, not just a bunch of overnight packages. Products, equipment, props, sets, and other things may have to be shipped both to and from the shoot.

- *Miscellaneous charges*—These are usually itemized later but a preliminary cost estimate needs to be included.

The client estimate is often presented during a meeting in which the producer or the executive producer describes the costs, line-by-line, and backs up the estimates with the assumptions they used to arrive at them. A creative from the agency is often present to describe the production concepts or defend a particular creative decision that affects the cost. When the estimate is approved and signed by the client, the agency can proceed with awarding the job to the production company, issuing contracts and purchase orders to other contractors, and move the project into preproduction—the topic of the next chapter.

SUMMARY

In this chapter, we described how the agency assembles a comprehensive budget for the production, which the client approves when it signs the client estimate. This step enables the agency to move production of the commercial forward into preproduction. During this client estimate preparation stage, the agency production team swings into action, working to obtain bids from other contractors and other vendors. It also works to obtain rights for music; negotiates with talent; and ensures that the commercial conforms to various rules, laws, regulations, and standards.

The agency production team is headed-up by an executive producer—a senior person who may have several producers who report to her. The agency producers are responsible for all scheduling and planning and for maintaining the budget during production. At this stage, they are responsible for gathering together all of the costs for the production and for getting commitments from various other contractors and vendors so that, should the production move forward, they can and will be involved.

Among the more complex issues that the agency producer deals with at this time are acquiring the rights to music and negotiating with any special or particular talent such as celebrities. The producer must also get network clearances on the commercial concept. This is preapproval from the network that, if the commercial is produced as described in the material presented by the agency, the network will air it. When the producer has assembled the final cost estimate, has commitments from important other contractors and vendors, has successfully negotiated for music and talent, and has network clearance, the estimate is presented to the client. When the client approves and signs the estimate, the agency has the green light to move the production into the preproduction stage.

DISCUSSION QUESTIONS

1. Why is it so important for the producer to nail down costs and obtain commitments from other contractors at this stage? What would be the problem if she estimates incorrectly, or fails to look into rights issues?

2. What happens if the network refuses to clear the commercial at this stage? What recourse does the agency have?

3. The Harlem Boys Choir records music for a Levi's 501 Jeans commercial and appears on camera singing it (see director Leslie Dektor's demo reel). Are these young men actors? Is their song considered dialogue spoken by the actors, or did the agency have to acquire the rights to the music recording?

RECOMMENDED READINGS

Davis, Michael H., Arthur Raphael Miller, and Michael H. Davis. *Intellectual Property: Patents, Trademarks, and Copyright* (Nutshell Series). Belmont, CA: Wadsworth, 2000.
Simon, Deke and Michael Wiese. *Film & Video Budgets,* 3d rev. ed. Studio City: Edmond H. Weiss; 2001.

NOTE

1. Scale talent is talent that will work for the minimum compensation as spelled out in an applicable union contract for talent, usually the Screen Actors Guild commercials contract.

CHAPTER SEVEN

PREPRODUCTION

There are two pretty different groups of people who know about James Wahlberg. One is the audience for the television show *South Park*. Wahlberg is the producer, animator, and was a partner in Celluloid Studios, the company that developed the whacky and popular animated series. The other is the advertising agency community that knows him as a live-action director with a knack for combining his footage with special effects, computer graphics, and animation. Wahlberg has created spots for *Power Rangers*, Kellogg, Eggo, Allegra, and *Fox Kids*—all of which feature a seamless combination of live footage and virtual reality.

Wahlberg can draw. While many directors write treatments and have someone else create a shooting board for the commercials they bid on and are awarded, Wahlberg takes things into his own hands. He has to in order to fully understand all of the production issues that a combination live–animated spot presents. By drawing every scene very carefully, he can visualize (and think through) not only how to shoot the live, but also how to create the animation and how to meld the two. After his company, Visitor, won the award to shoot the Kellogg's Frosted Mini-Wheats "Talk Show" commercial for Leo Burnett Advertising, he reinterpreted the agency board (see Figure 7.1) with his own rendition (Figure 7.2)—the shooting board.

In this commercial, the typical Jerry Springer-style talk show is parodied. The scene is a raucous live-action studio where the audience is allowed to pick sides and go wild. The guest is an animated Frosted Mini-Wheat, frosted on one side and plain wheat fiber on the other. The host, as all hosts do, tries to drum up a conflict between the two sides of the Mini-Wheat, each of which has its own personality—a sort of sweet versus fiber debate. The message of the spot is that you get the best of both with Frosted Mini-Wheats.

Sixteen storyboard panels drawn at the agency were sufficient to get the general concept, theme, and style across to and approved by Kellogg. But Wahlberg sketched more than forty panels in which he specified every single *shot*. He indicated framing (close-ups, long shots), camera moves like pans, and even how the talent would act. He added small details, such as what certain talent would wear. He even caricatured what some would look like, a touch that helps with casting. In about half the shots, the animated character interacts with the live environment and audience: He jumps up on a chair and back down again and struts up and down the stage. Wahlberg knew that during production, the animators would need to know what the live-action scene was going to look like so that they could create the animation to fit into it. Thus, the storyboard had to be quite detailed.

FIGURE 7.1   The storyboard from the Mini-Wheats commercial, produced by Leo Burnett Advertising; copies of this board were sent to various production companies for bids.

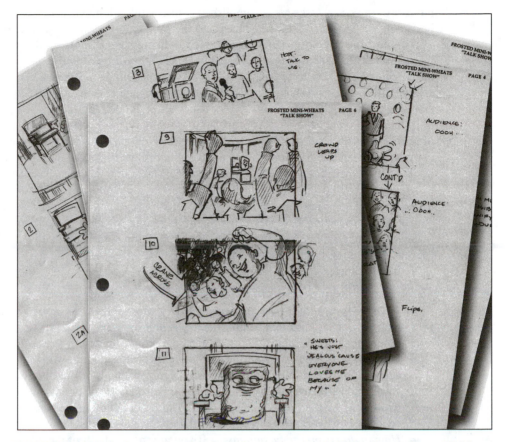

FIGURE 7.2 This is the storyboard, redrawn in much greater detail, by director James Wahlberg for the Mini-Wheats commercial shown in Figure 7.1. Every shot is depicted and even camera moves are indicated. When the director's bid was accepted, this became the working (shooting) board discussed at the preproduction meeting.

This storyboard was evaluated and broken down during preproduction; it revealed everything the agency producers, the production company, and the other contractors had to know about the commercial. They could see clearly what the set would look like, who was needed in the cast, what props were required, what wardrobe was needed. They could tell if there would be any stunts or other special effects. Everyone could see whether any affidavits or substantiations were needed, or if there was a danger that any copyright infringements might occur. In short, Wahlberg's storyboard made preproduction not only possible, but relatively easy to launch.

When the client estimate has been signed, which we covered in chapter 6, the commercial is ready to go into preproduction. This chapter covers that phase, which is when a number of important tasks are accomplished before actual filming takes place. At the very beginning of preproduction, the agency and the production company sign a contract for film production, and the agency signs contracts with other contractors for their work. Once the contracts are signed, the parties accept responsibility for certain preproduction tasks, all of which are critical to the successful start of actual filming. Some tasks are agency responsibilities, whereas other tasks are production company responsibilities. These responsibilities are normally defined in an agency spec sheet or contract.

Some of these tasks are part of the art of production, such as the design and creation of props, wardrobe, and sets. Some are legal, such as clearing the rights to music and other copyrighted material. Still others are management related—hiring the crew and talent; booking and scheduling stages, locations, and postproduction facilities. There are upwards to a hundred small details that collectively amount to a mountain of work for the agency, the production company, and the client. In the end, however, the who, what, when, where, and how of production have been thoroughly investigated, documented, approved, and planned. All of the planning details goes into a preproduction book that is distributed to everybody working on the commercial.

In this chapter, you will learn the following:

- *What the tasks in the preproduction phase are.* Most of the tasks have to do with planning, scheduling, and coordinating the live-action shoot and other production and postproduction details. Some of the tasks clear the production of any legal obstacles.
- *Who does the preproduction tasks.* Producers do most of the work; generally, the agency producer is ultimately responsible for all things related to copyright, network, and legal clearances, as well as being liaison with the client and approving the work done by the production company. The production company's producer is responsible for everything directly related to the actual shoot.
- *How to do the preproduction tasks.* If you are the producer at the client, agency, or production company, it's important for you to do what needs to be done efficiently.

Producers and future producers will find this material most helpful. Beware though, because you also will learn about some things that can trip-up a production when the preproduction phase tasks aren't done properly.

PREPRODUCTION TASKS, IN BRIEF

An outline of the general tasks that the advertising agency, the client, or the production company must do follows. The responsible party varies from one commercial production to another depending on the contractual arrangements between them and whether the spot is a major, national commercial or a local ad. Regardless, some version of these tasks will probably have to be done. The tasks are not listed in strict chronological order, but all of them are important prior to actual filming or recording of images. Incidentally, this is also a nice checklist for the producer.

MANAGEMENT TASKS

Award Contracts The agency producer awards the project and sends a contract to the production company. She also awards and sends contracts or purchase orders to the postproduction house and other contractors such as the computer animation (CGI) company, special effects company, and the music arranger–composer. She notifies any unsuccessful bidders, usually with a phone call.

Production Plan and Schedule The agency producer creates a production master plan—a day-by-day list of tasks, milestones, and due dates. The plan includes names of all who are involved in the production and who must be where and when. Travel arrangements are made at this time; she books flights, hotels, and ground transportation. The agency producer then provides each party with a preproduction book containing all of this information, and follows up continuously during production to make sure everybody is still on track. Interestingly, very few agency producers whom we talked to use sophisticated project management software to do their planning (which doesn't mean you shouldn't). Many use a calendar like the one shown in Figure 7.3 to schedule the main activities.

FIGURE 7.3 Production schedules and plans come in all styles, but one of the easiest to create, circulate, and understand is the calendar on which key activities and delivery dates can be marked.

Book Stage If the commercial will be shot on a stage—a controlled environment designed specifically for film production—the production company producer selects and schedules it for the shoot days.

Hire Crew The production company producer hires the crew needed for the shoot (see Figure 7.4), including the DP (cameraperson), riggers, electricians, grips, gaffers, and others.

Equipment, Props, and Wardrobe The production company producer rents or buys any necessary equipment, props, and wardrobe for the shoot and arranges for the items to be available on the shoot days.

Construction of Set The production company producer hires a company to build any special sets and buys, rents, or builds any set pieces and dressings (furniture, for example) needed for the shoot.

Client-Supplied Products For almost every commercial, the client must provide the product for the commercial. The agency producer arranges for delivery, storage, and handling of client-supplied product and props and finds out about requirements for packing and returning or disposing of the material.

FIGURE 7.4 This is the two-person camera/ sound crew that was booked to shoot local spots for Centro, a public transportation system in central New York; a few additional crew members were on hand to move equipment. Network commercials can have as many as twenty or more people on the crew.

Preproduction Meeting The agency producer schedules a meeting with all parties where details of the upcoming production shoot are discussed and approved. The preproduction book is distributed at this time.

LEGAL TASKS

Finalize the Legal Documents The agency producer makes sure that the commercial has all of the proper network clearances (only necessary for network commercials) and any substantiations and affidavits that might be needed. A *substantiation*—it promises that the claims are true—is needed if claims are made about the product in the commercial. An affidavit is needed if a product is demonstrated in the commercial; it promises that the commercial accurately depicts what the product can do. A signed affidavit is also needed when a nonactor makes a testimonial in a commercial; it affirms that he is telling the truth.

Clear Copyright The agency producer makes sure that all of the images, sounds, and other materials used in the commercial are free to use; that is, there are no copyrights or trademarks on anything that appears in the commercial that the agency may inadvertently infringe on when the commercial is released. Not only must copyright clearance be sought for the music and film footage itself, but it may be necessary to get clearance to show things that are in the *background* of a shoot—some may be copyrighted. Buildings, logos, paintings, sculptures, and other works of art usually belong to the original author (creator of the work), and permission must be granted to show such things in a commercial. Although some of these precautions are sometimes ignored when shooting local spots, nationally televised commercials are far too visible, and the stakes too high, to take a chance on using copyrighted material without permission.

Obtain Insurance Every production job must have insurance; this is a high-risk business in which people may be hurt, equipment stolen, or property damaged. The agency producer makes sure that there is a comprehensive insurance policy for her particular job by purchasing it, by notifying the agency's general carrier and getting it to issue a certificate of insurance, or by having the production company supply courage.

Obtain Permits The production company producer, who is responsible for things directly related to the shoot, must get any permits that might be required to shoot in public places and to block off streets, remove traffic signs, or generally disrupt an area while shooting takes place. Most cities have a film office (you can find them in the yellow pages or on the Web) that accommodates filmmakers. These offices send you the proper forms to fill out and arrange for city agencies (the police, for example) to block off streets or remove signage.

CREATIVE TASKS

Hire Casting Service, Cast Performers The agency producer (sometimes the production company) hires a casting service and provides it with guidance about who the agency wants for the commercial. Some talent will be on-camera, some will be voiceover announcers, and others who play bit parts or background parts are known as extras—they are barely seen. There are also roles for people whose hands or legs are special; they are literally hired just for their body parts. You often see them pouring coffee or smoothing on a body lotion in a close-up. The casting agency finds and recommends talent and sets up a *casting call*—an event where the agency producer, creative head, and the director can see all the possible talent and make their selections. The agency producer books—hires them and schedules their work days—the finalists.

Scout Locations, Determine Final Locations If the commercial is to be shot on *location*—on an urban street, on a farm somewhere, for example—the production company producer may use a location scout or find the right location himself. Tony Viola, art director on the Lubriderm "Alligator" commercials shown in this book, found that the perfect location for the shoot was in an art museum in Prague. It had the perfect clean, modern, well-lit interior; it doubled as a workout studio where Czech models were firming up alongside an alligator. Film commissions also have good locations in photo files, so a location scout can narrow down her choices without leaving the office.

Set Design Whether shot on location or on a stage, some set design will probably be needed. The production company art director or production designer generally designs the set where the film will be shot, specifying what is called the *mise en scène*—a French term for all those things that can be seen in the frame such as the set itself, set dressings, and props. Note that props are handled by the talent, set dressings are not.

Color-Correct Products The agency producer is responsible for making certain that any agency- or client-supplied products or packages are color-corrected for best film reproduction and that they are available on the set when needed.

Wardrobe Approvals and Fittings for Talent The production company producer usually arranges for the director to see and approve the wardrobe, and for the talent to be fitted properly with the right clothing. If the product is the clothing itself, the agency and client are more directly involved in this stage of creative decision making.

PREPRODUCTION TASKS, IN DETAIL

Some of the tasks in the preceding list need further elaboration, mainly because these are the tasks that are the most complex or potentially troublesome for the agency or the client.

The Production Company Contract

Once the client has signed the estimate, as described in chapter 6, the client is legally bound to the project and the agency can sign contracts for production services. The agency producer sends a contract to the production company that was recommended and approved by the client (see Figure 7.5). Advertising agencies have a standard contract in place with

Leo Burnett
Leo Burnett USA, Inc.
35 W. WACKER DRIVE, CHICAGO, IL 60601
Ph (312)220-5959 Fax (312)220-3299

PRODUCTION CONTRACT

To: Sample and void _____   Date: _____

_____   Contract #: _____

_____   Burnett Production Office: _____

Attention: _____   Job # : _____

Re: Production and transfer of _____ Com'l(s) for our client, _____ 's
                        (No.)   product_____

You, the undersigned Producer, after examination of the written specification sheet, scripts, and storyboards relating to the Commercial(s) coded as specified below, agree to produce as indicated in this Contract, and transfer such Commercial(s) in accordance with the Leo Burnett Standard Provisions Agreement previously signed by you and the Leo Burnett Company, Inc. which Agreement is incorporated into and made a part of this Contract:

1. Code Number	Title	Total Length in Seconds

2. Exceptions or additions to Standard Provisions are as follows: (if none, please so specify.)

3. Total price is $ _____

4. Price based on _____ Cost plus Fixed Fee _____ Fixed Bid

5. The Services of _____ are the essence of this agreement.
                        (Director/Editor)

6. This Contract is for transfer of all rights in Commercials (during and after their production) including but not limited to the right on the part of the Leo Burnett Company, Inc., and its assigns, to protect the same by patent, trademark and/or copyright. If requested, Producer agrees to cause Producer's employees, subcontractors or any other persons who in any way contributed to creation of the Commercials to execute any documents which, in Leo Burnett Company, Inc.'s judgment, are required or useful to establish, protect or enforce these rights. Producer warrants that it has full authority to grant all rights listed above. Rights purchased are as specified above unless expressly limited in writing on this Contract.

7. The provisions of Section 60-1.4 (a) of Title 41 of the Code of Federal Regulations (Equal Opportunity Clause) are hereby incorporated in and made a part of this agreement, such provisions shall, to the extent applicable, be binding upon Producer.

Accepted and Agreed To   Very truly yours,
                                          LEO BURNETT COMPANY, INC.
                                          Sample and void
_____
        (PRODUCER)

By _____

_____   By _____
        (TITLE)   TV PRODUCTION DEPT.

_____

Agency use only:
Standard Provision Agreement   Signed: Yes / No   Verified by: _____

Form 3-06 Rev. 8/02

FIGURE 7.5   Production contract.   This is the cover page of the standard Leo Burnett Advertising agency production contract; the other pages are filled with boilerplate warrants and indemnification clauses.

Courtesy of Leo Burnett USA, Inc. Reprinted with permission.

production companies they do business with regularly. These pro forma contracts spell out all the terms and conditions under which business will be conducted between the parties.

The terms and conditions of the general contract usually define the following:

- Ownership of materials
- Responsibilities of both parties
- Required technical standards for production
- The work-for-hire relationship between the agency and the production company—specifies what kind of working relationship the production company should have with itself and its employees, vendors, independent contractors, and any other suppliers.

This last one is important, because copyright law automatically gives ownership of certain elements that may be part of the production to the "author" of the work. The photographer, the artist, and the musician own their photographs, drawings, and music even though they are paid to create those works by the agency unless ownership is assigned to the agency by special agreement or by defining the working relationship as a work-for-hire.

The general contract also defines:

- Payment schedules
- When and how exceptions to the general contract can be made
- Various *warrants* and *indemnifications* that protect both parties

In a contract, a warrant is a promise and an *indemnification* is a reimbursement. The production company may promise (warrant) that it will hire only union actors and pay their fees and benefits. They promise to reimburse (indemnify) the ad agency if it is sued by an actor who is not paid properly. The production company must warrant that it has the rights to everything they will produce and that it will transfer those rights to the client. There are many such promises in a production contract.

The agency sends an unsigned copy of the contract to the production company. A responsible party at the production company (usually the executive producer) signs the contract and returns it to the agency along with an invoice for the first agreed-on payment for the job. The agency then accepts the contract by signature, returns a copy with the agency's countersignature, and processes the invoice for payment.

In small markets, and in particular when the local television station shoots the commercial, the production contract is simply incorporated into the agreement to buy the media time at the station. A small local production company will probably work with a purchase order or a simple letter of agreement. Although things on the local level are usually simpler, they are not casual. It is still important to define the relationship between the production entity and the client or the agency in writing.

Although it is common practice in the United States for agencies to issue standard contracts to production companies, in England and in Europe it is common for the production company to send a contract to the agency. In those countries, the terms and conditions have been negotiated between trade associations of the production companies and the agencies and/or the advertisers themselves. The trade association for the production companies in the United States—The Association of Independent Commercial Producers (AICP)—has attempted to promote the use of its own contract but has so far met with only limited success in getting it accepted by the advertising agencies.

It is common courtesy to notify the unsuccessful bidders on a timely basis that they did not get the job. The agency producer usually calls the production company executive producer or the production company rep and gives the bidders the bad news.

Other Contractors' Contracts

It is common practice that the agency contract, separately, for certain production tasks such as postproduction, music production, computer-generated imaging (CGI), and special effects. While years ago commercial production companies provided full-service production, including casting, postproduction, and CGI, most of these services are independent businesses today. Now, the production company simply delivers dailies (exposed, developed, and printed but raw, unedited film) and a corresponding picture negative along with any sound that was recorded during live-action filming. These elements are then taken by the agency to the contracted postproduction facility where the film is edited; animation and/or CGI material is integrated; and all sound effects, music, and voiceovers are integrated and mixed into a finished sound track. Chapter 10 covers editing and postproduction.

The agency producer issues a contract or a purchase order for contracted work to these suppliers acknowledging their bids or price quotes. Agency-issued purchase orders often have terms and conditions for doing business printed on them. If a contract is used, it will contain terms and conditions like those in the production contract. Even if you are producing a local commercial, the budget is small, and you think all of this is a waste of time, it is very good business practice to create a letter of agreement that has these details in it. As a famous Hollywood mogul once said, "An oral agreement isn't worth the paper it's written on."

Casting

The agency creative staff has some very specific ideas in mind as to how they believe the commercial should be cast. More than any other element of the visual language, the cast immediately telegraphs to the audience who the commercial is meant for, so getting people the creative staff and the client believe are *right* for the commercial is vital.

The agency usually hires a casting agent who estimates how many days will be needed based on casting specifications, storyboards and scripts provided, and discussions with agency creative and production staff. The agency producer issues a purchase order to the casting agent for the number of days needed for a particular commercial. The casting agent then starts the casting process.

On-Camera Talent. For on-camera talent, the casting agent begins by asking talent agents to recommend people for specific parts. If the casting agent has someone in mind, she will call the talent agent to see if the actor is available and does not have any conflicts about working for the client and the product of this commercial. Per the terms of the Screen Actors Guild commercials contract, on-camera performers and announcer talent cannot work for competing products.

The casting agent then calls in various talent and records them on a tape while they read and interpret the script. The agent compiles all of the talent on a tape and presents it to the agency and the director. These people then screen the casting reels and inform the casting agent which talent they consider right for the parts and would like to see in a live callback session. The talent selected for a callback will appear in person before the agency producer and creatives and the director. Again, the session is taped. The agency and director make a selection, many times a number one and number two choice, and present the tape to the client.

Prior to the callback, the agency producer must make sure that the talent is available and will work under the terms and conditions offered by the agency. The terms the agency usually offers are scale wages, as spelled out in the SAG Commercials Contract, but the talent can negotiate for additional compensation for the session fee and for reuse. When the client and the agency are in agreement on talent, the agency producer asks the casting agent to book the talent for the commercial; a booking is a firm commitment. The agency producer then contracts with the talent, usually through the talent's agent.

Voiceover and Character Talent.   Character voices are voices that actually replace the voices of the on-camera actors. It is not unusual for an actor who *looks* right for the part to not *sound* right. Voiceover and character talent are sometimes cast using a voiceover casting agent. Other times, the agency producer calls talent agents directly and asks for demo tapes, or she may provide scripts to talent agents so that they can have their talent read and record the script as an audition tape. An agency producer may hold voiceover auditions directly—calling in talent and recording them. The agency creative usually decides who should do the voiceover, and the agency producer then books the talent using the same procedure as for on-camera talent.

Celebrity Talent.   If special celebrity talent is cast for the commercial, a contract should have been negotiated with her agent or business manager prior to the signing of the client estimate. Celebrities command fees well in excess of the union scale, which can really impact the commercial budget, so the payment situation should have been resolved well in advance of the preproduction phase.

As soon as the client estimate is signed, the agency reaches a contractual agreement with the celebrity talent based on the negotiations. The contract spells out all the terms and conditions for the services the celebrity will provide, including the media she will appear in, the time period for services to be provided, the number of actual work days, and option terms for possible renewal or extension. In addition to these terms, the celebrity talent may want special treatment, such as appearances at events, promotional tours, and so forth; and/or special make-up people, special diets, travel allowances for a companion, and so forth. You have to negotiate all of these possibilities.

Class Discussion

Some celebrities have done well for their clients, such as Mike Meyer and Britney Spears for Pepsi, while others have caused some embarrassment—for instance, O. J. Simpson who pitched Hertz Rent-a-Car until his famous trial. Still other actors have actually *become* celebrities because of their involvement with commercials. Can you think of any? What might be the outcome of all three of these scenarios when contracts come up for renewal? What dangers are there for agencies and clients when using celebrities?

Legal Clearances, Substantiation, and Affidavits

During the preparation of the client estimate described in chapter 6, the producer got approval, or continuity clearance, from the networks or stations where the commercial is to be aired. During preproduction, and later during production, the producer must get any remaining legal documents signed and must watch out for any new legal encumbrances that may crop up.

As part of the preproduction process, all necessary clearances, substantiations, and affidavits must be obtained by the agency producer. All of these are basically written assurances that there are no legal obstacles standing in the way of the commercial being made or broadcast; or if it is broadcast, that there will be no legal challenges to its content, authenticity or truthfulness, or to the ownership of intellectual property in it.

Copyright Clearance.   Copyright clearances are required for the use of names, trademarks, or copyrighted items shown in the commercial. For example, if a commercial for an aftershave shows an airliner in the background with *USAir* on the tail fin, the producer must obtain USAir's permission to show its trademarked logo. It is the responsibility of the agency producer to note that a copyright clearance is needed and to take the necessary steps. She contacts the author or owner of the copyright and describes exactly how the copyrighted material will be used in the spot. The owner then determines whether it will benefit from the exposure, which is often the case, and whether to grant a license to show the copyrighted material.

A common and sometimes serious problem arises when the commercial is propped or shot on location. Signs, logos, paintings, automobiles, and even buildings in the background can lead to problems. On a set, posters or artwork in kids' bedrooms that are used as props are problem areas too, so the list of things the producer and production company must be aware of is very long.

Another possible problem is when a film or television show is shown on a television set within the scene of a commercial. Any footage used—shown on the set—must either be owned by the producer, cleared or licensed from the owner, or be footage in the public domain. In addition to clearing the footage, if any actors are shown, the producer may have to obtain releases from *them* separately. Televising people in a commercial is called commercial use and, without proper clearance, this can lead to an invasion of privacy action.

Historically, a person's right to privacy ended at death, so you could show the image of a dead person without fear of action; however, even this is no longer the case. Several states have enacted statutes that give heirs the rights to the images of their deceased relatives. This has been done primarily to protect famous people from being exploited without control by their heirs.

Substantiations.   Substantiations are needed for any claims made in the commercial about the effectiveness or capabilities of the product. If the commercial says that the product can mince an entire turnip in two seconds, this claim must be *substantiated*—the claim must be proved and the proof must be documented. The client is usually responsible for providing the documented proof of a product's effectiveness, which is often the result of product research and development. Some of the product claims that must be substantiated are tires that are supposed to grip the road or shed water effectively, automotive braking systems that are supposed to stop the car more safely, or laundry detergents that are supposed to get out grass stains with only one washing. Substantiations must be made *prior* to filming the commercial. It's actually illegal to try and prove a claim after the commercial is made.

There is a category of product claims that does not need substantiation, largely because the claims are so far-fetched that they are regarded as *puffery*. Two examples come to mind: The Keebler Elves, who are portrayed in commercials as baking the cookies you buy, do not have to be substantiated. No reasonable person believes that the product is baked by little animated critters who live in a tree. In a commercial for a four-wheel drive SUV, an ice-breaker with nine huge engines plows through the arctic when it suddenly cannot go any further because the ice is packed in around it. It's stuck. The crew lowers the powerful four-wheel drive vehicle, hooks up a tow chain, and the SUV tows the ship through the ice; this is puffery. It is so far over the top that nobody is expected to believe that the commercial depicts an actual product demonstration. A disclaimer is "supered" stating that it is a dramatization.

Affidavits.   If a nonactor testifies in a commercial that he or she uses a product and recommends it to others, the person must sign an affidavit promising that what was said is true. The agency producer has to obtain testimonial affidavits before the actual filming of the commercial. The affidavit itself is a document, usually a form signed by nonactors, which stipulates that they are telling the truth about their use of the product.

If a product is demonstrated, the actual product must be used and there can be no visual sleight-of-hand special effects or other techniques to improve product performance. The producer or other agency representative must sign an affidavit attesting that the demonstration was conducted faithfully and truthfully. The document describes the demonstration step by step; for example, an affidavit for a hair washing product must include the following:

- Name of the model
- Location of the demonstration
- What product was used, how much, and how many times
- Who actually washed the hair
- What kind of water was used
- Water temperature
- How the hair was dried and for how long
- Who set the hair
- How long after washing and drying was the film shot

As you can see, the producer must keep pretty good notes while shooting a product demonstration.

Clearances from Government Bodies.   The last type of clearance puts a special onus on the creative and production process because various states have very specific requirements about what can be said or shown in commercials for certain kinds of products or services.

Certain financial services, or automobile financing offers, must have lengthy disclaimers at the end of the commercial, which gave rise to the fast-talking voiceover and tiny, illegible type. There are different rules from state to state about what can be said or shown in beer advertising; most of them are codified by state and local governments, and rarely change.

The agency is ultimately responsible for everything shown or said in the commercial and must be vigilant about the legal clearances discussed here. The legal staff or the broadcast business or production business staff is aware of most requirements and will flag what is needed to clear a commercial for use. The most important thing to remember about clearances is to have all of them taken care of *prior* to the preproduction meeting, except for testimonial affidavits or demonstration affidavits, which usually cannot be obtained until actual shooting. However, even with relation to these, the agency producer should have assurances that the demonstrations will work, and that she will be able to sign the necessary affidavits.

Music Rights

We discussed the various kinds of music rights the agency must acquire in the last chapter. The producer works out the details of acquiring the rights while working up the client estimate but does not actually sign anything. During preproduction, the agency producer, sometimes through the agency's own music department or legal department if it has one, signs the paperwork that grants the rights to the music for the commercial and then pays for them.

Occasionally, when original music is needed, music tracks are recorded during the preproduction phase prior to the actual shooting of the commercial. This would be necessary if the film production itself is to be a music video and talent will dance or perform to the music. It would also be necessary if the commercial is to be animated and artists must animate characters in sync to a musical score. Otherwise, original tracks can be created during the creation of the commercial but prior to the client presentation. Music can also be "post-scored" as part of the editorial process; stock music is nearly always integrated during postproduction.

Location Shoots

During preproduction, the production company producer finds the location where the commercial will be shot, sometimes by hiring a location scout. Actual shooting locations are determined by the needs of the specific commercial, but even these can be finessed to meet the practical needs of the budget, schedule, or other parameters. Certain types of shoots, such as cars driving on highways and expansive, panoramic outdoor scenes, require locations; however, some outdoor scenes can be shot on a stage. House interiors can be shot on location or on a stage.

While having the "right" look is important to creatives, it is also important to economize whenever possible. If the script calls for multiple locations, the producer must determine whether a single location could be redressed or whether the crew must move to a different location. Any kind of move requires time and expense, which adds to the cost of production. For example, if a script calls for kitchen and backyard shots, the ideal situation is to locate a house that has both. If two separate kitchens are required, the producer should look for ways to redress a single kitchen rather than move the entire crew to a second one. Even on stage a set can be redressed rather than building two sets. The producer can also look for a prefabricated set with appropriate dressing rather than building a set from scratch.

The look of the location is the first priority, but not the only consideration when selecting the right place to shoot. All kinds of things must be considered, including neighbors, access, parking, area noise if sync sound is to be shot, acoustics for recording, permits, and permissions to make dress adjustments—changes to the location. Even if all of these things check out during location scouting, will the location have any problems on the shoot day? Will there be roadwork, a parade, or some other encumbrance scheduled on the street or in the area that will interfere with your shoot? The producer has to consider every possibility.

Location Permits.   With locations come the permit process. Normally, any film shoot that does not take place on a stage requires the permission of some civil authority, as well as the owner of the property. Let's address the property owner first. In order to use a private location, the production company must get permission to use the property, usually by having the owner sign a release. It is imperative that the producer be certain that the person signing the release has the authority to do so; this is an issue particularly on commercial property. A store lessee may not have the authority to grant permission to film in the building where his store is located. A store manager, or even the apartment/building manager, may not have authority—it may rest with the building's owner or actual business owner; that is, a homeowner can grant permission, but someone renting a house does not have such authority.

The location permit, if required, is obtained directly from the proper government authority by the production company producer; in major production centers, there are services that act as brokers for permits and walk the paperwork through the appropriate authority. The best way to find proper authorities is through the local film commission, a city clerk, or the chamber of commerce.

The permit not only grants permission, but spells out certain requirements that the production company must fulfill. A typical permit spells out shooting dates and hours; parking restrictions; requirements for fire department supervision; police supervision for public safety (usually not for production company security, which is normally handled separately); and special permissions for use of pyrotechnics, helicopters/airplanes, stunt driving, and so on. It is very important that the permit be properly drawn and complete as to exactly what is to be done. If any problems or complaints occur, or if accidents happen, the first thing any investigation looks at is was the shoot covered by the permit? For example, adding a helicopter at the last minute is a major error unless it is covered in the original permit or the permit gets modified.

Some municipalities issue permits for specific locations, while others issue multiple-location permits and/or multiple-day permits. Some jurisdictions do not charge for permits, others do. Some jurisdictions do not require a permit if the shoot is entirely on private property, others do. Local film commissions are an excellent source of permit requirements, as well as a lot of other area information. If a private permit service is available, it can also provide necessary information about permit requirements. If neither of these services is available, the local police department should be able to provide the information or at least direct the production company to the proper office.

Area location scouts are thoroughly familiar with permit requirements. When working at a distant location, it is always a good idea to use a local scout. Local scouts are familiar with current local conditions, rules, and foibles and can reduce wasted time and energy.

■ ■ ■ ■ ■

A SOBERING ANECDOTE

As a class film project, a group of college students decided to shoot a "robbery" at a neighborhood delicatessen. They notified campus security, got proper permissions from the owner of the building, and brought their equipment and cast to the location. A passerby saw the robbery, but not the film equipment, through a window and called the city police who had *not been notified* by the film students. The police entered with guns drawn, and the startled students dropped their fake weapons immediately. Had they hesitated for even a moment, something tragic could have happened.

Shooting on a Stage

A stage is usually a large building designed and constructed specifically for film production. Airplane hangars and warehouses also have been used as stages; these huge areas are fine, but other facilities, such as dressing rooms and electrical supplies must be brought in. Stages have very high ceilings, large loading dock doors, plenty of electrical power, and amenities for the cast and crew. The main advantage of shooting on a stage is the control that the filmmakers have over lighting, sound, set construction, and access, but there are other advantages as well. You don't have to worry about neighborhood restrictions and getting a permit for one. A set can be constructed on a stage to exactly meet the needs of the shoot from the point of view of both the desired look and the desired shots. On an interior location, the crew is limited by the existing physical structure, but on a stage, camera angles and shot selections are not restricted. Desirable camera positions can be taken into account during set design.

The production company producer selects the stage for the shoot based on its size, location, facilities, and amenities. During preproduction, the producer checks on these things: Are production offices and dressing rooms available, or will motor homes have to be brought in to meet these requirements? If sound is to be recorded, is it a soundproof stage? If cars or other large objects need to be shot, is there easy access? Is the stage clean so that you do not have to continuously touch-up products and props because of airborne dirt? Is the stage air-conditioned or will portable air have to be brought in? If food preparation is required, are facilities available? Is there a convenient place to bring in food storage and prep equipment? Is there room enough in the kitchen facilities area for the home economist/food stylist to work?

Foreign and Exotic Locations

Often, production takes place in remote cities or areas distant from the home of the advertising agency. There are major production centers in Los Angeles, New York, Vancouver, Toronto, London, and Sydney; and some very good facilities are available in Chicago, Dallas, Minneapolis, San Francisco, Seattle, Atlanta, Miami, Barcelona, Mexico City, Prague, Vienna, Budapest, Hong Kong, Singapore, and Johannesburg. An advantage to shooting overseas is the possibility of buying out the talent—making one payment that covers both the production shoot and reuse of the commercial. Another is the abundance of exotic locales—ancient cities and buildings, ruins, jungles, and mountains. The disadvantage of shooting in some of these foreign locations is the language problem. It is difficult to communicate with crew and to find talent who do not have accents to do on-camera sync lines. When shooting in some foreign markets, the key talent often must be brought in although the crew can be hired in major cities. When Leslie Dektor shot the Subtitles campaign for Ogilvy & Mather, he traveled with a crew of twelve and hired the rest in Europe.

While it's possible to produce quality commercials in secondary markets, one of the downsides is that there is a shallow pool of both performing talent and crew in them. In the major markets, such as New York and Los Angeles, there are many talented actors, musicians, and craftspersons to choose from.

Travel

Agency creative and production personnel attend most preproduction functions, including casting, location scouting, set construction, design approvals, and the preproduction meeting itself. Later, they attend the actual shoot and view the dailies. They not only attend, but often supervise, postproduction activities. *Where* all of these activities take place has an impact on the scheduling and cost of the overall production.

The agency producer prearranges travel for agency personnel and talent, including hotels and ground transportation if necessary. The production company producer arranges travel for the director and crew. In today's more cautious political climate, shooting overseas has become more troublesome. Added to the producer's list of preproduction chores is checking to make sure everyone's passports and visas are in order and that all equipment, props, wardrobe, and other production items will clear customs.

Booking the Crew

During the preproduction phase, the production company producer books a crew for the shoot. Typically, the trickle-down procedure is used when booking a crew; each key position is filled with people the director or producer chooses and each of those people chooses assistants who will work for them. The production company producer usually hires home economists, wardrobe stylists, riggers, key special effects people, choreographers, pilots, and other specialists; each of these normally specifies assistants to be hired. Historically, the assistant director is responsible for booking the crew; however, more recently on commercial shoots, the producer or production manager has taken this on.

Set Design and Construction

During preproduction, the production company art director or production designer—different functions on a feature film shoot but mostly used interchangeably on commercial shoots—prepares sketches for the sets to be constructed on stage or to dress a location. The agency creatives approve or make suggestions for modifications, then adjustments are made. When the design is finally approved, the production company producer hires a construction company to build the set.

Props and Set Dressings

Prop people purchase or rent props and set dressings for the shoot. It is very important for prop people to be aware of possible copyright or trademark infringements when selecting props, as discussed earlier. Some items may need permission or clearance before they can be used; specific toys and posters are nearly always issues in this area. Be careful about badges on uniforms, signage in backgrounds, products on store shelves, and car insignias—logos on automobiles. When showing supermarket shelves, whole islands may have to be restocked, sometimes with agency-prepared generic products to avoid copyright infringement.

Some commercials require the construction of special props. Are any mechanical devices required, and do you need specialists to operate them? If the prop can be considered a puppet, there may actually be union-rule implications about the puppeteers and reuse payments. Whenever a prop is designed and built, there must be a clause in the agreement with the prop maker that the client owns the prop and that there are no restrictions of any kind on its use.

Client-Supplied Items

In addition to the sets and props that are assembled by the production company, the agency or the client often supply certain items, including actual products, packaging, or special packaging that may have been color-corrected so it will look good on film. There are times when products can be purchased locally; sometimes clients want the product to be purchased locally so that the public sees what is actually available. Other clients spend a great deal of time having individual items sorted in a bowl to ensure that each little product part, such as a grain of rice, a kernel of corn, or a cereal flake, is a perfect representation of the product. A person who sorts product for optimum appearance is called a *flake wrangler.*

All clients have rules about how product can be handled. This can be as simple as how the hands of a clock must be set to properly show a logo, to how shoelaces must be tied, to how a product is handled by talent on camera. Some food companies refuse to have any animals in any scenes with their food. Auto service companies are very strict that their employees cannot touch the nonmechanical parts of a customer's vehicle. An agency producer must be aware of all of these issues and discuss them during the preproduction meeting.

It is indeed these little things that can make a production go sour. It can get down to the point of which of the model's hands pours product. A client once accused an agency of not shooting the commercial the way the storyboard represented the shot; the difference was that the hand model poured with the left hand rather than the right hand as was shown on the storyboard. The reason: the left hand allowed the product label to show because of the composition and blocking of the shot.

Wardrobe

The production company producer sees to it that wardrobe is designed and created, or purchased or rented. The producer can hire a wardrobe stylist to select the wardrobe; the stylist has conversations with the director to get some input as to the look she's going for with the wardrobe. For example, it should look right for the spot, but not dominate the spot and take anything away from the commercial message. There are companies that provide wardrobe for film shoots in most major markets, and the stylist or producer can contact them and specify what is needed for the shoot in terms of style, period, sizes, and so forth. The company usually brings a wide selection to choose from.

Wardrobe ideas are approved by the agency and sometimes by the client as well. Wardrobe fitting is usually done on the day prior to shooting. It is normal to buy or rent fashions in a couple of sizes and a variety of colors so final decisions can be made with a little flexibility right on the set. Some clients have business relationships with clothing companies. They may be part of a corporate conglomerate that owns both a clothing company and a washing machine manufacturer, for example. Such a business connection may determine what the wardrobe will be.

Many clients have specific policies about disposing of the wardrobe after the shoot. They may insist on renting as much wardrobe as possible, returning what can be returned, selling wardrobe to talent, storing wardrobe for future use (not really a good or productive idea unless it's a specialized costume), returning wardrobe to the client, or donating wardrobe to a charity (with a receipt to be sent to client).

The commercial may call for specialized costumes to be designed and made. As with props and other custom items for a production, the purchase agreement for the costume should assign ownership in the copyright to the client. This means that the client owns the costume design and the costume itself and can use it anywhere, anytime, without any limitation or additional payments being due to the designer.

Class Discussion

In a commercial for a wireless telephone provider, an average-looking guy walks around everywhere, appearing in the most unlikely places, asking an unseen collaborator, "Can you hear me now? (*pause*) Good." The message, of course, is that this provider has good reception everywhere. In one vignette, he winds up walking down the catwalk of a fashion show, surrounded by models in somebody's latest gowns. It's a funny idea. But was it costly? Whose fashions were those and did the client have to buy the rights to each one?

The Preproduction Meeting

As experienced filmmakers will attest, nothing about a commercial's production is more important than well-executed preproduction; and within preproduction, nothing is more important than the first preproduction meeting.

The agency producer should prepare an agenda for the formal *pre-pro* meeting, which should be attended by all appropriate production company, agency, and client personnel (see Figure 7.6). Because production is sometimes held in cities distant from either the agency or the client or both, teleconferencing or videoconferencing is frequently used to involve all necessary people.

The production company creates a preproduction book ahead of time and distributes copies at the meeting. It contains all the pertinent information, including scripts and storyboards; a complete production calendar; a postproduction schedule; contact lists for agency and client personnel, crew, talent with agent information, production vendors; and information on restaurants, hotels, transportation services, and banks. Any person or company that may be needed during production is included here. Everyone's travel schedule is included, along with maps and other necessary instructions to the stage or locations from the hotel where agency people stay or from the agency office. Normally, the approved budget is not included in the pre-pro book because this is considered confidential.

FIGURE 7.6 A preproduction meeting at Leo Burnett Advertising at which agency producer Bonnie Van Steen discusses the production shoot for a commercial for The National Cattlemen's Beef Association with Backyard Productions' producer Peter Keenan (*left*) and Blair Stribley (*right*), Executive Producer, Backyard Productions.

Courtesy of Leo Burnett USA, Inc. Reprinted with permission.

The typical preproduction agenda should include the following:

- General discussion of the purpose of the commercial—what it should accomplish
- Review of the storyboard and a scene-by-scene discussion of the shoot
- Review of the script
- Summary of all clearances, legal approvals, releases, affidavits, and substantiations that must be obtained on the set and who has responsibility for getting them
- Discussion about approval of locations or set construction and confirmation of permits
- Review and acceptance of casting
- Review of wardrobe and propping
- Assurances that client product is available, if required, and that packaging is approved
- Approval of production schedule
- Input about any concerns from any party

Obviously, there may be other issues for a specific job; these also should be addressed at the meeting.

A preproduction meeting should always be scheduled with enough turnaround time after the meeting is held, and before production begins, to allow for any adjustments needed as a result of discussions or issues brought up in the pre-pro meeting. Hopefully, the adjustments are not major. With proper preparation, you may never have to postpone a shoot because of an unresolved issue discovered during the preproduction meeting, but this has been known to happen.

By the end of the meeting, and absent any major obstacles or changes, preproduction is complete and everything is agreed to and in place. Now, on to the actual set or location and to the filming and recording!

SUMMARY

Preproduction is the planning stage for commercial production, when hundreds of tasks have to be completed before filming can take place. Some of these tasks are part of the art of production, such as the design and creation of props, wardrobe, and sets. Some are legal, such as clearing the rights to music or other copyrighted material. Still others are management related—hiring of crew and talent; booking and scheduling stages, locations, and postproduction facilities. The agency and the production company share many of the tasks that have to be completed during preproduction.

The main deliverable at the end of preproduction is a production "bible," or book, copies of which are distributed to everyone involved in the production at the agency, the client, and the production company. It contains all pertinent and relevant information.

DISCUSSION QUESTIONS

1. The agency producer is responsible for some things, and the production company producer for others. Who is responsible for making sure that a celebrity talent gets to the shoot on time? Why him?

2. Production is about to begin on a commercial for a clothing retailer. All of the featured clothes are manufactured by a clothing supplier. Does the agency need to get permission from the supplier to show clothing in the spot? Are there network restrictions on what kinds of clothing they can show?

3. You're producing and directing a local spot for a city's bus system. In one shot, the bus will pull up to a corner where a group of happy passengers climb onboard. In the background is a Subway sandwich shop—the signage will be clearly visible. Do you need to get permission from the sandwich shop owner to show the store in the commercial? From Subway's corporate offices?

4. In the same commercial, there will be a transit ad on the side of the bus for a local car dealership. The ad features a prominent picture of a Pontiac. Do you need permission from the car dealer to show his ad in the commercial? Do you need permission from General Motors to show the Pontiac?

5. In the same commercial, several real passengers (nonactors) will go on-camera to say how much they enjoy riding the bus to work instead of driving. What should the passengers sign for the producer?

CHAPTER EIGHT

SHOOTING THE COMMERCIAL

While writing this book, coauthor Larry Elin got permission from regional advertising agency Eric Mower & Associates (EMA), and its client Centro (the local public transportation system in Syracuse, New York) to shoot production stills and interview crew during the shooting of a commercial downtown. The spot was to feature Boomer, the Centro mascot—a guy dressed in a kangaroo costume. Centro had introduced the Boomer character two years earlier but only as a decal on the sides of the buses and in print ads. Because he had never been on television or radio, Boomer didn't have a voice or a personality. The commercial was designed to change all that; a comedian from New York City won the casting competition and would soon become the voice and persona of Boomer. He would wander around the Syracuse area, catching people off guard and humorously "selling" the idea of using the bus.

On the scheduled shoot day, Elin drove down to the location where he was greeted by the account executive, Pennie Gorney, and introduced to the client, the producer, the director, and a number of others. Equipment and crew were everywhere; the street had been blocked off and was guarded by city police and talent patiently waited their turn in front of the camera. Things were going more slowly than anticipated, and some talent scheduled for 11:00 A.M. were told it would be more like 1:30 P.M., or later.

Young director Sean Baker, and experienced producer Sandy Cohn were busy arranging props and directing talent for the next shot. They carefully arranged a borrowed Golf convertible and a huge Ford Expedition so that it looked like the two drivers were trying to wedge into the same parking space. In this scenario, some road hog in an SUV would try to steal a parking space in the hip Armory Square area from a couple of coeds, and they'd all wind up pointing at each other to give ground. Boomer would arrive and get the women to admit that none of this would happen if they'd just ride the bus. He'd also hassle the SUV jerk, just for laughs. The trouble was, they didn't have a jerk. Opportunity knocked when they looked over and noticed Elin watching from the sidewalk. "Hey, wanna be in this?" they shouted.

Elin became a member of the cast, pointing at the parking space he thought he was entitled to, following the directions of the director, and improvising when that seemed to be what Boomer was doing. It took about thirty minutes to shoot the vignette about the parking space, during which Elin took about twenty production stills from his seat in the SUV (see Figure 8.1).

Centro "Parking" :30

Boomer spots trouble: a parking conflict

Asks women if they'd thought of using the bus

Guy in SUV gets impatient - honks

Boomer ready to take him on...

FIGURE 8.1 One scene from the Centro spot, in which a coauthor appears as an extra in the final frame. About half the performers in this local spot were amateurs, and the crew was much smaller than on a shoot for a national commercial.

Courtesy of Central New York Regional Transportation Authority and Eric Mower & Associates. Reprinted with permission.

A couple of weeks later, Elin was invited to attend the editing session at Daily Post in Buffalo, where art director Kevin Tripodi and writer Pete VonDerLinn, worked with editor Andy Donovan on the Avid 9000 Image Composer to edit the spot. In the intervening days, the agency and the client had come to realize that they had shot so much material, and so much was good, that they could actually make *five* commercials. The additional editing costs were approved by the client. There weren't any storyboards or scripts, just a lot of footage that featured an ad-libbing Boomer getting great reactions from potential bus riders. Tripodi, VonDerLinn, and Donovan were literally winging it as they created entirely new commercials from the raw footage.

Although not typical of how network commercials are usually designed and produced, EMA's work on the Centro spot is a classic example of the intrepid and creative work often done on the local and regional level where budgets are smaller, crew members wear two or more hats, decision making doesn't go through multiple levels, and even onlookers may be pressed into service.

In this chapter, we cover shooting the live-action footage for a typical national commercial. In other chapters, we discuss animation, special effects, computer graphics, and the sound elements that may be part of a spot. The actual shooting of the live-action commercial may take only a few days, or less, depending on the design of the spot and the skill of the producer, director, and crew. If preproduction was handled properly, all of the plans, schedules, bookings, hires, clearances, permits, budgets, approvals, and other details are complete, so the shoot itself is largely a matter of following the plan. Of course, everyone must bring his or her special skills, gifts and talents to the shoot, and everybody must be prepared to be a little flexible and adjust to unexpected changes. A bit of luck is always needed when using new and untested shooting techniques, or to survive the weather, noise, crowds, traffic, the health crises of important cast or crew members, and other elements, which commercial makers have little or no control over.

Here, we take the reader to a typical shoot and discuss the activities of the director, the producer, and the crew. We get inside the head of the director and examine the decisions he makes while shooting film. We detail how the agency and the client remain involved throughout the shoot but do not interfere unnecessarily with the work of the director.

In this chapter you will learn the following:

- The chronology of the live-action shoot—what happens and in what order
- Who does what on the live-action shoot
- What special skills the talent and crew have
- The visual language—how frame composition, camera angles, lighting, and other aesthetic elements are drawn into the film by the director and the crew
- Communications on the set—what common protocols keep the shoot running smoothly
- How to apply all the information here in your productions

CHRONOLOGY OF THE SHOOT

A typical shoot may last only several days or up to a week, depending more on how much preparatory work is needed before actual shooting. The shoot normally includes the following main tasks:

- Build days—when a set is constructed from scratch, perhaps on a sound stage, or a location is redressed or modified for the commercial.
- Pre-light day—when the lighting director, director, and DP work out the lighting design (the effect they want the lights to have on the "look" of the shots) and lighting set-up (what lights are needed and where to create the design). Lighting is very complicated, and filmmakers always spend time trying to get it right.

- Shoot day(s)—when the crew and talent and others needed for the shoot are called and scenes are filmed one by one.
- Breakdown day—when the set is disassembled, cleaned up, and props and dressings are returned or put into storage.

Each of these involves certain people working on specific tasks. We get into the details of these production days in the following sections.

Build and Pre-Light Days

As described in the previous chapter, the agency and the production company have set everything up for the shoot day(s) through preproduction planning, as follows:

- Locations have been selected and contracted for
- Permits have been obtained
- Stages have been rented
- Sets have been designed and constructed
- Location dress is on the trucks and ready to roll in
- Talent has been cast, contracted, and called
- Equipment has been rented and checked out
- Film and tape have been purchased
- Crews have been booked

Obviously, not all elements are needed for every shoot, but nearly everything is needed on most shoots. For example, some stage requirements are not needed on location shoots and vice versa, but there may still be "stage construction" to dress a location that needs improvement (see Figure 8.2).

On most shoots there are *build days,* when a crew of carpenters, painters, and set decorators construct the set, and a *pre-light day,* when the director and her crew set up lights and the director and DP (director of photography) adjust camera positions before the actual shoot. During build days, carpenters and other craftspeople hired by the production company build sets to the specifications of the storyboards and other drawings, designs, and blueprints provided by the set designer. When the set is completed, the director blocks his shots—determines where the camera should be, how it can move, where talent will be, how actors will be lit. The DP and the gaffers light the set in the various ways called for by the shots planned for the next day. In this way, the lighting decisions are made before the full crew and talent are on the set. Lighting can take a long time, so it is pointless to have a lot of people standing around while this is going on. Although the set construction will have been based on drawings and plans done weeks in advance, seeing the set for the first time often dictates minor changes to the original planned shots.

On a location shoot, there are often *load in/dress days*—bringing in equipment and setting props and location dressing for a special look over and above the existing space. This may involve the embellishment of a kitchen; propping the bedroom; or bringing in greens, bushes and shrubs, to dress out the backyard. The location scout may have found the perfect general store out in the middle of nowhere, but it may have been abandoned for years. The production company has to redress the store to make it look like it's still operating, including

FIGURE 8.2   A location shoot in Los Angeles, in this case a private home. Trucks arrive early for set dressing and pre-lighting.

Courtesy of Leo Burnett USA, Inc.

painting, stocking products on shelves, putting up signage, placing period furniture, and adding window treatments—the works. It is not unusual to repaint a road so that the asphalt is perfectly black with new striping. Roads are nearly always watered down to make them look better. Removal of highway guardrails and signage may be done to ensure that the passing scenery is pristine. All of this has to be returned to normal afterwards.

Other preparations involve props. Some of these preparations can be done on the pre-light or build day, others just before shooting, and still others between every take. As long as prop adjustments do not affect a product claim or a product characteristic that is being demonstrated, which could raise legal issues, many embellishments are used to make things more photogenic. Food stylists sometimes paint foodstuffs to perfection; they are effectively "making up" the product just like a makeup person makeups talent. Acrylic ice cubes are used because they look better and do not melt. Glycerin replaces other liquids for pouring qualities and stability. Sets are cooled down so food will steam as it is served.

The Look of the Set

As one looks around a shooting set or location, it is difficult not to be amazed by the amount of equipment: a camera with a spare camera body, a second camera for capturing action simultaneously, numerous lenses to capture the scene just as the director visualizes, lights, and grip equipment to cover any possible situation (see Figure 8.3). Other equipment includes video assist to see an instant replay of a scene that has been captured on film, stabilization devices for allowing handheld action shots, cranes for overhead shots, jib arms to allow special moves, dollies to give mobility, camera cars and helicopters for following action, specialized rigs for mounting cameras on overhead wires or on little "toy" trucks to film babies or dogs from a low-angle perspective. It's not possible to list everything that may be on a shoot. As we said, every commercial is a prototype and has its own special equipment list.

Some equipment may need to be custom-made for a shoot. Recall shots in films you have seen, from rock climbing to car chases to beautiful close-ups of talent to underwater sequences. Some of these were shot by camera operators suspended from mountainsides or helicopters in specially constructed scaffolds and harnesses.

In addition to the equipment and props for filming or taping, other facilities and resources are needed to support the crew and talent. There may be a classroom space for child actors, or camper dressing rooms for production offices, wardrobe changing, and putting on makeup. A camper may serve as a bathroom, although there are specialized vehi-

FIGURE 8.3 Lighting equipment fills the backyard of this location for a commercial to be shot for the National Cattlemen's Beef Association.

Courtesy of Leo Burnett USA, Inc.

cles called honeywagons for this purpose. There may be a catering truck on a location to feed the crew and talent, although some caterers work out of a car trunk.

THE CREW

A crew on a high-end, high-budget spot can easily consist of forty to fifty people plus the talent. The crew and talent are booked by the production company producer and the agency producer, and their arrival times at the stage, location, or a transportation pickup point (if transportation to the shoot is provided) are scheduled by the assistant director. Calls—the term used for the time and place the crew and talent are to show up—are often staggered because some crew are needed long before others. For example, prop people, grips, and electricians (gaffers) are needed before the sound or makeup people. The assistant director is nearly always the first person to report and the last person to leave a set or location because his responsibility is to the director for every detail before, during, and after the shoot, except the actual shooting itself.

Departure times from the shoot are also staggered. Some of the crew associated with talent, such as costume and makeup and welfare workers for child actors, can be released before the shoot is wrapped for the day. After they leave, a "short" crew remains to do insert, product, and package shooting, or to shoot a plate, or a background. A *plate* shot is a shot of a scene that will have other elements—products, objects, or even people—matted or composited into it.[1]

The Typical Commercial Crew

In a previous chapter, we described the roles of the producer and the director from the production company, and the roles of the various representatives from the client and the agency. For shoot days, a group of professionals and craftspeople are hired to manage filmmaking details, handle lighting and electrical needs, run the camera and sound-recording equipment, lift and move things around, and provide transportation services. All of these crew members belong to unions that have contracts with the commercial production industry. The principal unions are the International Alliance of Theatrical Stage Employees (IATSE), The National Association of Broadcast Electrical Technicians (NABET), and the teamsters. Actors and actresses are members of the Screen Actors Guild (SAG) and/or AFTRA.

Pay scales, benefits, work hours, job responsibilities, break times, and other working conditions are spelled out in union contracts. The roles and responsibilities of crew members are so explicit, and exclusive, that members of one union are not permitted to do anything on the set that members of another have jurisdiction over. Only teamsters (members of the AFL-CIO) can start a vehicle, even if it will be driven away by an actor. Only gaffers can handle electrical equipment, including plugging in a coffeepot for the caterers. Union members are well aware of these rules of conduct, but the novice producer may not be. You should avoid asking crew members to do anything unless you know what they are allowed to do—it can get embarrassing if not downright testy.

Any commercial shot in a major market, such as New York or Los Angeles, must be shot with a union crew and with union talent. Commercials shot in foreign cities, and certainly in third-world countries, are not under union jurisdiction, and most local commercials in small markets are not union shoots. That's what made it possible for a college professor to appear in a Centro commercial.

The normal shoot day in New York or Los Angles is ten hours, and rates are set to this time frame. While there are scale rates for all union categories, commercial crews normally work on an *overscale* basis—everyone is paid more than union rate. It is normal for the electricians (gaffers) to be paid about 50 to 60 percent overscale. A commercial director of photography can receive 4.5 times scale. This is because the DP is considered a creative position as well as a technical position, so DPs are paid for both services.

A shoot day may extend to a 12-hour day, which may have been budgeted on the original estimate. For some shoots, 14- or even 16-hour days are allowed. Crews normally get paid time and a half for hours 11 and 12 and double-time for more than 12 hours (actually they get time and a half for more than 8 hours but this is automatically computed into their overscale "base" rate for timecard and legal purposes). Union talent (SAG or AFTRA talent) gets paid time and a half for hours 9 and 10 and double time thereafter. Union contracts for both talent and crew specify required time off between release time on day one and report time on day two—known as *turnaround time*.

Long workdays are required in order to get the proper morning and evening light on exterior locations. This is really important for automobile shoots because it is the golden light—the light just after sunrise and before sunset—that provides the exquisite lighting of the product.

It is common practice to have snacks and meals available at a set or location. This keeps the crew and talent together and ready to go back to work as soon as the lunchbreak is over. By contract, breaks can be shorter if food is available at the set or location, which of course makes it possible to squeeze more work into the shoot day. The cost of providing the food is more than offset by the increase in efficiency and morale; however, the producer should be careful about excesses in this particular area.

Although union rules may seem stifling and inflexible, the unions themselves and the well-defined roles of their members make it possible to assemble a crew of complete strangers and begin work immediately, with professionalism. Commercial film production is the child of feature film production, which has a 100-year history of success; the union division of labor is both an outgrowth of that and a contributor to it. The following sections discuss some of the key crew members.

Assistant Director. The assistant director (AD) is the director's firstmate who acts as a second pair of hands and a second mind. She is responsible for almost all of the details of the shoot except directing the actors and the crew while the camera is rolling. Many of those duties involve doing whatever the director wants her to do while the shoot is taking place, including prepping the next shot, informing members of the crew or the talent to be ready, or checking on the delivery of lunch. If the production crew does not include a production manager or a production assistant, the AD takes on those duties too. The basic duties are organizational; she is often seen wearing a hands-free cell phone and carrying a PDA, a clipboard, a walkie-talkie, and a hundred keys hanging from her belt. The AD schedules the crew calls and provides each crew member with instructions about when and where to show up, whom to report to, and when to leave.

Director of Photography.   The director of photography (DP) is responsible for capturing the precise look of the commercial on every frame of film. This involves determining the position of the camera in the shot; the composition (framing) of the shot; the lighting on the subject(s) and the background; the depth of field; the camera's f-stop and shutter speed; the type of film to use; how the camera moves, tilts, pans, dollies, or trucks; and what equipment to use with the camera to accomplish all of this (see Figure 8.4). The DP is both a creative master of the visual language and technically adept with cameras, lenses, film stocks, lights, and peripheral equipment such as tracks, cranes, and Steadicam harnesses (see Figure 8.5). It is increasingly important for the DP to be conversant with digital cameras and digital effects, particularly when a shot will eventually include both the live action he shoots and the computer-generated effects added later.

Because of the DP's responsibility—the final look of every frame—the DP has authority over lighting and directs the gaffers on the positions for lights and other lighting equipment. The DP also determines what kind of camera, camera motor, tripod, or other camera control equipment is necessary and needs to order all of this ahead of time.

DPs often develop reputations for certain kinds of filming. Some have a flair for shooting underwater, others shoot tabletop extremely well, some can light and shoot romantic and glamorous scenes, others are experts in action-oriented shots and can shoot everything while hanging out of a helicopter door. Sometimes the director of the commercial acts as his own DP, but it is the rare individual who has the artistic and technical talent to be the DP and also direct actors.

FIGURE 8.4 Director Kevin Smith sets up a shot; many directors are also DPs.

Courtesy of Leo Burnett USA, Inc.

FIGURE 8.5 Steven Del Monte, a video shooter for Electronic Field Productions in Rochester; holds his Sony BVW-D600 Betacam SP camera while discussing a shot with talent; he works on many local and regional commercials and shot the Centro spots.

Courtesy Central New York Regional Transportation Authority & Eric Mower & Associates. Reprinted with permission.

First Assistant Cameraman. The first assistant cameraman reports to the DP and is usually responsible for checking film equipment to be sure it is in good working order before the shoot, and for keeping film magazines loaded with film during the shoot. After a magazine of film has been shot, he removes the exposed film from the magazine and labels the can properly for the lab.

Gaffer. The gaffer is the chief electrician who is responsible for setting the lights. Based on instructions from the DP, who is choosing the camera position and viewing the scene through the viewfinder, the gaffer positions the correct kind of light in the right position. He uses the various combinations of gels, filters, barn doors, and other lighting tools to achieve the desired effect. The gaffer does this with every light for every shot. His assistant is called the *best boy;* now you know to whom that strange film credit belongs.

Grip. As the name suggests, grips handle camera mounts, rigs, and nonelectric lighting reflectors. They move things around to where they are needed (but not electrical objects or vehicles). Some grips are responsible for pushing, pulling, or lifting camera equipment such as camera dollies or cranes, and do so while the camera is rolling.

Art Director and Production Designer.   The production designer is responsible for the overall look and design of the set with input from the agency art director. The production designer specifies what changes may be needed on a location—additional set dressings, plantings, or other stuff that should be brought in to make a location look right.

Prop People.   Prop people are responsible for renting or purchasing props for the shoot, usually under the direction of the production designer, so they get the right things; they handle these props during the shoot. They keep an inventory of everything so that no one leaves with a momento. After the shoot, prop people return everything to the owners.

Specialized Additional Crew

Many commercial shoots require specialists for certain tasks; for example, a Vegas-style musical extravaganza may need a choreographer, graphic artists, riggers of all types, stunt coordinators, and pyrotechnicians. Other shoots may call for baby wranglers, animal trainers, food stylists (home economists), and fencing coordinators. A recent shoot had a grill-effects technician for a shot of cooking on a barbecue. There are specialists in every area. A dog thief?? The *Los Angeles Times* described him as the prop man's prop man—the person who can find anything that even the prop man can't round up—hopefully, legally.

The specialties are as broad as the required needs and the needs are as broad as creatives' imagination. In today's production world if you can conceive it, it can probably be done either in live action or with the help of digital technology, and there are the specialists ready and waiting to make it happen—all for a day's wages.

If the product requires special handling during the shoot, the client supplies technical personnel to actually work with the product on the set. It is important to involve these tech people in the planning and preproduction meetings so that they understand exactly what the product must do during the shoot. Technicians must be on standby during the shoot to make certain the product works properly, especially during demonstrations.

Sometimes products have to be disassembled but can't be easily reassembled. Not only would the technical experts assist in doing this, but they would also reassemble the product between takes. Products used during shoots normally cannot be returned to the client in a condition that would allow reuse (or reselling) after the shoot. This is especially true with things such as automobiles, appliances, computers, and other durables, particularly if the product had to be modified for the shoot.

Safety on shooting sets and locations is a big concern. Union contracts and prudent management and insurance carriers specify that every shoot needs to have comprehensive coverage. If the shoot involves any risky performances, there should be a medical technician and an ambulance on standby. If action is to take place in water, there nearly always is a lifeguard on duty. If stunts are involved, a stunt coordinator tests the equipment and works with the talent to ensure that all possible safety steps are taken. Stunt doubles are used for actors in situations where specialized skills and athleticism are required. This can be for driving sequences, scenes involving pyrotechnics, or any sequence for which a skill is needed and/or an element of danger is present.

THE DAY OF THE SHOOT

The crew arrives and, under the direction of the AD, they finish anything that hadn't been done during the pre-light day. On commercial shoots, the director usually prepares a shooting board or a shot sheet that spells out exactly what shots will be done on each day and in what order. Occasionally, because of creative suggestions that come up during shooting, there may be some changes from the shooting board or shot sheet (see Figure 8.6). But, everything agreed to during preproduction must be shot. If the creative suggestions involve extra costs, the agency or the client has to approve them first.

The shooting board and shot sheet guide the assistant director as she reviews setup requirements with the crew. They may go about setting dolly tracks, positioning dollies, setting up the camera, checking out lights, placing props, dressing or setting stage pieces. Film magazines are loaded and things are generally positioned for the first shot. While this is going on, talent is wardrobed and made-up. The director works with the talent, discussing the roles and reviewing the scripts.

As things are generally positioned, everybody is ready for the first walkthrough, assuming the shot uses talent. Normally, scenes involving talent are shot toward the beginning of the day and nontalent shots are done near the end of the day, unless there is a specific reason to alter this plan. If children are in the cast, the shoot must be scheduled to accommodate child welfare requirements such as schooling, breaks, and the length of the workday.

Directors work in different ways but generally once the technical elements are in place, the talent walks through the first scene as the director and crew fine-tune light settings, positions, line delivery, timing of the scene, and so forth. Then the first "take" is shot—the film rolls, the director yells "action," and the first scene is shot.

And reshot.

Shooting Ratio

Commercials have the highest shooting ratio—the amount of recording medium (film or tape) that is shot compared to what will be incorporated into the finished production—of all filmed entertainment. A :30 commercial, projected at 24 frames per second, uses 45 feet of 35mm film—16 frames per foot. A 1,000-foot roll of 35mm film, therefore, runs about 11 minutes. It is not at all unusual for a commercial shoot to consume 5 to 10 rolls of 1,000-foot 35mm film, or more than 100 times the amount to be used in the final cut. If the final shot is supposed to look like it is happening in slow motion, the film is shot at a faster speed, which requires even more film. By comparison, normal television shows shoot 3 to 4 times the final production length, and feature films use as high as 8 to 12 times final film length.

There are three reasons for this high shooting ratio. First, remember that there is a finite time for a commercial message to be delivered, normally 30 or 15 seconds. Since time is short and every frame must be a poster—technically and artistically excellent—perfection is the only acceptable option. Performances must be excellent too. This means many takes to reach the level of perfection demanded of the client, the agency, and the director. The second

New York Times :30   "Sense of Detail"   Shot Log

	NOTES	TimeCode	Length	FIN
FS/CU Man in background, food in foreground.	Shallow focus on food.			
CU Ingredients				
CU Grabbing vegetables				
CU Chopping				
CU Frying				
MS Frying				
MS Putting Ingredients in the pan				
CU Ingredients in the pan				
CU Stirring				
FS Man at counter -- out of focus				
CU Selecting Spcies				
CU Smelling spices				
CU Putting spice in pan				
CU Taking a spoon out of pan				
CU Tasting from spoon				
MS Turning page on paper				
CU *FG*-newspaper, *MG* pan in focus, *BG* man collecting something				
CU pan sizzling				
CU man tasting				

FIGURE 8.6   The shot sheet, or *log,* is a list of the shots the director has decided he needs to get, usually specifying the composition, framing, and any other notes about how it will be used. This shot log is from a student project—a commercial for the *New York Times.*

Courtesy of David Thomson.

reason is to provide the editor and the agency creatives with coverage—plenty of alternate footage to choose from for flexibility in editing (see chapter 10, Postproduction). Finally, reshoots are very expensive, even to correct a tiny detail. Normally, it is not possible to schedule less than a day of shooting no matter how little extra needs to be shot. Even with special deals, a shoot day can easily run from $75,000 to $125,000 in a major production market. By shooting extra footage, and paying attention to details diligently, it is unlikely something will be missed, making a reshoot unnecessary.

Shooting to the Board

As noted in previous chapters, the director's specialty is storyboard and script *interpretation*—applying the elements of the visual language to tell a story in which every single frame, and everything in it, has meaning. Scribbled on the wall in a washroom at a sound stage in Hollywood was the astute observation: "The main difference between pornography and erotica is the lighting." Likewise, the main difference between a well-executed and a poorly executed television commercial (or any film project for that matter) is in the camera framing, composition, angle, movement, and focus. It is in the lighting, shadows, and highlights; in the performance of the actors; and in the editing, pacing, and sound. Some of these elements are influenced by the cost and quality of the equipment used, but more importantly by the creative choices the director makes and the time he takes to get all of them right, on every shot (see Figures 8.7 and 8.8).

So how does the director think? What does he know that the rest of us don't? What makes him the director? There are four things: (1) The director can understand the message the agency wants to communicate; (2) he can visualize the exact images that will communicate that message; (3) the director can master the technology needed to create the images; and (4) he leads and instructs everybody else involved in the shoot so that what they do as individuals contributes to the whole production. The director is the conductor, the chef, the architect, and the engineer all rolled into one.

The director got the job in the first place because he demonstrated to the agency and the client that he understands what they want (and through his demo reels and reputation, that he could probably pull it off). During the bidding process, he described his vision in phone conversations, a written treatment, and meetings. Now on the set, the director demonstrates his acumen with the technology, his leadership of the crew and talent, and his control and mastery of the visual language.

HOW THE DIRECTOR THINKS

Here we are going to take a little detour from our description of the shoot day to get inside the head of the director, to explore what kinds of aesthetic judgments he makes during the shoot. He has already played a role in casting, selecting wardrobes, defining the overall look, and perhaps in selecting music. This was all done before shooting started. During the shoot, he is, of course, directing the talent and trying to get the best possible performances out of them, and capturing it all on film. While shooting the action, the director makes a hundred small decisions about the camera and the lights and fills every frame with precise and deliberate meanings.

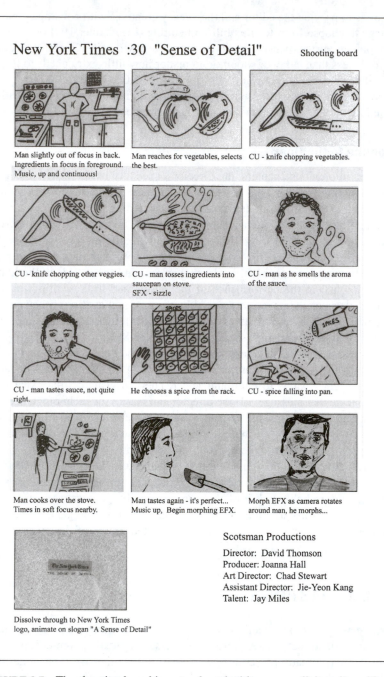

New York Times :30 "Sense of Detail"   Shooting board

Man slightly out of focus in back. Ingredients in focus in foreground. Music, up and continuous!

Man reaches for vegetables, selects the best.

CU - knife chopping vegetables.

CU - knife chopping other veggies.

CU - man tosses ingredients into saucepan on stove. SFX - sizzle

CU - man as he smells the aroma of the sauce.

CU - man tastes sauce, not quite right.

He chooses a spice from the rack.

CU - spice falling into pan.

Man cooks over the stove. Times in soft focus nearby.

Man tastes again - it's perfect... Music up, Begin morphing EFX.

Morph EFX as camera rotates around man, he morphs...

Dissolve through to New York Times logo, animate on slogan "A Sense of Detail"

Scotsman Productions

Director: David Thomson
Producer: Joanna Hall
Art Director: Chad Stewart
Assistant Director: Jie-Yeon Kang
Talent: Jay Miles

FIGURE 8.7   The shooting board is a storyboard with more explicit and specific renderings of what each shot will look like; this storyboard is from a student project, a commercial for the *New York Times*.

Courtesy of David Thomson.

New York Times :30 "Sense of Detail"

Establishing shot kitchen
Music up

CU lucious vegetables

CU hand selecting veggies

CU slicing and dicing

CU ingredients into pan

MCU checking the paper

CU putting in more spices

MCU getting out spoonful

Follow spoon - taste

Scotsman Productions

Director: David Thomson
Producer: Joanna Hall
Art Director: Chad Stewart
Assistant Director: Jie-Yeon Kang
Talent: Jay Miles

Morphing effect on face

Pan across "Dining Out" -
dissolve to "Dining In"

FIGURE 8.8 These frames are from the finished student commercial for the *New York Times*. Notice how the director interpreted the storyboard in Figure 8.7; he chose to shoot the commercial in letterbox format, to flip the images, to eliminate a couple of shots, and to shoot nearly everything tighter.

Courtesy of David Thomson.

The director controls the tools of the filmmaking trade in exactly the same way as a painter controls her tools. Like the portrait painter, the filmmaker starts with three-dimensional subjects—(the set itself, props, and human actors)—that must be rendered in a two-dimensional medium. The filmmaker's canvas is the film frame—a rectangle of space with a four-by-three aspect ratio. The filmmaker's brush is light and his eye is the lens of a camera. In addition to controlling space, and everything in it, in ways that closely resemble what the painter does, the filmmaker controls motion, time, and sound (see chapter 9).

Let's examine the camera and the lighting, and discuss how the director uses them to create meaning in every frame of film in his commercial. This discussion focuses on the aesthetics of the visual language, not the technical or mechanical approach to create the effects.

How Film Is Seen

Almost everyone in modern, Western society has shared a common experience during the consumption of filmed entertainment. The average eighteen-year-old American has watched something like 20,000 hours of television and a hundred or more films in theaters. We are, most of us, expert film watchers. We are aware of the rhythm of the three-act film structure. We react similarly to the storylines and plots, the development of the main character, the arc of the story, the pacing, and the music. We don't consciously think about this while watching a film (or a commercial), but we know quite a bit about camera angles, framing, lighting, music, and other film elements and how they make us react—the message each element conveys, individually and collectively.

An entire theater filled with teenagers will jump out of their seats at the exact same moment even though they all knew the guy with the chainsaw would show up at that very instant. They were tipped off by the eerie music, the bottom-lighting on the soon-to-be victim, the high-angle shot that made her look vulnerable, the quick cut to a rustle in the bushes. It didn't matter that the actress seemed to be oblivious, even secure, while walking alone in the woods at night because all of the other elements created tension and apprehension. It was, they whisper to each other, "like, creepy!" The director knew how to use the visual language to make the scene creepy, and everything in the frame contributed to the message he wanted to convey. And, he didn't put anything extraneous in the frame that would confuse or distract one from the message.

We experts (meaning *everybody*), consciously or not, spend most of our time watching film and decoding every single thing in every single frame, shot after shot, scene after scene. Camera framing and angles, composition, lighting, pacing, music, and many other visual language elements have specific meanings to us, universally, unambiguously. This truth makes it possible for skilled filmmakers to employ these aesthetic techniques to get the desired result: a terrified, thrilled, laughing, crying, believing or disbelieving, angry, or cuddling audience.

The Three-Dimensional Subject

One of the skills of the director is to sketch out, or look at an existing storyboard panel—two-dimensional rendering—and visualize the three-dimensional space that needs to be created (or located), which, when photographed, will result in a similar image. The director can *see,* in his mind's-eye, what the space, props, and actors will look like from the point of view of the camera. As he knows, no other point of view matters.

The director is aware of everyone's tendency to try to make sense of—identify and justify—everything in a shot: "Why is that tricycle over there on the sidewalk?" "Why is that person walking by in the background?" "Why is there a pot bubbling on the stove?" "What's that Led Zepplin poster doing on the wall?" "What does it all *mean*?" we ask ourselves. Unless it does have meaning for the message of the commercial, the director makes sure it isn't in the shot. He can imagine what should be there, how the audience will interpret it, so he makes sure that it *is* in the shot.

Because the director carries this vision around in his head and can articulate it, he directs the location scout to find, or the set designer or production designer to create, a space where the shots will be possible. The director arranges the camera, talent, props, and set dressings in this space so that the resulting filmed image approximates the two-dimensional concept. This process is called blocking the shots, and the director often draws a *blocking diagram*—a sort of blueprint—to show where objects are located in the physical space, and where the camera should be/could be located to get the required shots (see Figure 8.9).

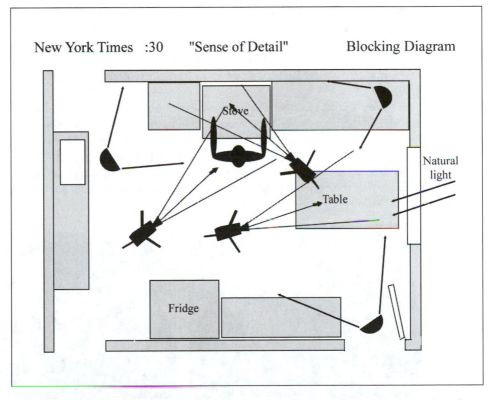

FIGURE 8.9 The blocking diagram shows the location of props and the actors and where the camera will be positioned. From such a diagram, the director can visualize what the shot will look like from the point of view of the camera. This blocking diagram is from a student project—a commercial for the *New York Times*.

Courtesy of David Thomson.

Shot Composition

The director must now think about shot composition—not only what things are in the shot but also what those things look like in the frame—for each of the camera setups. The director must decide on framing, angle, focus, and movement.

Framing the Shot. The director frames a shot when he decides whether it will be a wide shot, a medium shot, or a close-up, and what will be the center of attention—the *subject* (the product or talent) of the shot. Framing a shot is based on the shot's purpose. In general, wide shots, also called long shots, are about geography; they are used for establishing the whole environment in which a commercial is taking place and the subject's place in it. Whether a shot can be considered a wide shot or not is based on the subject of the shot. For example, if the subject of the shot is a Mercedes Benz, a wide shot may show the car from quite some distance as it negotiates curves at a high rate of speed on a mountain road. A wide shot in which the subject is a bowl of Cheerios might take in the interior of a kitchen, with the bowl on the table in the breakfast nook.

Medium shots are close enough to the subject so that it is recognizable, but also wide enough so that the background is also discernible. Another name for a medium shot is the 2-shot, so called because a typical medium shot tightly frames two people sitting next to each other, from about the waist up. The purpose of the medium shot, particularly when shooting people, is to be tight enough on the subjects so that you can see the expressions on their faces, but be far enough away to show their body language as well (see Figure 8.10).

The close-up is a *tight shot*—the subject almost fills the frame. In extreme close-ups, the edge of the frame crops the subject. The image in an extreme close-up could be a facial feature such as a mouth or an eye. The purpose of the close-up is to show emotional detail. You have probably heard the expression, "The eyes are the window to the soul." It's absolutely true, especially in filmmaking. Close-ups provide the audience with views that are so close that the eyes of the actor betray her inner-most thoughts and feelings. When the

FIGURE 8.10 The shot on the left is a wide shot, establishing that the talent is in his backyard grilling a steak; the right shot is a medium shot, showing the talent interacting with the product.

Courtesy of the National Cattlemen's Beef Association and the Cattlemen's Beef Board.

subject is the product, the shot is so tight that the audience can see highlights on drops of milk slipping off the corn flakes, or watch the tire tread cut through a drift of snow like it was just shaving cream. Commercials tend to have lots of close-ups, not only to get up close and personal with the product and the actors using it, but also because the commercial will be on a television screen—a relatively small piece of real estate in the average living room. Close-ups look great on television, but the audience tends to squint at long shots and with time so short, establishing shots are often cut first.

The director sets out to control the experience of the audience by composing and framing every shot, keeping in mind how each shot will be deciphered by the audience. Most directors think about the editing process while shooting. They concern themselves with how one shot will logically lead to the next, and then to another, with the audience grasping the story the shots tell. Almost all well-shot and well-edited commercials work as silent movies. Try it sometime—turn the volume down and watch. Do you still get it?

Camera Angles. When we talk about camera angles, we are referring to the angle formed by the physical difference in height between the camera and the subject. In a *high-angle* shot, the camera is higher than the subject, and pointed downward. For a *low-angle* shot, the camera is lower than the subject, and pointed upward. An *eye-level* shot puts the camera and the subject at about the same height. The camera angle communicates a subtle but sometimes powerful message about importance to the audience. A high-angle shot can make the subject look small, vulnerable, and unimportant. A low-angle shot can produce the opposite effect for exactly the same subject.

German filmmaker Leni Riefenstahl, who was hired by the Third Reich to shoot pro-paganda films (persuasive films) during the 1930s, was a master of the camera angle. Her first films were romantic, adventurous mountain-climbing films shot in the Alps, and there she learned about the emotional effect of high-angle shots of climbers filmed from above, with miles of distance and a valley floor below them. They always looked like they were in trouble. The same climbers shot from below, with nothing but the sky and the summit above them, looked triumphant. Whenever she filmed Adolph Hitler, who was not a tall man, she always positioned the camera below his shoulder level; as a result, he always looked commanding even when most of his subordinates were actually taller than he. She did the same in a film about the 1936 Berlin Olympic Games. All of the German athletes looked heroic, everybody else less so.

Directors are always aware of camera angle and the effect it will have on the audience; it is second nature. Even though students readily grasp the idea of camera angle, and usually remember it long enough to pass a test question, many beginning students forget it entirely on their first production assignments. It is often possible for the instructor to tell which member of a three-student production team was the camera operator while watching a film assignment by noting how high the camera was during the shoot. Most students instinctively set up the camera on a tripod at a height that is comfortable *for them,* and shoot from there, without regard to the message that angle conveys.

Focus. The term *focus,* known to all, refers to the sharpness of the subject in the image. It is a decidedly photographic and film term, because the director controls it with the lens he decides to use. The director uses focus (and lack of focus) to draw the audience's attention to the subject, and to render unimportant—in fact unobservable—other things in the composition. In theater, such a thing is not possible. Everything on the stage is in focus for everyone in the audience as they choose, as their eyes dart around. In theater productions, the most important performer is usually wearing something special to set her apart from the others, or she moves to the front of the stage, or a spotlight follows her around, or all three.

Using certain lenses that produce a shallow depth of field—an area some distance away from the camera in which things are in focus—the film director can cause objects both in front of and behind the product or talent to be blurry (out of focus), while revealing the subject in complete sharpness and fidelity. Anything in front of or beyond a certain distance is out of focus. Focus therefore can be used to make important things "pop out." Lenses with long focal lengths—telephoto lenses—have the shallowest depth of field (the area where things are in focus is small) and therefore the lens of choice to use focus to draw attention to the subject. Wide-angle lenses, the kind one finds on disposable cameras, have the deepest depth of field, which is why they never have to be focused by the average consumer snapping graduation photos.

The director can also use focus to create emotional images. Slightly out-of-focus images, combined with certain lighting setups, can produce ethereal, ghostly effects. The glamour shot is a slightly out-of-focus close-up of a beautiful woman lit with what are known as eye lights, which produce twinkles in her eyes. Many cosmetic commercials use the glamour shot effectively because the wistful, romantic imagery it conveys is precisely the message of most makeup, hair, and lip gloss spots.

Movement.   Cameras have legs; at least, they do as far as the audience is concerned. They move with omniscient freedom and power through private places to show us whatever we need to see. They seem to bounce around, looking here, and then there, never wasting any time as they show us the next important bit of information and help us piece the story together. Much of this kind of story movement is created using cameras that don't actually move at all. The apparent movement is created in editing as the editor cuts shots together.

On occasion, however, within a shot, the camera moves gracefully within the action as if on wheels, or it flies above it as if with wings. This kind of camera movement within a shot communicates something very different to the audience than editing locked-off shots. When the camera moves, the audience moves with it. The camera becomes a subjective element in the film, as opposed to an objective window through which the audience observes the action. When the camera moves, the audience becomes aware of its own involvement in the film's action. This is a powerful tool for engaging the audience with the product or the talent using it. The camera can move in the following ways:

- A *pan* is when the camera rotates sideways as though turning its head.
- A *tilt* is, as the word implies, a tipping of the camera up and down.
- In a *dolly* shot, the camera moves forward or back to show the subject closer or to move away from it. Don't confuse this with a zoom, which can have a similar net effect but look much different.
- A *zoom* is done by changing the focal length of the lens.
- In a *trucking* shot, the camera moves sideways.
- In a *crane* shot, the camera is raised or lowered off the ground.

■ In a *handheld* shot, the camera moves with the cameraperson, who walks (or runs) and moves within the shot as though part of it. When she does not use any special equipment, this usually results in the shaky camera style, which originated with the documentary but was made popular in television shows such as *NYPD Blue*. If she uses a *Steadicam*—a harness that keeps the camera steady even when jostled about—the handheld shot is smooth as silk.

Because moving shots always affect the audience in some way, the director uses them only to produce the effect he actually wants. It isn't always desirable to draw the audience into the scene. Like everything else the audience sees in the commercial, they will ask themselves: "Why am I moving closer to that car?" "Why am I turning to the left?" "What's over there that's important?" "Why are we suddenly flying over the swimming pool?" If you create these questions in the minds of the audience, you had better have an answer for them.

Students should simply experiment with the camera, and spend time thinking about shot composition and the effect framing, angle, focus, and movement will have on their message. Eventually, this will become second nature, especially after you become familiar enough with the equipment. It is difficult to behave artistically while struggling mechanically.

Lighting

If the camera is the eye of the filmmaker, light is his paintbrush. Once the director has composed his shots with camera placement, framing, angle, focus, and possibly movement, he has what a painter would regard as merely a rough sketch of what the image will look like. It needs highlights, midtones, and shadows, which the director creates with lighting. The director is concerned with two things with regard to lighting: (1) How to light the set and (2) how to light the subject. Placing lights in such a way that both the set and the subject are lit properly takes a great deal of skill and time, which is why lighting is usually done during the pre-light, the day before a shoot. Students often have disadvantages—no experience, little time, only three lights in the college-issue lighting kit—when trying to light a set. However, if you take the time to experiment with the lighting kit, use ambient and available light, and use some creative ingenuity, you can get surprising results. You need to know what to aim for, however; we describe design options and what they usually communicate to the audience next.

Perhaps more than any other visual element, lighting creates the mood of the shot. What is known as *high-key* lighting is bright and evenly lit. Subjects and backgrounds are lit equally, often with few shadows. We see this type of lighting in television programming, such as situation comedies and game shows, and it is nearly always used when the desired effect is light and breezy. Generally, it is used to create a welcoming, wide-open atmosphere and for the happy homemaker and children commercials—household cleaning products, breakfast cereals, games, toys, and candy.

High-key lighting has a tendency to flatten the image, giving little importance to anything in the shot. It has the effect of diminishing the three-dimensionality of the subjects and the set. The lighting designer can get high-key lighting outside during mid-afternoon on a sunny day with little or no assistance from artificial light. An interior, however, will require fill-, key-, and backlights and usually lots of them.

On the other end of the spectrum, classic *low-key* lighting features deep shadows, dark areas in the background, and pools of light illuminating important subjects or parts of the set. We tend to associate this kind of lighting with more serious moods, dramatic and romantic. Because parts of the image are dark, and perhaps in full shadow, the lighting creates a sense of apprehension, even tension, in the audience. Low-key lighting makes the scene have more dimension and depth with unseen possibilities. Shadows are abrupt and shadow lines can be run right across the talent's face.

Between these two extremes is a wide spectrum of lighting possibilities. Somewhere outside these extremes, both of which rely on a lighting design and a light set-up, is the use of available light—making no attempt to create the lighting but using whatever naturally occurring light is available. This could be sunlight, moonlight, car lights, nightlights, firelight, candlelight, or a flashlight. Again, only by trying things can you know what it will look like and whether it conveys the message you want. Even experienced art directors, DPs, and lighting directors experiment with the camera and lights and regularly discover new visual language techniques.

The director gets into a *zone,* a creative mental state that enables him to see in his mind's-eye what the shot should look like. He knows what needs to be done with the camera, the lens, the lighting, the talent's performance, and the shoot's other elements to get that vision on film. Much of what the experienced, or particularly talented, director does is instinctive and experiential. For him, it's as much second nature as driving a car.

BACK TO SHOOTING

We now return to the chronology of the shoot. All of the shots that use the same set-up are usually shot at the same time, even if those shots use different actors or will appear, chronologically, at different times during the commercial. This is to take advantage of the time and effort that goes into setting up for a shot. When all of the shots at a particular location with the same lighting are completed, the crew adjusts whatever is necessary to set up for the next series of shots. This continues all day, with specified breaks and lunchtime, until the day is done.

Composite Scenes

Increasingly, live-action films are composited during postproduction with visual elements created using digital, computer-generated animation. The director needs to be cognizant of how the special effects will be added and must communicate with the special effects artists during the shoot. A good example is a Lubriderm commercial shot for J. Walter Thompson and its client, Pfizer, by Eric Heimbold (see Figure 8.11).

The commercial was designed to allow placing a computer-generated crocodile into live-action scenes of a workout center, where beautiful women were exercising and getting massages. The crocodile was "one of the girls" but her skin was so parched that she looked like and felt like she had tough, scaly skin. While shooting the commercial in the Czech Republic, Heimbold had to leave space in the frame for the alligator to be placed in the

FIGURE 8.11   The Lubriderm live-action commercial had to be shot in such a way that the computer-generated alligator could be composited (combined) with the live scene later, during postproduction.

Courtesy of Pfizer, Inc., permission granted by J. Walter Thompson U.S.A., as agent for Pfizer, Inc.

scene and had to communicate things such as camera location, lens, light positions, and other information to the computer graphics animators. This enabled the animators to match their crocodile with the live-action moves frame for frame.

Waiting Is Working

To the casual observer there may seem to be a great deal of sitting around on a set during the shoot day, but everyone must be ready to respond to the director's instructions, decisions, changes, and emergencies at a moment's notice. The home economist must have pies ready for photographing when needed. Talent must have fresh makeup, possibly for each take. Creases in wardrobe must be ironed out and props must be in proper place for each take. Of course, all the people who need to support all of these functions need to be available and ready with the support materials they need—makeup cases, needle and thread, wax for the table, and so on at all times.

Dailies

At the end of the day, film is taken to the lab, developed, and a one-light print—a *daily*—is struck. Nowadays, the negative is transferred to videotape, and that tape is the daily. Dailies and the negative are usually inspected by the DP before anybody else gets a look, then the director, the agency, and the client screen them. Although final decisions about what specific *takes* to use in the edit session are not made at that time, remarks like "There's a good one" or "I like the way she winked" are usually made, and a kind of consensus emerges.

If a shoot is more than one day long, the dailies are screened either the night before or the morning of the next day of shooting. That way, if something unforeseen occurred during the previous day, scenes can be reshot. Film cameras are equipped with video equipment that simultaneously captures on tape what is filmed, so the production company has a real-time video record of every scene that is shot. But other problems can arise with the film itself, including light leaks, bad film stock, and screwups at the lab. Also, as you can well imagine, viewing the film is an emotional high for the people who have been working on the project for weeks or months, and they "get stoked" for the rest of the shoot when they see how good the footage looks.

THE ROLE OF THE CLIENT AND THE AGENCY

On almost every shoot, representatives of the client and the agency business and creative staff attend. The agency producer, along with the creative team, is directly responsible to the client for ensuring that what needs to be filmed is, and in the manner the agency envisioned. Directors have ideas about what would be best for the spot, but it is up to the agency to insist that what was approved by the client is shot. Even though there is usually no need for micromanagement by client and agency representatives, their input, decision making, and approval may be called on at any time.

Possible Changes

While all details should be planned before the shoot, it is impossible to anticipate everything that may come up, so the client and the agency must be on the set. Just as with creative development, which we covered in previous chapters, production is not a mindlessly linear process—it is *iterative*. Production does not always move smoothly from start to finish. You try something you thought would work, it doesn't, and you create a new approach. It isn't at all unusual for a new idea to develop during a shoot—an idea for a new shot, stunt, camera setup, a new line by one of the talent, or a myriad of other things—which will enhance the commercial but cost more money. The client and agency representatives can give approval for a cost overrun and can also clarify legal or company policy issues. For these reasons, it always behooves the client to be certain that the individuals who represent the client either have the authority to make decisions or have ready access to whoever can make decisions.

COMMUNICATIONS ON THE SET

This gets us to the issue of communication. There is a protocol, or pipeline, for communications on the set, which is generally acknowledged by everybody present (see Figure 8.12). At the highest level, the agency producer and creative director discuss business and aesthetic issues with the director, respectively. Because it is her responsibility to ensure that everything the client expects is achieved, the agency producer talks directly to the director, usually to keep track of what is being shot and how it will be used in the spot. The agency creative director talks directly with the director, usually to ensure that the director still understands what the creative vision is and is making those choices that will bring it about. If any decision is made that will effect cost, time, or the storyboard during those conversations, the agency producer is brought in. Other agency and client personnel communicate through the agency producer.

FIGURE 8.12   On the set, protocol calls for the client to communicate with the director through the producer. The people working on this shoot are (*left* to *right*): agency producer Bonnie Van Steen; Leo Burnett agency producer; Backyard Productions assistant director Kevin Howe; Page Miller represents the client, The National Cattlemen's Beef Association; Backyard Productions line producer Peter Keenan; Backyard Productions Kevin Smith, director.

Courtesy of the National Cattlemen's Beef Association and the Cattlemen's Beef Board.

When director Leslie Dektor shot a pool of commercials for IBM in Europe, Roy Schecter, the brand producer for IBM, was the responsible party representing the client. If Schecter wanted to communicate an idea or ask a question of Dektor, he talked to the Ogilvy & Mather agency account executive. The account executive then spoke to the agency producer, who spoke to the creative director, who spoke to Dektor. All of this, even while they were within two feet of each other. "Without this protocol, the director would be bombarded with questions from everywhere," said Schecter. "But after a while, they just said to me, 'Why don't you ask him yourself?'"

The director gives instructions to his assistant director and the assistant director talks to the rest of the crew. The director talks directly to the director of photography, and of course directs the actors, often in the same sentence: "Walk slowly toward the car while we dolly in the same direction."

All senior crew people talk directly to their own assistants. The DP gives directions to his camera operator (if included in crew), his camera assistants, and to the key grip or first gaffer who, in turn, communicate directly with their own assistants. This protocol ensures that all communication is directed in an orderly manner and that the people responsible are in the information loop and can make intelligent decisions. There is nothing more harmful than stopping a shoot while people are trying to make a decision or, worse yet, trying to find someone who is not at the set and needs to be involved in a decision. Even on a firm-bid basis, delays for this type of a problem can lead to extra agency and client expense.

BREAKDOWN AND WRAP

After days of shooting, but only after all the dailies have been viewed and approved, the production company and its various vendors carefully take down and remove anything they brought to the stage or the location. Rented wardrobe, props, and equipment are returned, trash is swept up and discarded, and client-supplied material is properly returned. Both the agency producer and the production company producer have paperwork to tend to. Crew, talent, vendors, and suppliers must be paid; time logs and invoices need to be collected, checked, and approved by one or the other. The film negatives and prints are delivered to the agency producer, who hangs on to the material until the creatives at the agency are ready to view everything and begin planning for the postproduction session.

SUMMARY

The live-action shoot is the culmination of weeks, sometimes months of work. Agency people, who live with the creative and production process from beginning to end, often marvel at how a creative concept begins with a brief statement of purpose from a client, and winds up with a hundred people on a set, cameras rolling. And before they know it, it's over after only a couple of days.

This chapter covered the chronology of the live-action shoot, which begins with days of prebuilding dressing of the set, and pre-lighting for the camera. The director and the DP block the shots and the DP and the gaffer do the lighting setup, a process that can take all day to get right. All of this is done before the crew and talent arrive.

On the day of the shoot, the assistant director manages the schedule and the crew and talent, making sure that they are where they are needed, when they are needed. In major markets, the members of the crew belong to various unions that have jurisdiction over the various tasks on the set; for example, only a gaffer can handle lighting equipment and only a teamster can handle a vehicle.

The director has a special gift for visualizing how to arrange the set, the subject, the camera, and the lights in three-dimensional space so that the resulting image, recorded in two dimensions on film, packs a powerful message for the audience. He uses frame composition, which includes framing, angle, and focus, to convey subtle but important information to the audience. He lights the scene to establish mood. Although some of what he accomplishes is made possible by having very good equipment, none of it is possible without his skill with the visual language.

The crew moves from one shot to the next, making sure that every planned shot is filmed and reshot to get the best take possible. As a time-saving measure, all of the scenes that use a particular camera and lighting setup are shot at the same time, before moving on to a new setup. There are times when special effects like animation will be composited with the live-action scene during postproduction. The director has to consult with the special effects coordinator or the animator so that what he shoots can be combined with the other imagery later.

Dailies are viewed as soon as the film is developed and printed. Although final editorial decisions aren't made then, it is usually clear to the group what shots are the best. If anything went awry during the shoot or the film processing, the group can see if something has to be reshot.

During the shoot, the agency and the client are on the sidelines. If they have questions or comments for the director, or if the director needs approval for a change from them, they all communicate through the producers. In fact, there is a communications protocol that applies to the whole crew to avoid a cacophony of voices with opinions, ideas, questions, and debate.

At the end of the shoot, the production company breaks down the set while the producers take care of the remaining paperwork, mainly paying people. The agency producer holds on to the finished film negative until postproduction.

DISCUSSION QUESTIONS

1. During the shoot, the director looks through the viewfinder and gets what he thinks is the perfect shot in every respect, but there is a billboard in the background with some other ad on it. What are the options for the company, agency, and client? Is this a copyright problem, or can this be fixed during postproduction?

2. Watch a commercial from a director's demo reel. Watch it without sound, and observe the visual language. Considering the composition and lighting, what are some of the subtle messages the director created with framing, angle, and focus? Based on the lighting, what is the mood of the commercial?

3. The high-end, high-budget commercial has all the time, crew, and money in the world, but the locally produced spot for the corner hardware store has little money and time. What could the producer/director do that has nothing to do with cost to bring production value to the shoot and improve the spot?

RECOMMENDED READINGS

Brown, Blain. *Cinematography Image Making for Cinematographers, Directors, and Videographers*. Boston: Focal Press, 2002.

Gross, Lynne S., and Larry W. Ward. *Electronic Moviemaking*. Belmont, CA: Wadsworth Publishing, 2000.

Herlinger, Mark. *The Single Camera Director*. Denver: Western Media Products, 2000.

Viera, Dave. *Lighting for Film and Electronic Media*. Belmont CA: Wadsworth Publishing, 2000.

Zettl, Herbert. *Television Production Handbook*. Belmont, CA: Wadsworth Publishing, 2000.

NOTE

1. The term *matte* refers to an optical film effect that combines (or composites) an image from one piece of film with another image from a second piece of film. All of the spacecrafts in the original *Star Wars* films were shot separately, then matted over shots of star fields. Even though nearly all compositing today is done digitally rather than optically, the term is still used.

CHAPTER NINE

SOUND, GRAPHICS, SPECIAL EFFECTS, AND ANIMATION

"You've heard that old expression, 'Like shooting fish in a barrel'?" asks Bill Kroyer. "It's supposed to describe something that's easy to do. But let me tell you, the hardest thing I ever tried to do was shoot fish in a bowl." Kroyer was describing what was supposed to be a relatively simple live-action shoot that turned into a challenging special effects shoot. It was eventually rescued with computer graphics. His production company, Rhythm & Hues, had been hired by the SicolaMartin Agency to shoot a spot for Novell that was a combination of live action and computer graphics, and Kroyer, because of his expertise as a special effects coordinator and computer graphics wizard, was selected to direct.

Novell wanted to get across the idea that the computer software giant could join together entities that had been kept apart because the technology they were using was different, and incompatible. Novell wanted to convey that it could bridge the gaps and distances between disparate computing systems and make everything work like they were all under the same "virtual" roof. The agency's concept was a spot that would open with a number of small fish bowls, each with a single tropical fish swimming around (see Figure 9.1). The fish could see each other through the clear water and glass but could not communicate— they couldn't network with each other. Of course, the fish symbolized all those computer users who were all using different systems.

"The action of the commercial was that there would be this one intrepid fish that wanted to communicate with the rest of them. He would jump from his bowl to another bowl. At the end of the spot, we were going to have all of the fish swimming in one big bowl to show how Novell could unify all these different systems and you can communicate with each other easily," Kroyer explained. So R&H got together eighteen fish bowls, a small school of tropical fish, cameras and lights, and a crew on a sound stage. The bowls were all arranged so that from a particular point of view, it looked like they stretched for miles. "You would think that all you'd have to do is point the camera at the fish, and that would be it. They'd swim around and you'd get the shot," Kroyer added. "Wrong. Every time we turned the camera on, these fish would disappear. They'd swim over to the sides of their bowls where the light refraction made them hard to see. They'd sink to the bottom of the bowl like they were dead. It was absolutely amazing. It looked like eighteen empty bowls."

Novell, Inc. :30 "Fish bowls"

Spot: Fish bowls
Client: Novell, Inc
Agency: SicolaMartin
Production company:
      Rhythm & Hues
Director: Bill Kroyer

FIGURE 9.1 The storyboard designed at SicolaMartin Agency in Austin, Texas, for Novell, Inc., called for fish to jump from one bowl to another in an effort to network with each other.

Courtesy of Novell, Inc.

To try to solve this live-action problem, Kroyer had all the stage hands and grips on the set get big swizzle sticks and churn the water in unison, and then step out of the shot together, on cue, so he could shoot the fish swimming around. It didn't work. As soon as the crew ran from the field of view, the fish misbehaved again, and sank to the bottom. The talent, so to speak, refused to cooperate. The live-action shoot needed a digital solution.

Kroyer shot each individual bowl separately (it wasn't that hard to get one fish at a time to behave), which resulted in eighteen shots of individual bowls. He then took the live action back to the Rhythm & Hues studios, to the company's computer graphics special-ists. Each shot was digitized, then each piece of digital footage was manipulated to place the bowls in different locations in the frame. Some bowls were "moved" farther away, over to the left or to the right, and so on until they had bowls located all over the frame with co-operative fish swimming around. These shots were then digitally composited into a single master scene. Even then, they had to add a number of computer-generated fish to make the thing work (see Figure 9.2).

FIGURE 9.2   Shots from the Novell commercial as executed by Rhythm & Hues; some of the fish are real, others are computer generated.

Courtesy of Novell, Inc.

Bill Kroyer is one of the new breed of directors who can shoot live action as well as direct computer graphics. His digital solution to the sinking fish problem, as clever as it is, actually plays out over and over on many commercials. Computer graphics and animation, and digital special effects, compositing, and other tools are in wide and routine use throughout the industry. Experienced directors like Kroyer can think on their feet, and use technology to solve unusual problems like bashful fish. The process of designing and producing computer animation is covered in this chapter, as is sound, animation and special effects—all of which have entered the digital age.

With few exceptions, all commercials have sound and graphics, many have special effects or animated scenes, or are entirely animated. This chapter covers the design and production of these audio and visual components, as well as other special concerns that they give rise to.

In this chapter, you will learn the following:

- The purposes of the three tracks of sound, and how they are created
- Sound recording tips for low-budget or student productions
- The purposes of graphics and animation, and how they are created
- The steps involved in producing computer-generated and handdrawn animation
- Suggestions for trying your hand at graphics for your low-budget or student commercials

SOUND BASICS

There are three elements in the sound track—dialogue (or voiceover), music, and sound effects. During the live film shoot, dialogue is recorded simultaneously, but separately from the film or video on special audio recording equipment. It may be used as is, or it may be replaced later during rerecording sessions in order to obtain better quality or better performances from the actors. On occasion, entirely different actors are used for the voice recording and their performances are dubbed over the picture in a process called *automated dialogue replacement* (ADR). Music is used in the commercial to create mood, as it is in all forms of filmmaking. It serves many other purposes as well—we cover these later in the chapter. As we discussed in chapter 6, the agency is responsible for either hiring an arranger/composer to create new music or acquiring the rights to existing music. Sound effects are used to add realism, and all kinds of them can be acquired from sound effects libraries or by hiring a technician—a *Foley* artist—who can create sound effects from scratch.

Sound Design and Recording

When commercials were first produced during the days of live television, some of them consisted almost entirely of sound—these were the days when television was regarded as "radio with pictures." Then commercial producers discovered that television is a visual medium, and in their exuberance over shooting epic films, they nearly forgot the relative importance of sound. So little regard was given to sound that microphones (mics) were buried under clothing, very little time was spent creating sound effects, and music was thrown in at the last minute. Sometimes mics were located on booms far from talent so as to be out of frame. This, of course, resulted not only in poor pick-up of talent voices, but also unwanted ambient sounds were picked up. Even though poor sound quality resulted, it mattered little because the speakers on home televisions were of equally poor quality.

Today, sound systems in the home have reached theatrical quality and consumers' expectations for good, CD-quality sound have grown. Digital television now carries digital-quality sound, and many households subscribe to digital cable radio. Many consumers are online, and they openly trade and download music and burn their own CDs. The advent of music on television, and its popularity with a major segment of the consumer market, has raised the bar for sound quality across all media, including television commercials. Commercials are also released theatrically, which puts additional pressure on the sound production process. Theatrical sound requires encoding for the translation of sound processing by companies' systems such as Dolby, THX, and Sony, among others. These sound formats are now already on DVDs and some VHS tapes.

Agencies and their clients have found themselves in a more competitive situation, and they have felt pressure to create commercials with superior sound quality. The industry has responded with much-improved microphones, recording equipment, mixing and editing systems, and more professional attention to the details of sound production. Even equipment used by local television stations to produce local spots has improved because of better digital equipment, both for recording and for editing and mixing.

The Purposes of Sound

As in other forms of filmmaking, there are three components to the commercial sound track—dialogue (human voice), music, and sound effects. Each has specific purposes in filmmaking, with a bit of overlap. The commercial's sound designer, often the agency's creative director, thinks through how she will use these components to her best advantage; these creative decisions then drive the production methods that follow.

Typically, the dialogue track serves four purposes: (1) to reveal backstory (exposition), (2) to reveal character, (3) to provide information, and (4) to move the story forward. Well-written dialogue can accomplish all four, often using very few words. A character in a commercial may say something like "He hasn't been the same since the divorce..." to a friend at the watercooler, as a coworker shuffles by listlessly. With those words, the viewer now knows that the guy got divorced (backstory, information), things were better before (exposition), his friends notice this, and they are concerned (reveal character). The viewer is interested in knowing where all this is going and continues to watch (move the story forward).

Many commercials employ *expository narration*—the off- or on-camera announcer who explicitly describes the benefits of the product or service. Some commercials feature off- or on-camera testimonials by nonactors who describe, in their own words, the benefits of the product or service. In all of these cases, the speaker must be convincing, appealing, and trustworthy. Writing and casting—tasks undertaken well before sound recording—are key to the success of the narrated commercial.

Dialogue may be used for other purposes. For instance, a cacophony of voices, jumbled together—*walla walla* in filmmaking parlance—is actually a sound effect used to suggest a crowd. Only if one or more of these specific purposes is served should there even *be* dialogue in a commercial or any other film, and the decision to include dialogue is obviously a creative one.

Music has several purposes in a commercial. Music is the primary sound for creating mood and emotion in a commercial, as it does in all settings in which we listen to it, including during films and television shows, at concerts and nightclubs, in church, on the radio, and at home. We all react emotionally and psychologically to music in ways that are universal and cross-cultural. For example, a single bugle playing taps during a funeral is an emotionally stirring experience, while dissonant and electronic music is often associated with danger or evil, generally leaving most listeners feeling on edge.[1] Even though we all react to music in much the same way, our tastes differ mightily and we are attracted to certain kinds of music that others dislike. Music, then, can be used to attract certain audience demographics to a commercial and at the same time, while not exactly turning the others away, suggesting to them that "this may not be for you."

The style, pace, beat, orchestration, and arrangement of the music can create not only the mood of the commercial (happy, sad, melancholy), but also establish time and place. Bluegrass music places us in the country, jazz in the city, and wooden flute music sometime in the ancient past. It is a very powerful tool for those who use it properly to convey a message.

Commercial music is also used for product branding, largely because music can be so memorable. Many clients adopt a particular piece of music, sometimes only a short riff, and merge this music with their product or service as part of its television identity. Coca-Cola, Pepsi, and McDonald's restaurants are examples of products closely associated with particular musical scores. When this branding relationship between music and product is exceptionally close and well-established, the music often drives creative decisions about the content, pacing, and overall attitude of the whole commercial.

Sound effects add realism. Cars starting, guns firing, doors slamming, rain pounding on the roof are examples of sound effects that help create a sense of something happening, even when those things are not *seen* on the screen. Watch almost any episode of the television series *Law and Order,* and pay particular attention to the ambient (background) sounds you hear while the detectives question witnesses or suspects inside Manhattan apartments. You will hear, sometimes almost imperceptibly below the sounds of those people and things in close proximity to the camera, the sounds of the city—the din of traffic, car horns, a siren. Persistent background sound is known as *ambience.*

Sound effects heighten the experience by punctuating visual events with the expected aural cue. In commercial production, as in all film production, sound effects are often actually exaggerated versions of the real thing, added later to accompany only those visuals that need emphasis or to suggest something unseen. Real sounds can be distracting, on the one hand, and less effective than unreal sounds that are added later in a larger-than-life way. The sounds of breakfast cereal falling into a bowl, milk pouring over it, and the crunch of a spoon thrust into the mix by a hungry child are added during postproduction and are greatly exaggerated in both volume and clarity by the sound designer.

Sound effects can also be used as transitional devices. In much the same way that a dissolve can be used to visually bridge two shots, a sound that begins at the end of one shot can continue through to the beginning of the next. Imagine a shot of a woman stepping out of her car in the driveway and shutting the car door. The sound of the door is heard just as we cut to inside of the house, where her husband hears the *rest* of the sound effect and turns his head toward its source. This has the effect of connecting the two shots temporally and helps the viewer understand the relationship contextually.

Not all commercials have all three sound components, and some may even be completely silent. Silence in fact is the fourth component of sound, often providing a contrast between the sound-laden tracks of dialogue, music, and sound effects and the moment of silence when the listener/viewer can ponder what she has just experienced. The responsibility for recording or acquiring the various sounds needed for the commercial can fall to the production company, the agency, or both depending largely on the design of the commercial and the production methods chosen for it.

Dialogue Recording

If the commercial has dialogue, the most important consideration during production is that it be heard and understood later, when the commercial is aired. The proper recording of dialogue—not only well-acted but of high technical quality—is of paramount importance. As described earlier, dialogue may be on-camera or off-camera and may involve actors, nonactors, and/or announcers. The location of the commercial shoot and the presence of other, unwanted or unneeded, sounds must also be considered. All of these possibilities present production issues that must be anticipated and planned for.

For example, when a commercial is shot on a set in a sound stage, the production company has much more control over the sound environment than it has while shooting on location. The sound recordist mikes the talent carefully and records the dialogue during the film shoot in synchronization with the film. There is special recording equipment, both analog and digital, that recordists use to lock the sound recording equipment with the film camera so that the film and sound get recorded simultaneously.[2] The resulting dialogue track can be used exactly as it was recorded with little or no fixes or changes. On location, however, the production company may have no control over environmental (ambient) sounds—air conditioning, street and crowd noises, dishes rattling—that may be recorded at the same time as the dialogue. All of these could occur while shooting a spot in a restaurant. Although the ambient sounds may actually add to the gestalt of the commercial later, there is no way to control when the sounds occur and their volumes relative to the recorded voices.

Regardless of where the shoot takes place, the sound recordist can use almost any variety of microphones to capture the spoken word, including boom, lavalier, omnidirectional, shotgun, and wireless (see Figure 9.3). Each actor in the shot can be miked individually to obtain the best results. During preproduction, the recordist determines which mics to use, basing the decision on what the shot calls for, what the actors will do in the shot, and what conditions at the shoot allow him to do. He may mike two actors carrying on a conversation while riding side by side on horseback with a shotgun mic mounted at the end of a boom. However, if the shot is too wide to get the boom in close enough, the recordist may use wireless mics on both actors.

When you mike your productions, you generally have access to four kinds of microphones, one of which you should never use. Most film and television students have access to digital video cameras and equipment these days, and some of them (the VX 1000, for

FIGURE 9.3 Microphones in common use today: (A) The Sony C-48—a capacitor mic with variable pickup patterns; (B) the Neumann U87—a capacitor mic, similar to the Sony C-48; (C) Sony Lavalier—a small omnidirection mic (some are more directional) with built-in high-range boost to picking up the human voice; (D) a capacitor mic—used in the studio, mostly for instruments; (F) the Electra Voice RE 20—a dynamic, unidirectional mic used mostly for the human voice; (G) the Electra Voice RE 16—same as the RE 20, but the RE 16 is designed for field use while the RE 20 is used in controlled studios; (H) the Sennheiser 816—a hypercardioid mic designed to give greater mic-to-source response.

example) have mics mounted right above the camera body. This microphone is notorious for picking up more camera sounds than voice. Don't use it unless you plan to replace that voice later.

For the student, the main difference between these microphones is in the pickup pattern, or the space around or in front of (sometimes behind) where the mic can "hear." The shotgun is a *supercardioid* mic, which means it can pick up sounds that come from a narrow space right in front of it and from some distance. It will also pick up some sounds behind the mic, but only from close to it. A shotgun mic pointed at an actor's mouth will pick up what he says, but not the sounds coming from other sources to his left and right. It could pick up sounds coming from directly behind or in front of him.

An *omnidirectional* picks up sounds all around the microphone, including sounds made by the person holding it. A lavalier (a tie-tack) is a small microphone that can be fastened to the clothes of an actor. It will generally pick up only what the actor wearing it says but can also pick up the rustling of clothes.

Every shot you plan may need one or the other or all of these microphones if what you record is the audio you have to use in the final spot. Have a person listen to the recorded audio very carefully while shooting, and rely on that person to tell you if you have captured the audio you'll need for the final production. Although it is fairly common in student film productions for the camera person to wear headphones and listen to the audio recording simultaneously, this is not a good idea. In fact, it is a good idea for the sound recordist to not watch the video or film recording but to just listen and focus on the technical and aesthetic quality of the audio recording.

Dialogue Replacement

When the budget allows, dialogue that was recorded while shooting on location is rerecorded in a controlled environment using the ADR technique (looping); it is also used to replace an actor's voice for creative, rather than technical reasons. An actress, for example, may have the right appearance for a particular commercial, but not the right voice. During the live shoot, she will speak her lines as though the recording will be used, but her voice will later be replaced by the voice of another actress performing in an ADR session.

During an ADR session, the film or tape of the commercial is projected for the actor, who is positioned in front of a microphone wearing headphones to listen to the current synchronized sound. Normally, this is done in a sound studio. The actor attempts to repeat the lines with exactly the same cadence, inflections, and acting as was originally captured on film. When it works properly, the new voice recording is lip-synced with the film so that it is impossible to tell that the voice has been dubbed over the original.

If the commercial has *voiceover*—the speaking character is not on camera—the agency records this narration at a special voice-recording session using a sound booth in a tightly controlled environment. In most cases, the announcer track is produced during the postproduction process; sometimes this is handled by the postproduction facility. If multiple voices are recorded, they can be recorded together to get natural interaction between them, or they can be done separately and mixed later. Voiceovers can even be recorded together, but from different geographic locations, through the use of high-quality, digital patch hookups. The two (or more) actors can hear each other during the recording. Normally, even if two or more actors are recorded simultaneously, they will be recorded on separate tracks for better flexibility and enhancement later.

One of the advantages of recording voiceover during postproduction is that it gives copy flexibility until the last possible moment. While it is ideal for all final copy to be approved prior to the preproduction meeting, sometimes this is not possible. There may be copy adjustments up to the very last moment for legal, technical, creative, or marketing reasons.

When a commercial has animated characters who talk on-screen, character voices are recorded in the same way but *before* any animation is produced. In many cases, voice actors are videotaped while they are giving their voice performances, and these videotapes are given to the animators who can use them as guides for facial expressions and gestures.

The dialogue sound track for the animated commercial is recorded and edited first, and sometimes mixed with the music, in effect, creating a radio commercial. The sound track is transferred to the magnetic stripe on 35mm film; then the animation director or an assistant does a frame-by-frame analysis of the voice tracks on the film and produces an exposure sheet.

An exposure sheet tells the animator which frame of film matches up with a syllable an actor uttered during the recording session. For instance, the exposure sheet can inform the animator that the character begins saying the word "buttermilk" in frame 128 and finishes it in frame 152. In between, he made the "tuh" sound, the "er" sound, and the "mmm" sound. The animator uses this information to draw or, in the case of computer animation, program the proper character mouths, facial expressions, and body language (pose) for each frame to correspond with the sound on that frame.

All dialogue tracks are recorded on either analog or digital recording systems but nearly always edited and stored on digital systems.[3] Dialogue tracks are approved by the agency and kept until the final mix during postproduction.

Music Acquisition and Recording

In chapter 7, we described how the agency, during preproduction, either acquires the rights to existing music or hires a composer/arranger to create new music for the commercial. Even when the agency acquires the rights to use existing music, it may be necessary for a composer/arranger to create a new arrangement specifically for the commercial, often to accommodate the spot's :15 or :30 time frame. Sometimes the lyrics of an acquired song are changed slightly to work better with the intent of the commercial. Both of these require additional rights and clearances from the copyright holder.

The agency generally hires an arranger/composer for a commercial by reviewing demo tapes or CDs submitted and selecting the one whose past work most closely matches the style of music needed for the spot. Agencies have long-term relationships and experiences with certain composers, so often work with the same one over and over again.

The design and intent of the spot may require a single musician, a small ensemble, a band, or a full orchestra. There may be vocalists in any number, or there may be a single well-known recording star hired by the agency specifically to appeal to a certain audience. Many commercials feature such stars on camera, performing in :30 music videos that pitch the product. Pop star Britney Spears' appearance in Pepsi ads during the 2002 Super Bowl is an example.

One of the first considerations is whether the music will be prescored—written, performed, recorded, and mixed *before* the commercial is shot—or postscored. If on-camera talent will either perform to or lip-sync to the music, then the music track should be prescored. The graphic tag line, especially if animated, may also depend on the music and that may force the music to be prescored. On some occasions, the visuals shot by the film direc-tor should be done with the music in mind; in those instances, the music will be prescored. In almost all other cases, music is postscored. It may be necessary to score the music track whenever a heavily booked star talent is available, which could be anytime before, during, or after the film shoot.

If the music is to include a song, one of the first tasks of the agency will be to write the lyrics (or hire a lyricist) and get approval of it from the client. This step is especially important if the agency has long-term plans for the music and the lyrics. The lyricist may have to write lyrics that will incorporate a slogan or tag line developed by the agency. The composer/arranger and the lyricist usually work together in order to arrive at the musical composition and the lyrics simultaneously.

Modern digital music technology makes it possible for a single arranger/composer to create music that sounds like a much larger group of musicians working in a sound studio. Using such tools, the arranger/composer usually creates a selection of possible tunes, which include the lyrics, and plays them for the agency, which "down selects" to the one it likes. The composer/arranger then polishes the composition, hires the musicians and vo-calists (if necessary), books a sound studio, and records the final musical track. Like the dialogue track, the composer/arranger delivers the final music in digital format to the agency for approval and safekeeping until the final mix.

Sound Effects Acquisition and Recording

Sound effects, often abbreviated *SFX,* are always added during postproduction, although they may be selected from a sound effects library or created by a Foley artist at anytime before or during filming if the sound designer knows what will be needed. There are a number of sound effects libraries, some on CD and others online. They all catalog the sounds so that simple textual search terms can be used to locate sounds. The designer can play the sounds and select the most appropriate one. Most libraries charge a license fee on a per-use basis or offer the use of the entire library to customers for an annual fee.

If the sound designer cannot find an appropriate sound in a library, the agency can hire a Foley artist to create the sound from scratch. Foley artists use clever and inventive techniques to create sounds, often taking delight in fooling the ear of the listener. These artists use special sound studios filled with, well, *junk* that can be banged, smashed, shaken, or slammed to create a sound. Increasingly, Foley artists also use electronic and digital devices to create sounds or to manipulate sounds they have already recorded.

In these ways, the agency produces and collects a number of tapes, CDs, or digital sound files that have dialogue tracks, music tracks, and sound effects. When the live-action footage and other visual elements are also completed, the elements are taken into post-production, which is covered in the next chapter.

Low-Budget Alternatives

You can create and mix very acceptable, in fact professional quality, sound for your pro-ductions if you start out with the right design—using sound for the proper purposes—and then use the right equipment to record and mix it. Even with a limited number of microphone choices, if you use the mics you have for the right situation and are careful with placement, levels, and take the time to record retakes when necessary, you can start out with good raw material for the mix. CD libraries, if your school has one, or any of the online sources for music we described in chapter 7, should net you some appropriate and usable (best of all, free) music and sound effects. You can also create your own Foley stage with available microphones and a room full of noisemakers.

Mixing sound—controlling levels, editing tracks, syncing with pictures—can be done best on digital systems such as Final Cut Pro or the Avid (see chapter 7). Two commonly used sound software products are Pro Tools and SoundEdit 16, both of which allow you to import any number of sound files and control many different sound characteristics. A free sound editing software program, PlayerPro 5, can be downloaded from www.download.com. There are others, but we have found this application to be quite good for student productions.

GRAPHICS BASICS

Graphics are used at the end of the commercial to identify the product or service and the client, and they may be used during the commercial for artistic purposes, to illustrate an important point, or to make a product statement. Sometimes graphics or captions are required by law, a disclaimer or warning to viewers "not to try this at home." Special effects are used to enhance the visual experience, to create fantasy, or to recreate something that would have been difficult or impossible to shoot live. Computer-generated images (CGI), in particular, are used to create scenes or events that at one time would have been shot live at great expense or risk. This is because computer graphics can look photo realistic, which means that the images created by the computer are difficult to distinguish from photographs of real things, such as the fish created by R&H for Novell. Many newer model cars seen in commercials today are actually computer generated. Also, using various digital effects, postproduction equipment, and software enables existing images to be retouched, changed, supplemented, color corrected, and repositioned. The animator uses tools similar to Photoshop to enhance animation with even more flexibility. Explosions, fires, and other pyrotechnic events are routinely created by computer and composited with live action during postproduction (see Figure 9.4).

There are many forms of animation, and each is selected and used for purposes that range from creating cartoon characters to creating characters that look surprisingly real, but behave like cartoons. Handdrawn cel animation, computer-generated three-dimensional animation, and stop-motion animation are three common techniques used for commercial production.

Whenever a commercial requires graphics, special effects, or animation the agency must be aware that each raises certain unique design and production considerations. For example, the client often provides logo or brand art, or even a design "bible" that must be adhered to by the studio that creates a logo tag for the commercial. If special effects eventually need to be composited with live action, plans must be made to engage the special effects supervisor in the live shoot so that the two visual elements can be coordinated and combined later. The voices of animated characters must be recorded before the animators

FIGURE 9.4   Modeling/R&D technical director Hans Rijpkema (*left/background*) and visual effects supervisor Bill Westenhofer (*right/foreground*) are working on the CGI version of Lou the talking beagle for the feature film *Cats & Dogs*.

Courtesy of Rhythm & Hues Studios, Inc. Reprinted with permission.

can draw (or program) the lip movements, facial expressions, and body language of the animated characters. Creation of new animated characters may cause intellectual property rights issues to come up.

GRAPHICS, SPECIAL EFFECTS, AND ANIMATION DESIGN AND PRODUCTION

During the creative development of the commercial, the agency art director created a storyboard that was presented to the client and approved. Besides illustrating the live-action shots needed, the storyboard included drawings (in some cases, computer-assisted drawings) of graphics, special effects, or animation in the spot. Of course, some commercials are entirely animated. With few exceptions, all commercials end with a graphic of the product or service and often with the name of the client and other pertinent information. Although short (less than four seconds), these graphics are occasionally animated in some way or have some effect that draws one last bit of attention to the product and the brand.

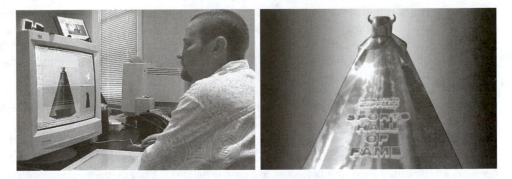

FIGURE 9.5 Scot Kaitanowski, animator at J. R. Animations in Buffalo, New York, constructs and lights a CGI logo for The Greater Buffalo Sports Hall of Fame.

Courtesy J. R. Animations and The Greater Buffalo Sports Hall of Fame.

Other graphics also may be included in the commercial for product identification, comparison, or legal purposes (see Figure 9.5).

When the design is approved, the agency shops for a graphics or animation studio that can produce these visual elements. The search begins, as it does for the selection of the film director and the music composer, by looking at demonstration reels. When the agency narrows the selection down, it prepares a bid package and asks the studios for prices and a delivery schedule. The agency art department sometimes creates a more detailed storyboard of the needed graphics or animation so that bidding studios can clearly understand what is required for the job. The bid package includes a timetable for production, sample art, approved logos, and perhaps blocking diagrams or other more technical information. If the visuals have to be composited with live action, the agency would expect the graphics studio to work very closely with the live-action director, so the bid package will contain even more detailed information about that.

The studios bid on the graphics and animation for the commercial by submitting a cost and time estimate. Sometimes, they also submit another storyboard with fresh ideas about the graphics or animation, or pitch these ideas to the agency during a meeting. Eventually, the agency selects the studio based on price, schedule, creative ideas, track record, and fitness for the particular spot. The selected studio produces the visual elements, usually at the same time live action is shot. If the graphics aren't too complicated or time-consuming to create, they may be produced by the postproduction facility after the live-action shoot.

Producing Computer-Generated Images

With the exception of classical, Disney-style character animation and other styles of the art of handdrawn animation (see next section), nearly all graphics, special effects, and three-dimensional animations are produced by computer. There are two types of studios where this takes place: (1) the full-service CGI production studio that specializes in computer graphics, and (2) the postproduction facility that has some CGI capability. When the graphics require a great deal of creative input, creative development, character design, motion capture, complex compositing or shot matching, writing specialized software, or other very involved processes, a CGI production studio will be used. If the work involves title design and placement, transitional effects, repositioning, or repainting existing materials, the creatives may look to the post house to do this work.

CGI studios create two-dimensional (flat) art and/or three-dimensional objects (or characters), and they animate both kinds of art entirely by computer (see Figure 9.6). They can output their animation to film or tape, provide files on CD-ROM or DVD, or send the picture files to a post house via the Internet. They can achieve many different "looks" with their systems, from the simplistic and flat characters of the *South Park* television series, to the glitzy logo treatments for NCAA football, to the nearly photo-realistic automobiles in many car commercials. Many characters that were formerly created by models and stop-motion, such as the Pillsbury Doughboy or the Kellogg's Frosted Flakes Tony the Tiger,

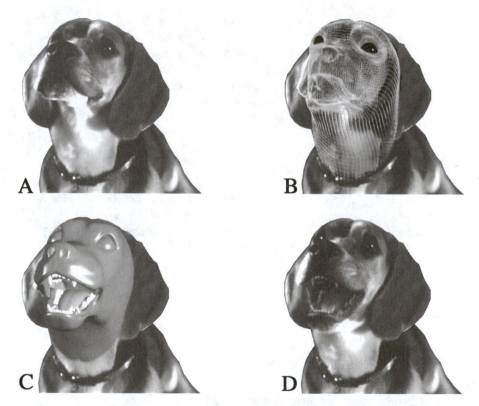

FIGURE 9.6 Computer animators begin with a real model, in this case a beagle (A), and construct a wireframe model of the dog's head (B). They then cover the wireframe with polygons and apply lighting to shade the face (C). The animators have applied textures to the polygonal model, giving the dog an uncanny, photo-realistic face (D). Now, they can animate the CGI dog, even make it talk if necessary.

Courtesy Rhythm & Hues Studios Inc. Reprinted with permission.

are now created and given life through computer animation. Although many software programs enable the creation of computer graphics (most of which work on consumer-grade PCs and Macintoshes), they are all based on the same fundamental principles.

Creating computer graphics for commercials involves the following five basic steps regardless of who is producing the work and what equipment and software are being used:

1. Create the object, whether a three-dimensional character or a two-dimensional logo (i.e., modeling)
2. Animate the object, as well as the camera and light sources
3. Light the object, including applying various properties (e.g., textures) to the surface of the object
4. Render the frames
5. Output the finished animation

All of these steps take place in the virtual world of the computer, but the results appear on the computer monitor. The agency can see these steps, and if it wants, approve them every step of the way.

Unlike live-action filming, which takes only a day or two, computer graphics and animation can take weeks. The agency rarely hangs around while graphics are produced. Instead, the CGI producers send various stages of the graphics to the agency for review and approval. The studio may send a CD-ROM or DVD with the images or animation, or they may actually put the images on a server so that the agency can FTP the files to their own computers.[4]

Modeling. In order to create the object, whether a logo, a product, or an animated character, the animator (a *modeler* at this point in the process) needs some kind of visual designs; approved art; or even a real object, such as a clay model of the character, to digitize. The source art may be provided by the client, the agency, or the art director of the studio. This should be established early on during preproduction. The modeler uses various hand-held tools, such as a mouse or a light pen, on the source art and inputs data into the computer. The data defines the surface and edges of the object in *3-space*—in a three-dimensional coordinate system. There are devices that can scan objects and collect the same data automatically. A likeness of the object appears in near real time on a computer screen, usually in what is called wireframe, as it's scanned, allowing the modeler to make adjustments and corrections along the way. Because the definition of this object in the computer includes not only the front, visible surface of the object, but also all of its sides and the back, the object can be rotated and viewed from any point in space.

Animation. Once the object is constructed, the animator can position it in space and move it over a number of frames to other locations, thus creating animation. By repositioning all of these parts frame after frame, parts of the object can move independently so that the animator can create a character that waves his arms, moves his lips, and walks toward the camera. The animator can control the surface of the object so that the character squashes and stretches in natural-looking ways. The animator works from the storyboard, sound track, and exposure sheets provided by the agency and creates the animation to those specifications.

Sometimes computer-generated work is integrated into live-action scenes. This usually involves a great deal of coordination between the live-action director and the CGI director. Many times a CGI representative will be on the live-action set to give or collect technical information about the shoot. This could include any aspect of the live-action shoot such as lighting, blocking of talent, design painting, and placement of rigs or other items that may effect the ultimate placement and look of materials that will be digitally created later and integrated into the scene. The agency provides the animator with the resulting footage, which the animator can display on her computer screen along with the computer-generated object. She can then match the position of the object with the live-action scene to ensure that it has the proper perspective. In this way, a computer-generated Pillsbury Doughboy, for example, can appear to be standing on somebody's kitchen table.

A process known as *motion capture* helps animators program an animated character to move realistically. In this process, a real human wears sensors on important parts of his body—at all of the joints and at the ends of every limb, for example. He acts out a certain motion in front of special cameras that collect positional information from the sensors as he moves. This positional information is then applied to a computer-generated character that has been constructed with the same joints and limbs so that the CGI character now moves exactly as the human did.

Lighting.   When the objects have been modeled and animated, the agency usually sees test footage of the animation and approves it before the next step—lighting and texturing. In this third step, the animator places hypothetical lights in the scene with the object. She assigns various properties to both the object and to the lights, including color and intensity. She can cause the object to have a high or a low degree of reflectivity, making it appear to be either shiny or flat. She can *texture map* the object, by covering it with the equivalent of wallpaper. The wallpaper texture could be wood grain, fabric, chrome, or even human skin. It could also be the package art from a box of corn flakes, applied over a CGI box, which has already been animated to dance and strut cross a live-action kitchen counter. When the computer-generated animation gets composited with live action, special care must be taken to match the lighting on the CGI object with the lighting in the live scene, in order to suspend disbelief that these are in fact in the same world together. The computer animator can heighten the illusion if the CGI object casts a shadow on the live-action set.

Rendering and Output.   When the agency has approved the look and the animation of the CGI object, the studio commits its computers to *rendering,* by calculating, every frame of animation. Depending on the complexity of the scene, the resolution of the images, the number of frames, and the speed of the computers used, this may take hours, even days. Afterwards, the frames are checked again to see that no artifacts have been introduced during the rendering stage. The final animation is either output to film, digital tape, CD-ROM, DVD, or stored on a hard drive until the agency is ready for it.

Other Purposes of CGI

Very high-end CGI studios have many other graphics techniques and special effects software and can produce images of fire, smoke, water, flocks of birds, vegetation, and many other believable (or, more to the point, *unbelievable*) effects. Reaching those end results, however, almost always involves some version of the five steps just described.

Typically, these forms of computer animation are used to add effects to live-action scenes, and since being developed, they have replaced many live dangerous and/or destructive techniques. Computer graphics can be used to create effects that were once simply impossible. As of this writing, computer animation is used for effects such as buildings burning, explosions, monsters and creatures, vehicle and aircraft accidents, enormous crowd scenes, and morphing. Yet another important computer graphics application, not quite as sexy but very important, is correcting live action. It is possible to repaint—delete or add significant elements—a scene, including removing rigging (i.e., the cables and wires used to support or suspend something in the shot). Originally riggers prided themselves on how well they could conceal rigging; nowadays, they actually paint the wires so that they are *easier* to see and electronically remove during postproduction!

Computer graphics can distort images to prevent identification and be used to insert or remove signage (e.g., in a televised baseball game behind home plate where none exists in the stadium itself). (By the way, do you know that the first-down line that appears in bright yellow during football games is electronically inserted and only visible to the television-viewing audience?) An added bonus of these electronic fix ups for the agency has been lower insurance premiums for film shoots. Screwups can now be fixed electronically, which is much less expensive than reshooting film.

Each of these effects may require that something special be designed or provided by the agency; during preproduction, it is incumbent on the agency producer to determine what is needed by the studio so that it can create the desired effects in a timely and efficient manner.

Producing Handdrawn Animation

The art and craft of handdrawn character animation has changed little in the past eighty years or so, or since Disney and others perfected the cel process. There are computer applications that perform what is called *in-betweening,* although most of these are not favored by animation purists. Some animators now draw animation directly on a computer, eliminating the need for paper and cels. This makes it possible to colorize the pictures; combine them with the proper background; and output directly to film, tape, or digital file. The process of animation, however, has not changed at all. The following are the ten steps in the creation of handdrawn cel animation:

1. Storyboard
2. Character design
3. Exposure sheets
4. Layouts
5. Background painting
6. Key animation
7. In-betweening
8. Clean-up
9. Inking and painting
10. Filming

An animated commercial is initially designed at the advertising agency when it writes and storyboards the spot and gets client approval. The creative concept behind the spot usually governs the animation style, and in the world of animation, there are many. One style that people are familiar with is the Disney-style, as exemplified by the classic films *Snow White* and *Bambi*. Other styles include the modern look of UPA's *Mr. Magoo* and *Gerald McBoing Boing;* the flexible, metamorphic style of Fleischer's *Popeye;* and the crude, simple style of *South Park*. The agency reviews demo reels of animation studios looking for a studio whose work matches the style of the commercial. It may send bid requests to several studios and award the contract based on price, schedule, track record, and other factors.

If the commercial uses existing characters, such as the Keebler Elves or Tony the Tiger, the agency provides character designs, turn arounds, and color keys to the animation studio; otherwise, the animation studio will have to design characters as part of its scope of work. Character designs are detailed drawings of the character, showing it in different poses and with various facial expressions and mouth positions. Turn arounds show the character from the front, a three-quarter view, from the side, and from behind. *Color keys* are color versions of the character, indicating the color of the flesh, eyes, hair, clothing, and even the inside of the mouth.

Keep in mind that a character is not necessarily a person or an animal. It can be a flower; a product box; or any object that will move, talk, and have a personality and life. Sometimes the design can be taken from an existing source such as an illustration on a package or a drawing from a book (which you, of course, must have rights to). There will be significant input from creatives, possibly agency research, and from the client. Another issue may come up in this process; if the character is a company trademark, care has to be taken that the character design for animation does not jeopardize the trademarked character.

The animation studio generally executes a more detailed storyboard, breaking the spot down into individual scenes and drawing in more detailed backgrounds. Based on this storyboard, the studio makes a layout of each scene. A *layout* is a detailed sketch of the background of the scene—a sort of blueprint—which is used by the background painter to paint the background and by the animator to draw his characters in over the background. In this way, if a character reaches out and touches something on the background, the animator can draw this without actually having the finished background. The agency provides the studio with the sound track for the spot on 35mm magnetic film, and the animation director or an assistant analyzes the track and makes exposure sheets, as described earlier in the chapter.

When the animator has a layout, exposure sheet, and character designs, he can begin drawing key poses, also known as *key animation*—rough, but accurate, life-filled drawings, which show the first and last positions of a character in an acting gesture. An assistant animator uses these drawings to determine what should go in-between, then the assistant draws these. The key poses and the in-betweens are sent to clean-up artists who trace the animation using clean, perfect lines; these are the final animation drawings. Meanwhile, a background painter uses the same layout to paint the background over which these character drawings will be placed and shot onto film.

If the character is to be composited over a live-action background, perhaps even interacting with live characters, the live action must be shot first and the character animation must be *rotoscoped* over it. During this process, each frame of live-action film must be exposed onto a large-format, black-and-white material known as a *stat*—sheets that have peg holes just like animation paper. The animator places a stat on his animation disk, puts a sheet of drawing paper over it, and illuminates the setup from below. He can see the live-action scene through the paper and draw the animated character in the right place, in the right size, for each frame. The drawings then go through the same process just described. When the finished animation is combined with the live action, it is a frame-by-frame match.

At this point, the clean-up animation can be scanned into a computer, where the now digitalized drawings can be filled with color, combined with the background, and output to film or tape. Or, the drawings can be copied onto cels and painted by hand, then filmed using an Oxberry animation camera—although doing it this way is very rare these days. During this process, the agency gets several opportunities to see animation *pencil tests,* (the un-colored drawings are filmed) oversee the background painting, approve intermediate steps along the way, and make moderate changes or improvements. The animation process is time-consuming, so the agency should be made aware that drastic changes will impact both the schedule and the budget.

Low-Budget Animation Alternatives

Clearly, unless students have animation talent themselves or have friends who do, including animation in a student commercial project can be problematic. Television stations do not, as a rule, offer animation services to their local advertiser clients, because even local animators can be expensive to use. However, computer-graphics software that was developed for Web applications can be used to create animation for television.

Flash, for example, has been used by our students to create animated logos for their projects that are as good or better than work we have seen on television. The program is an inexpensive software package, very easy to learn, and is quite powerful. One of our students taught himself how to use Morph, which is a program that allows you to begin with one image and gradually, over time, completely change it into another image. Another taught herself how to use Electric Image, a three-dimensional software package, which she used to create and animate a company logo for her class project. Later, a local nonprofit organization hired her to make a logo for their commercials using the same software.

Although we acknowledge that many schools do not yet have computer labs and software like what's mentioned here, so much freeware is available for simple but elegant projects that we are convinced any intrepid student can find and use downloadable software to embellish a project. A great place to look first is www.download.com.

SUMMARY

In this chapter we covered the purposes of and production techniques for sound, graphics, special effects, and animation. Sound has always been an important component, dating back to the beginning when the first commercials were little more than radio spots with a reader standing in front of the camera. For many years, after commercial producers realized that television is a visual medium, the audio portion became less important—the visual impact was emphasized. But in today's MTV/MP3/digital sound world, sound is now extremely germane to the television commercial, especially to reach the all-important 18- to 49-year-old demographic. They love quality sound.

Likewise, new digital production techniques for graphics, animation, and special effects, which the audience has come to expect in its motion pictures, now proliferate in television commercials. Computer-generated images are now used to create characters, products, pyrotechnics, animated logos, and graphics for almost every national spot. In addition to covering these elements for the national spot here, we suggested ways that students can make the most of limited resources to include multitrack audio, animation, and graphics in their productions.

With regard to sound, there are three tracks, each with a specific purpose. The dialogue track is called that because it features the human voice. Dialogue is used to communicate information, to provide backstory and exposition, to reveal character, and to move the story forward. It should only be used if it does one or more of these things. The dialogue track may feature a voiceover, an announcer, actors or nonactors who give testimonials. Sometimes, the final dialogue track is recorded at the same time the film or video is shot, but at other times, the dialogue is rerecorded after the film is edited, a process called automated dialogue replacement. This usually is done when the original recording is not clear and crisp, the performance isn't acceptable, or unwanted sounds were recorded. If the dialogue features the voices of characters who must be animated, it is recorded first so that animators can use it to create their drawings in synchronization with what's being said.

The sound track is used to set the mood of the commercial. Although most people react to music in similar ways (music may be calming and romantic, loud music may have more of a dramatic effect), we all have different tastes. The music you select for your commercial should be the music that most closely matches the mood you want to evoke to the audience you want to reach.

Sound effects are used to add realism, though they can also be used to create actions that are heard, rather than seen, with wonderful results. Sound effects are used to create ambient sounds that suggest to the audience a sense of place, size, and perspective. The impression of a crowded restaurant can be created by just using the proper sounds, even when the commercial is being shot in the corner of an empty one.

On high-end commercials, a sound designer is often involved in mixing and editing the final sound track—combining the dialogue, music, and sound effects tracks. On low-budget and student productions, the producer or director does the honors. There are a number of very fine digital tools, which run on PCs and Macs, for the purpose of editing and mixing multitrack audio, including the Avid, Final Cut Pro, Pro Tools, SoundEdit 16, and a number of free software packages, most of which are available on www.download.com.

Almost all of the graphics, animation, and logo treatments in commercials today are computer generated. Full-service graphics studios provide design and production services for graphics and animation, and even local television stations have some graphics capabilities. Agencies bid out the work for graphics and animation just as they bid out for the live-action shoot, music, and postproduction. They choose the studio that has demonstrated that it can create the necessary work for an acceptable price and meet the deadline. The agency or the client may have to provide certain things to the studio, such as original art, logos, character designs, and other material. If the animation or graphics have to be combined with live action in some seamless way, the special effects supervisor or animator should to be consulted during the live-action shoot.

In computer graphics studios, regardless of which software and hardware are used, the process of creating the images is fairly similar. Objects are modeled, animated, lit, textured or colored, and rendered; other steps may be called for because of a particular need, but these are the basic ones. At traditional cel animation studios, the process is much more complex and time-consuming because every single frame must be drawn by hand. Computers are used now for some of the work such as coloring the final drawings and sometimes for creating in-betweens. But, image creation is still a hands-on craft.

Computer graphics software and the computers the programs run on are becoming less expensive and easier to learn and use. A lot of software is available at no cost to anyone with the time and inclination to download it and teach it to themselves. The student who wishes to improve his work, and the television commercial producer who wants to offer something more to her local retail advertising clients, have many low-cost options.

DISCUSSION QUESTIONS

1. You shoot a number of customer testimonials for your local hardware store commercial as they leave the store. They say great things, but the quality is bad because your mic picked up street noises. Can you use ADR to replace the voices?

2. You want some music for your commercial and come across a site from which you can download almost anything. You find just the right tune, but you know it's from a CD released by a major label. Can you use it, even after you have modified it and mixed it with dialogue and sound effects so that it's almost unrecognizable? Does it make a difference if you are a student and nobody will see this spot but the others in your class and the professor?

3. You have to create character animation for a commercial, and the voice of the character is a celebrity who cannot do a voice recording until just a week or so before the commercial is due. That doesn't leave enough time to animate! Why is this a problem in the first place? What are some solutions for this problem?

RECOMMENDED READINGS

Goulekas, Karen E. *Visual Effects in a Digital World: A Comprehensive Glossary of Over 7,000 Visual Effects Terms,* 1st ed. New York: Morgan Kaufmann Publishers, 2001.

Kuperberg, Marcia. *Guide to Computer Animation for TV, Games, Multimedia and Web.* Boston: Focal Press, 2002.

Laybourne, Kit. *The Animation Book,* rev. ed. New York: Three Rivers Press; 1998.

Meyer, Trish, and Chris Meyer. *After Effects in Production,* 1st ed. Southampton, UK: CMP Books, 2000.

Phillips, William H. *Film: An Introduction.* Boston: Bedford/St. Martins, 1999.

Rose, Jay. *Producing Great Sound for Digital Video* (book/CD ed.). Southampton, UK: CMP Books, 2000.

Wright, Steve. *Digital Compositing for Film and Video,* 1st ed. (with CD-ROM). Boston: Butterworth-Heinemann, 2001.

NOTES

1. Phillips, p. 177.

2. There are technical aspects of this involving timecode and other methods of locking sound with picture that are beyond the scope of this book; we suggest the book *Audio in Media* by Stan Alten.

3. The precise digital format varies from one company or project to the next. Some like audio CD; others prefer a higher sampling rate than audio CD provides.

4. FTP, File Transfer Protocol, refers to the ability to send data files from one computer to another via the Internet.

CHAPTER TEN

POSTPRODUCTION

In a charming townhouse near the fashionable and artsy Allen Street district of Buffalo, New York, Pete VonDerLinn and Kevin Tripodi kick back in leather easy chairs and nibble corned beef sandwiches. This is the editing session where the two creative directors—one a writer, the other an art director at Eric Mower & Associates—are posting six commercials for the Centro public transportation system in Syracuse. On the opposite side of what was once the formal parlor, Andy Donovan plays the Avid Media Composer 9000 like a virtuoso.

Donovan, a senior editor at the *Daily Post,* is busy actually *creating* a scene. During filming, the crew got a great shot of the Centro mascot, a kangaroo named Boomer, walking in front of a recognizable landmark on the Syracuse University campus. Students walked by in both directions and remarkably, none of them looked surprised to see a six-foot-five guy in a furry costume hoofing it to class (see Figure 10.1). What was missing was the product—a city bus. So Donovan was *compositing* a bus that had driven past earlier into the Boomer scene; it took a little while. Donovan used the *animatte* tool in the Avid to trace around the bus in each of the eighty-five frames (the number of frames it took for the bus to drive through the scene); then he had to indicate that the bus was visible but the area around it was invisible, or clear. When the two scenes were composited—the bus was placed over the scene with Boomer in it—he had a totally new scene.

VonDerLinn and Tripodi liked the new scene, and Donovan continued to cut and edit the spot together. He would play it back after adding a new clip so that the creatives could adjust the transition, timing, or pacing. From time to time, Tripodi or VonDerLinn would ask for a shot to be flipped, or color-corrected, or to be time-shifted a little. Donovan would oblige, usually with just a few keystrokes (see Figure 10.2). Within an hour, the spot was roughed out, and the trio went on to the next spot. At the end of two days of editing, they sent the digital master to the agency where the spots were screened for the client, who then made a few requests for changes for the final cut.

The last phase of commercial production is postproduction, when all of the visual and audio elements that were shot on film or video; recorded; animated; or generated on a computer are edited, mixed, synced, and composited to create the final commercial. Special effects and graphics are added. Scenes are color-corrected or digitally manipulated and may wind up looking entirely different than the original source material. The final commercial is output directly to digital videotape, and sent to the networks, the cable channels,

FIGURE 10.1   The bus leaving the scene in the frame (*left*) was added to this shot by the editor using the Avid Media Composer. The camera then zoomed into the Boomer character.

Courtesy of Central New York Regional Transportation Authority and Eric Mower & Associates.

or to individual television stations for airing. In the very near future, commercials will usually be sent as digital files to servers at the networks, stations, and cable channels.

Postproduction is one of the most important parts of the creative process. Although all of the visual and audio elements are carefully shot and recorded, it is only when combined with each other that they form a powerful persuasive message. While editing, the creatives determine the basic storyline by deciding which shots from among hundreds should be used in the commercial and the order in which the audience will see these shots. They decide how the chosen shots will be *paced*—how fast or slow the audience will perceive them—and what kinds of *transitions* (cuts, wipes, dissolves) will be used to connect one shot with the next.

While compositing, the creatives add nuance and excitement to the storyline by combining certain visual elements with others. A computer-generated character can be composited with a live-action scene so that it looks like it is interacting with a real child eating breakfast cereal. Such a scene would have required extremely careful planning and coordination during the preproduction and production phases or compositing would be next to impossible during postproduction. Or, a simple graphic tag line may be composited over a satisfied customer, a fairly routine task. Special effects can be added to scenes, or the footage itself can be finessed, altered, or filtered. Audio tracks—music, sound effects, and voice—are mixed or *layered* (each track is carefully balanced) and synchronized with the visuals.

Nearly all of today's national and regional commercials are finished at *post houses*—special facilities that have sophisticated equipment and talented editors and technical directors to accomplish the myriad of postproduction tasks. Typically, it is the agency producer and the creative director who supervise the final assembly, sometimes with a client representative present. More often, the final commercial is screened for the client after it is done.

The agency sends all of the visual and audio elements to the post house ahead of time; there the elements are digitized, if they are not already in digital format, and stored on a computer hard drive. After all of the elements are in digital form, a postproduction session is scheduled during which the agency supervises the editing of the visuals, the mixing and syncing of audio, the addition of certain effects and graphics, and the correc-

FIGURE 10.2   Daily Post's Andy Donovan uses the Avid Media Composer 9000 to edit six commercials for Eric Mower & Associates and its client Centro.

Courtesy of Central New York Regional Transportation Authority and Eric Mower & Associates.

tion of any problems. All of this is done on a computer using special software tools that have been developed over the past ten years. Because the visuals are in digital form, the editing can be accomplished in a nonlinear fashion—images and sounds can be easily inserted or removed anywhere in the assembly process. There is no loss of quality as they are manipulated over and over again; when the work is complete, the final commercial is output to digital tape, or to 35mm film if the spot is to be shown theatrically.

This work occurs in real time—an editor or technical director does everything while seated at a console under the direction of the agency creatives seated right behind her without having to wait for delayed electronic processing. Digital effects have provided creatives with a new visual and audio vocabulary with which to finish their commercials, and these capabilities are augmented constantly.

This chapter goes into greater detail about the processes and the tools of commercial postproduction. We also delve into the past a bit because most of the basic art and aesthetics of postproduction were developed during the early days of film editing; those fundamentals are still the heart and soul of postproduction. Postproduction techniques have evolved dramatically over the past few years to the point where much more of the finishing touches are added, even created, on a computer during postproduction sessions. The tools and talents of postproduction specialists are an impressive marriage of technological advances and creative skill, but it wasn't always this way, as we discuss in the next section.

In this chapter, you will learn the following:

- The principles of editing that were "discovered" during the early days of film; most are still used today
- What these principles are, and what the editor and creative director aim for during the editing session
- The technology that has pushed postproduction beyond editing, so now many more finishing, fixing, and even production-like things are done to the commercial
- Postproduction services continue to drop in cost, enabling regional and local advertisers to create commercials with effects and graphics that would have been impossible until quite recently
- The difference between analog and digital media, and why digital is more flexible, powerful, faster, and results in better quality
- The steps involved in postproduction, from digitizing the elements to outputting the final commercial to tape

Postproduction as we now know it evolved over a long time and continues to change. In order to understand the process, a little history about what led up to today's digital post house is necessary.

FILM EDITING'S YESTERYEARS

When movies were first produced, it was not necessary to edit the film. A camera was pointed at a stage where a live performance took place. The objective view of the performance was similar to the view that someone in a live audience would have had—a locked-off view, which provided a medium-long shot of the entire area where the performance took place. The camera seldom moved, the actors simply changed positions in front of it. The performance stopped when it was time to load more film or to correct a gaff; the actors waited in roughly the same spot as where they stopped; and when the camera rolled again, they acted again. This is still called in-camera editing.

Eventually, filmmakers experimented with the subjective camera. They moved the camera into the scene with the actors and filmed close-ups, medium and point-of-view shots. The film audience was no longer bound to their seats but rather floated into and within the world of the actors. Filmmakers experimented with camera angles, shot composition, lighting, and camera motion. The performance was no longer shot as though it were live theater; it stopped and started repeatedly while the filmmakers moved the camera and lights. This, of course, resulted in far more footage than was needed, and all of these shots had to be cut up and assembled by hand in an editing process. Filmmakers became editors, and soon were experimenting with transitions, pacing, action, reaction, and montage.

These efforts gave birth to the idea of the visual language—the notion that images shot, lit, and edited a certain way could convey messages above and beyond the message in the acting or the dialogue. The combination of how the actors behaved and how the camera saw them was greater than the sum of the two. The visual language became an extremely powerful storytelling formula. Filmmakers awoke to the importance of editing. While shooting film, they had to think ahead about how they would "edit" the film—what shots they would need and how they would cut and pace the shots later. The editing process that would come later actually drove directorial decisions made during the film shoot, and still does.

At the end of each shoot day, negatives were taken to the lab where they were developed and prints were struck. These prints were called dailies or rushes because they were printed copies of the day's shooting. The editor held the prints up to the light and viewed them to make decisions about the actual picture assembly.

In the early 1920s, a machine called the Movieola was invented. It had a small projection light behind a glass screen, and 35mm film could be run through it. Although originally devised to be a device for viewing films at home, filmmakers soon adopted it to view the dailies and make editing decisions. Industry demand inspired the addition of a sound head, and later the adoption of several film and sound heads so that several different strips (film scenes) could be viewed and laid out for cutting. These machines, when properly maintained, are real workhorses. The basic machine was in use way past the introduction of electronic editing in the late seventies and early eighties and was a common site in film production companies even during the 1990s. Two other companies (Kem and Steenbeck) introduced the *flatbed* system, which has more sophisticated reel management and faster speeds (see Figure 10.3).

FIGURE 10.3 A six-plate flatbed editing system. Cutting film was once the only way to edit a commercial, but it has given way to digital nonlinear

Film editors used the Movieola and flatbed systems to view the positive prints of the film and to make selections of individual takes, which they generally cut off the main reel of film and hung in a film bin. They would then assemble their film by splicing the film back together in the right order. Editors could splice the film with tape, a fast and easy way to join together two pieces of film, but it resulted in a splice that could be easily seen when the film was projected. They could then view their film on the system; make additional decisions, which often meant cutting the film again; and sync-up the sound track with the visuals. This version of the film was called a *rough cut* because it was not the final, finished product but rather a first draft, or representation, of it. The film was usually covered with dust, scratches, fingerprints, and tape splices of course. When the editor, the director, the agency, and the client were happy with the rough cut, it would be sent to a *negative cutter*—a person who specialized in *conforming,* or matching, the negative with the rough cut. The negative cutter would work much more carefully and use a hot splicer to make frame-accurate, invisible splices (see Figure 10.4). This negative would then be used to strike a final print of the commercial.

Although very time-consuming and error-prone, this editing process was the *only* way to create a finished film for about fifty years. During that time, the art and craft of editing evolved, until the basic aesthetics and principles of editing were fully understood. New editing technologies, such as videotape in the 1970s and digital techniques in the

FIGURE 10.4   The film editor cuts the film and splices it together to construct his edited film. Many college's film programs still teach film editing in this way so that students learn editing aesthetics before they learn digital systems.

1990s, have added nothing new to the basic principles of editing although new effects and tools have expanded the idea of postproduction from merely editing to much more.

Film Opticals

Even though filmmakers knew the art of film cutting and created compelling stories during the editing process, the technology of film effects was often an obstacle. Creating simple transitions, such as dissolves, involved making two strips of film negative, spliced in such a way that a scene on one strip overlapped a scene from another. Other effects involved making high-contrast mattes and other film elements that required extremely accurate registration (matching sprocket holes) between multiple strips of film. All of these processes are known as *film opticals* because film had to be optically exposed, developed, and printed again and again to arrive at the final negative.

An optical printer, a large and expensive machine, was used to reexpose these various film elements and make a new negative that was a composite of all of them. The whole process was tedious, time-consuming, costly, and error-prone. It took place in a film lab, and the results weren't seen by the agency or the client until after the work had been completed the night before. The reexposure and reprinting of film degraded the original footage with each generation. Scratches, dirt, registration errors, and misjudgments on exposures and frame counts caused almost every first attempt to be repeated. Postproduction, which should have been a mostly creative endeavor—telling the story with visuals—was instead largely a technical exercise. The "special effect" of postproduction was often getting the job done at all.

ANALOG TAPE EDITING

The film industry usually changes or adopts new technology for only three reasons: (1) it will save money, (2) it will save time, or (3) it will allow something to be accomplished that used to be impossible. The switch from the earlier ways of editing film to postproduction on videotape provided television commercial producers with all three.

While the first attempts to edit electronically came about in the mid-1960s, it was several years before it became a routine in the commercial industry. Electronic editing came about because of the slow but steady acceptance of magnetic videotape. Videotape was first used not as a production tool but rather as a storage medium. It allowed time shifting in the delivery of network programming to adjust for the three-hour time difference between New York and Los Angeles. It was initially regarded as a storage medium because it could capture a program immediately, including a filmed program, and then play it back three hours later to the audience on the West Coast.

Few in the industry, however, thought that the quality of tape matched 35mm film, so it was rejected as a production medium. It was fine for recording "live" shows but was undesirable for shows with higher production values—movies of the week, drama, even sitcoms—although many of these eventually were recorded on tape. The tape-versus-film debate continues to dog the production industry, even as the tape itself has become digital.

Interestingly, it is precisely because images captured on digital tape look so crisp and perfect that some people still prefer the look of film!

Tape made a fine storage medium. Prior to tape the only way to preserve live television was to shoot film off the face of a television picture tube—a process known as a *kinescope*. As soon as tape was used to capture and store images, the need for tape editing came about. Some of the characteristics of tape, and the way that it held images and sounds, made "cutting" tape impossible. It could not be held up to the light and viewed as film could be, and the pictures and sounds that synced together were not actually lined-up on the tape.

A major element of editing is syncing sound with picture. Historically, picture and sound elements were kept separate during editing and only combined during the final compositing of the material. An early attempt to edit tape was to place a liquid on the tape to "see" the synchronization pulses that differentiate one frame of video from the next. The liquid helped to visually define the magnetically stronger sync-pulse from the other magnetic video information on the tape. The editor then placed the tape under a microscope and made a razor blade cut on the aligned sync-pulse—this was a time-consuming and cumbersome process at best.

By the mid-seventies, the Society of Motion Picture and Television Engineers (SMPTE) developed a method to keep track of frames on videotape, the SMPTE timecode. There are thirty video frames per second in the standard NTSC television system. The timecode system places a time reference (in hours, minutes, seconds, frames) on each frame of a videotape, providing each frame with a unique identifier. This makes it possible to search for individual frames by specifying the timecode—reference number. There is even space within the code design to enter some separate specific information about the frame. As computers were introduced, programs were developed that allowed editors to work at a keyboard and enter the timecode for cuts and dissolves. The computer then controlled the videotape players, making the assembly process completely automated.

Another technical development at about this time was an improvement in the film-to-tape transfer process. Up until then, the equipment designed to transfer film to videotape did not produce a tape that was of acceptable quality for further editing. Unacceptable movement within the video's frame—jiggle—was introduced into the transfer while the film moved through the mechanical gate of the optical projection equipment. This was a real problem when two video elements were later composited, matted together—for example, a title over a background—because one element would move or jump around while the other would remain rock steady. If you had a still of a package on video and live-action footage of a table in the background, it was impossible to place the package on the table by compositing without the background jiggling perceptibly. The equipment for film-to-tape transfer was not designed for precise registration but had been adapted from other uses—that is, film projection. In response to industry demand, the Rank Cinetel was invented to solve the jiggle problem and some other companies followed suit. Soon, transferring film to tape for editing and effects creation was routine.

Even though the proper technology existed to transfer film to tape, and to edit the tape using timecode, ad agencies did not fully adopt videotape editing until they suddenly discovered that it could significantly shorten the editing time. Being able to use tape was a critical improvement over editing film, which took longer and was more susceptible to error. Remember, commercial completion is time-critical because media buys, which usually cost far more than the production of the commercial, are made long before the commercial is completed. The commercial must be completed before the first "air date" or else there is nothing to show and a hefty investment in media is lost. Ad agencies adopted videotape editing to mitigate the threat of late commercials, and soon virtually abandoned film editing.

Videotape simplified the postproduction process, and analog postproduction and editing facilities sprang up in the major commercial production centers in the early 1970s. Commercial producers could shoot on film, develop their negative, and take it to a postproduction facility where the negative (or a positive print) could be transferred to videotape. Once in this form, seasoned videotape editors would color-correct the tape scene by scene, fixing errors but also enhancing any footage that needed more of this or less of that. Supervised by the agency, they could edit the tape and insert any kind of transition in real time. They could add graphics, captions, and other text. Eventually, post houses, as they were (and still are) called, added more equipment and services, including "paint systems," which enabled them to create graphics, and digital systems, which enabled them to create three-dimensional animation.

The final commercial was edited together on analog tape during sessions that often took hours and hours for a :30 spot. Although the process was less time-consuming than optical film techniques, the analog systems were *linear*—the final commercial was assembled scene by scene—and any change or mistake meant starting all over from the top. In addition, the technology introduced a generation loss of quality with every transfer of tape.

Growth of Postproduction

The wide acceptance of videotape editing for television commercials, as well as shows, also gave birth to the idea of postproduction as we now know it. Videotape editing facilities added more services as demand for these services grew, and as competition between the facilities forced them all to adopt new technology or perish. The facilities added equipment to color-correct poorly exposed film footage. Other equipment made it possible to *chroma key* two visual elements together—a type of matting that previously required a long and complicated film process. They added graphics departments that could create titles and captions. The facilities themselves became stylish boutiques where agencies brought their clients for comfortable postproduction sessions, replete with leather couches and catered meals.

DIGITAL POSTPRODUCTION

Today, we rarely physically cut and splice film, although it is still sometimes done with a negative, and even the analog videotape systems seem quaint. The cutting, splicing, transitions, and special effects are done in a nondestructive and nonlinear manner with digital technology on a computer. The commercial filmmaker can shoot on film, have it developed by the lab, and take it to the digital post house. There it is digitized—each frame of film is scanned by a device that converts color and intensity (or brightness) information on the film into digital data. If the commercial is shot on analog or digital videotape, the producer skips the film lab step.

When a picture is digitized, it is scanned by a device that divides it up into an array of dots called pixels (picture elements), usually numbering 640 dots wide by 480 dots high, although the picture can be divided into more pixels: there is no real limit. The device measures the color and brightness of each dot and converts the information into a binary number. If the array, or resolution, of the picture is 640 by 480, there are 307,200 pixels in each frame that will be stored in this binary format. Once a film has been digitized, it can be logged, edited, composited with other visuals, synced to sound (also digitized, edited, and mixed), and output to digital video or scanned back onto film. This takes little time, errors can be readily fixed, the process is nonlinear, and, since the binary code that represents the images and sounds never degrades, there is no generation loss of quality.

Analog-versus-Digital Media

In the late 1970s, digital media emerged as computer technology became more ubiquitous. Computers became less expensive, more powerful, and easier to use, a trend that continues. Entrepreneurs began writing software programs that were useful to filmmakers. Several companies began creating three-dimensional computer animation, while others began using computers to control the video editing systems described in the previous section. Even film labs began using computers to control development and printing processes. As technology caught on over the next two decades, more and more equipment and software were developed to handle both sound- and picture-making tasks until all things digital began replacing all things analog. To understand and appreciate the significance of digital technology to the capture, creation, manipulation, and transmission of images and sounds, it is important to understand what analog means and what its limitations are.

Film and magnetic videotape, as well as vinyl recordings and magnetic audio tapes, are analog. The visual and audio information contained in them are stored and/or played by signals of continuously varying values known as waves. Differences in the values from one moment to the next are interpreted and constructed by our physical senses as sight or sound. For example, a natural analog signal is the sound caused when a tree falls in a forest, and you are nearby to hear it. As the tree crashes down, it disturbs the air around it in different but continuous waves from one moment to the next. The now vibrating air affects the air nearby in the same way, sending a wave toward you, the listener. When the vibrating wave of air, with differences in its intensity following along behind it, makes contact with your eardrum, your hearing mechanisms interpret the wave of vibrations in a certain way, and your brain constructs a sound from the information delivered to it. "Ah," you say to yourself, "that sounded like a huge tree!" The answer to the famous question, by the way, is no—if a tree falls in a forest and nobody is there, it does not make a sound. It just makes the air vibrate; a tree that falls in a vacuum doesn't even do that.

All analog signals are similar to the natural analog signal just described in that they consist of continuous waves of information that can only be "heard," or interpreted, by the correct receiver. An FM radio receiver can only receive, interpret, and play an FM sound signal; the same is so with AM radio, NTSC television, a magnetic audio cassette recording, and so on. Because the information is stored as, and travels in, continuous waves, it is not easy to change any discrete aspect of the wave without changing the entire wave. Plus, any change to the wave is almost always destructive or degrading.

Digital signals, on the other hand, are made up of discontinuous—either on or off, present or not present—pulses of electrical current. In a sort of blast from the past, digital technology is actually a throwback to Morse code, which was information sent over a wire in the form of an electrical signal that was either present or not present based on how the sender tapped a key. These two states (on, off), delivered in predetermined sequences, represented letters of the alphabet and a string of these sequences created words and sentences. On the receiving end of the Morse code signal, a human converted the on/off pulses back into the letters they represented. But, back in the 1800s, there was no way to store these signals.

Flash forward to the present. When the electrical signal is present, it represents the number 1, and when it is not present, it represents a 0. Gathered together in the proper, agreed-on order, these two digits can represent larger numbers, and the larger numbers can represent letters of the alphabet, symbols, mathematical algorithms, or even colors or sounds. The entire computer universe is based on this extraordinarily simple, yet flexible and powerful, notion that 0s and 1s, arranged in the proper sequences, can represent anything we want them to. Digital information is also called *binary data* because it is represented by using only two characters which are an electronic reference, off or on. These references in combination can be building blocks for image or sound materials.

If you have followed all of this, the advantages of digital media over analog may be obvious. Only one type of signal containing binary data is needed to represent any kind of information—text, mathematical, images, or sounds. Only one type of machine is needed to create, control, manipulate, store, receive, or send the information—a computer. All or any discrete part of the information can be changed at any time by simply changing some of the binary data, and no matter how many times you change the binary data, you never destroy the fidelity of the media it represents. Computers were poised, then, to solve every problem filmmakers have ever had during the postproduction process and, for the most part, they have. We have looked at the steady evolution of the tools, but let's look at the creative editorial process too, both the audio and the visual elements. We'll deal with pictures first, and our discussions will focus (pun intended) on commercials.

THE POSTPRODUCTION PATH

As mentioned earlier, editing is only one of the tasks of postproduction. Creating certain visuals, modifying visuals, and compositing visuals with others are also postproduction tasks that may be needed in addition to editing of live-action film. The editor also edits and manipulates the sound track during postproduction, controlling the various tracks and creating a final mix. Figure 10.5 shows a flowchart of the possible path of live-action footage, computer-generated effects, animation, special effects, and sound during the postproduction process.

Let's examine the case of a commercial that is all live action, ending with a logo tag. In this simplest of examples, much like many local commercials and student projects, the live-action footage would be digitized, the logo would be scanned into the computer, and the entire postproduction process would probably consist of a nonlinear digital editing session.

The Postproduction Path

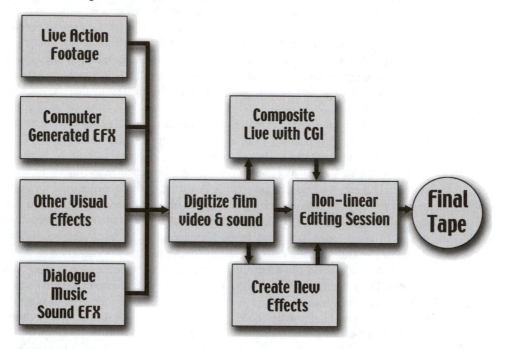

FIGURE 10.5 The postproduction path. Raw live-action footage, animation, computer graphics, and sounds are brought to the post session, where everything is digitized; many new effects can be added at this time.

In the case of an effects-heavy commercial involving computer-animated characters interacting with live-action characters over a background, with additional effects added at the last minute, nearly all of the steps on the flowchart would be taken. The steps are all explained in the sections that follow, beginning with the selection of live-action footage for postproduction.

Prescreening the Dailies

When the live-action commercial is shot and the negative is processed, dailies are struck and viewed by the director, agency, and client. During a multiday shoot, film is usually processed every day and dailies of the previous day's shoot are viewed in the morning. If there is something wrong or missing from the previous day's shoot, or if something new is thought of because of what the creative team sees, the successive days are used to fix or add more shots. During the shoot, the director probably indicated to the script supervisor, or a production assistant, whether the take he just finished was any good, and that information was written into a log. During the review of the dailies, the creative team uses the log as a guide and selects the *hero* takes—the ones they think they will want to use in the final commercial. These are separated out from the rest and, along with any other visual and audio material to be used during postproduction, are sent to the post house.

Film-to-Tape Transfer, Digitizing the Elements

At the postproduction house, the film elements, and any other analog material for the commercial, are usually transferred to tape first and then the tapes are digitized. More and more post houses can digitize the film negative rather than transferring it to tape first, which only introduces a generation loss of quality. While the operator digitizes the footage, she digitizes it shot by shot and *logs* and *saves* each *clip* as a separate *clip* in a *bin*. The developers of the digital editing systems chose terms like clip, log, bin, and other film editing lexicons to create a *metaphor* for the user. Because these terms are familiar in film editing, operators can quickly identify and learn the purposes of the various tools on the computer.

When footage that has sound with it is digitized, the sound tracks are treated by the computer as separate *clips*—the sound is separated from the picture and stored as an independent file. This gives the editor a lot of flexibility, enabling him to lay down a sound track and place any visual clip with it, not just the one it came with. The operator gives each logged clip a unique name and other descriptive information that will help the editor find the shot when it is needed for compositing, color-correction, and editing.

All of the source material—film negatives or prints, CGI tapes or files, sound files or CDs and tapes, and flat reflective art are put away and protected. They can be brought out again and be redigitized if necessary.

Color-Correction

Any digitized element can be color-corrected, brightened, and cleaned up—this is the *color-correction* session—using digital paint system tools at the post house before the edit session. New effects can be created with existing elements using computer effects programs such as Adobe's After Effects or MacroMedia's Flash. A scratch on a negative can be removed, a color film can be made to look like it was shot in black and white, and vice versa. Live-action characters can be *colorized,* while the background they appear on can be *posterized.* The variety and number of possible visual effects that can be added to digitized visual elements are great, and growing. Of course, none of these effects in and of themselves necessarily improve the persuasiveness of the commercial, and many agency creatives have to constantly remind themselves of the primary directive—Sell the product!—and avoid the temptation to create an effect simply because they can. The agency producer should be on the alert for runaway costs. Postproduction houses usually charge by the hour for their services, and each service probably will add extra cost to the hourly rate.

Compositing

Compositing is the marrying of certain picture elements with others. In most cases, it is combining two elements that could not have been shot together but must appear as though they were. As explained earlier in this chapter, this was once a long and tedious optical process involving multiple strips of film, mattes, and expensive optical printers. The early *Star Wars* films contained many, many composited scenes done using optical processes; George Lucas used digital compositing techniques in his more recent films. Many commercials combine live action with computer-generated backgrounds, characters, and effects, and in most cases, the two worlds—the real and the virtual ones—have to appear as one. When the design of the commercial calls for compositing visual elements together during postproduction, steps are taken during preproduction and production to make sure that the elements are created in a way that will allow compositing. This process was described in chapter 9. When all of the scenes needed for the final edit have been digitized, color-corrected, and composited, the final editing session can be scheduled.

Nonlinear Editing

On the first day the agency creatives, the editor, and perhaps the client gather around a digital editing system such as the Avid Media Composer—a special purpose, high-end, non-linear digital editing system—and begin to do an offline edit (see Figure 10.6). An *offline edit* is the first acceptable cut, but not likely the final cut of the commercial. The term

FIGURE 10.6   This close-up of the computer monitor of a nonlinear editing session using Final Cut Pro shows various windows on the screen, including one for the timeline and multiple tracks of video and audio. The editor can simply drag and drop a clip of film or audio anywhere along the timeline.

offline once referred to using a particular type of equipment that historically yielded a less than broadcast-quality product; only an *online* edit was of broadcast quality. Today, the only difference between offline editing and online editing is how the final result will be used. An offline edit always yields a product that is not intended for broadcast; an online edit yields the final commercial.

The editor accesses the clips stored in the virtual bin, and assembles them along a timeline displayed on the computer screen in accordance with the design of the commercial, using the best possible takes of each scene. Computer editing systems allow the editor to have multiple parallel timelines, and the editor can easily make sure that the material on one timeline dissolves into the material on another, that the material on one timeline is matted over another, and so forth. The systems provide a library of preprogrammed transitions, wipes, and other effects the editor can insert with a single keystroke. The digital editor can shift the clips to begin and end sooner or later, completely remove a clip, and/or add a new one in the middle of the whole project. Because this process is nondestructive, different versions of the edit can be tried and each saved for reference, and the editor can view every decision immediately. The term *nonlinear* is characterized by this ability to add or remove clips from the middle of a timeline that may have hundreds of clips already specified.

In the prior-to-digital days, transitions, title insertions, and other effects were pretty well locked in once done and any changes, even moving a title up or down a little, involved much time and money; editing was linear. Once a shot was cut into the sequence of shots, it was very difficult to swap it out or change it in any way without dismantling the whole thing. Transitions that were once assembled in an optical camera with intermediate elements are now as simple as a couple of keystrokes on the computer or maybe a mouse click to a computer short cut.

Sound is added and synced to the picture on the nonlinear editing system in the same way. Special tracks are reserved for the sounds, which can be locked to or disengaged from film clips on other tracks. So when the editor moves a film clip by dragging it along its track, the appropriate sound track moves along with it, if he wants it to. The editor can create and use as many individual tracks as he wants or needs. He can select all or any part of a sound clip and adjust or modify many different sound attributes, including its relative volume, pitch, reverb, and so forth. The editor can cause the sound to fade in or fade out, listen to creative decisions instantly, and undo them and try again if they aren't right. With proper planning, followed by a session that can include many iterations and a bit of trial and error, nonlinear editing can result in at least one and usually several versions of the commercial.

EDITING AESTHETICS

The primary purpose of postproduction is to edit the various shots into a linear sequence of pictures and events that tell a story, and, as we said earlier, the principles of editing (the how-to of editing) are pretty well established after nearly a century of experience. The television commercial leans heavily on editing to select out the usable footage from a mountain of raw material to tell a persuasive story in exactly thirty seconds—that's 720 film frames or 900 video frames. How does the editor think? What guides her decision making?

First and foremost, the editor is directed by the commercial's design as it was sold to the client—there is no escaping that. The design of the commercial will call for one of the two basic types of editing—continuity editing or montage—and possibly a combination of the two. Second, she can only work with the material she has: the live-action footage, the computer graphics, the music, the sound recordings. Third, she only has thirty seconds, or less, in which to create her story. Beyond these constraints, the editor actually has a great deal of creative wiggle room while editing a story or a montage.

Continuity Editing

Continuity editing involves selecting and using shots that, when edited together, tell a continuous story. Each shot reveals a little bit of the story, piece by piece, until the end is reached in a relatively logical progression of images and words. Feature films, television shows, and documentaries are all edited in this way. This kind of editing is evident in certain commercial themes or concepts—the slice-of-life, the product demonstration, testimonials. These commercials have a beginning, a middle, and an end, and very often they have a structure that closely matches the three-act structure of the screenplay. The first act sets up the premise—what is the problem that the main character must solve (the conflict); the second act is the confrontation—how the main character deals with the problem; the final act is the resolution—how the main character wins in the end. Naturally, in a commercial, the product plays the major role in resolving the conflict.

In continuity editing, the editor controls three very important aspects of the audience's experience. First of all, the editor controls the experience of the audience by controlling what the audience knows and the order in which the audience knows it. She does this by deciding which shots to use, and in what order, to parse out the information (storyline) bit by bit. The second thing she controls is the audience's sense of time. The editor can compress time, without hurting the continuity of the story, by her shot selection. The third thing she can control is the audience's mood or emotion. This she can do mainly with the pacing of the shots and the transitions between them. Let's examine each of these next.

Shot Order.   As we discussed in earlier chapters, the film audience is on a constant hunt for meaning. Viewers watch every shot and scan for information to keep with them. They piece the story together as each shot reveals a little more about what is going on. Sometimes a shot leaves the audience with a question, which they expect to have answered in subsequent shots. Even when shots are just thrown together with no specific order to them, experiments have shown that people actually create their own meanings from a haphazard collection of shots. This propensity is valuable when we watch the other kind of editing—called *montage*. Russian filmmaker Lev Kuleshov intercut a man's stoic face with shots of a bowl of soup, a woman in a coffin, and a child playing. The audience was astonished at how well the actor seemed to react to each very different image. It did not realize that the actor wasn't reacting to any of the shots and that in fact the same shot of the actor was used each time. The audience created its own meaning from the shots.[1]

Because every shot carries with it a piece of the story puzzle, the order of the shots affects our perception of what the final story outcome will be. If the shots are presented in a different order, our anticipation of the final outcome will follow a different path, and our experience will be quite different. In his book, *Film Directing Shot by Shot: Visualizing from Concept to Screen,* Steven D. Katz uses a very clever example to show how a small number of shots, ordered differently, dramatically changes the experience of the audience.[2]

Consider the three storyboard frames, perhaps from a commercial for an antilock braking system, in Figure 10.7a. In this sequence, the audience sees (shot 1) that a car is headed at full speed toward an intersection where a woman is preparing to cross, pushing a baby stroller. The audience is the first to know that some kind of catastrophe is about to happen. They aren't sure why the car isn't slowing down until they see that the driver is looking off to his left (shot 2), perhaps distracted by something. They still don't know what will happen next. Then they are relieved to see the horrified woman notice the car at the last instant (shot 3), perhaps accompanied by screeching brakes. Figures 10.7b and 10.7c show the shots in Figure 10.7a in different orders. What are the stories now?[3]

From the examples in the figures, you can see how the order of shots can affect our experience of the same basic event—order matters. In the first example, the audience knows that there is trouble brewing, but none of the characters in the story do. We are in a high state of anticipation and dread. In the last example, we don't know what is going on

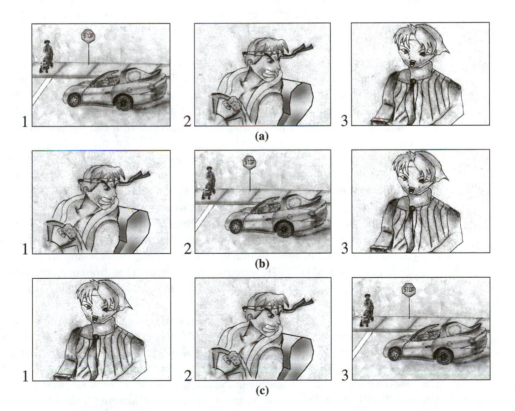

FIGURE 10.7

until the last shot, when we see what the woman is excited about. Our anticipation is replaced with wonder.

Compressing Time.   The audience accepts the omission of shots, particularly when they can imagine what occurred by the context of the action around the missing piece. This simple fact enables the editor to leave out events the audience can assume occurred. For example, a family is shown piling into a car on its way to Burger King. The car starts down the driveway; in the next shot, they are at the drive-in window. The audience does not need to see the family's entire drive, or any part of it, to accept the fact that they drove some unnamed and unimportant distance to get their lunch.

Time compression is especially important to the commercial editor who has only thirty seconds in which to tell an understandable and convincing story. She cannot afford to fill time with even a single frame that does not contribute to the message. Commercials for lawn care products that begin with weedy, patchy lawns and finish with lush, green carpets of grass compress months of time. Commercials for laundry products in which filthy trousers are plunked down into the washer and then emerge sparkling clean compress an hour. The editor makes certain that the context for the missing information is there; the audience does the rest with its imagination.

Another way that the editor can compress time is with a certain kind of montage editing, called American montage, described later in the "Montage" section.

Pacing and Transitions.   *Pacing* refers to the apparent speed of the commercial; it is a function of both the speed of the action in each individual shot and the length of the shot in screen time. The editor paces the commercial to create emotion and control the mood of the audience. You may remember that music is the mood-setting component of the sound track, and that rhythm set by the visual pace, the result of film cutting, is often in sync with the beat of the music.

In a Mountain Dew commercial, a young extreme-sports-type on a dirt bike chases down a cheetah across an African plain. The cat is running full tilt, and the biker is speeding along in pursuit, kicking up a cloud of dust behind him. The editor cuts from the cat to the biker, to a point-of-view (POV) of the cat, to a ground-level shot as they both rocket past. In 30 seconds, there are more than 40 shots. The pace of the action and the cutting is frenetic and pounding for about 24 seconds until he catches up to the cat, stares it down, and thrusts his whole arm down its throat. After a moment of searching around in its gullet, he pulls his arm out and voilá! He's recovered his can of 'Dew from deep in the maw of the big cat. This fast pace, set to equally rapid percussion music, creates a high-energy, adventurous mood.

Cuts are used as the transition for fast-paced editing, while dissolves are used for slowing things down and smoothing, or we could say *soothing,* things out. In a commercial for organ donations, Leslie Dektor's sensitive, slow-motion, black-and-white film footage of a child tossing a ball into the air dissolves to a shot of doves taking off. From the doves we dissolve back to the ball landing in the hands of another child. He used a long lens and got a shallow depth of field to create an ethereal, almost haunting look. The voiceover, two parents, describes how one child's tragedy became another child's hope.

Montage

If continuity editing tells a story by putting shots together in a logical progression—one easily decoded by the audience using its intellect—*montage* is editing that relies almost entirely on subsurface meanings. The audience relies more on its instinct or intuition to understand the meaning, which is generally the result of all of the shots taken as a whole rather than the sequence of messages built, one onto the next, in continuity editing. Feature films often use montage to show a great deal of activity in a short period of time. A large number of shots, usually cut to music, show pioneers clearing the land, building cabins, plowing fields, harvesting crops, exchanging approving smiles, getting married, having children, and building a town. A half century of growth is condensed into fifty seconds of brief, but telling, glimpses of how they tamed the wilderness.

The word *montage* comes from the French word for *build,* and it originally referred to all forms of editing. During the 1920s, Russian filmmakers, such as Sergei Eisenstein and Vsevolod Pudovkin, experimented with and wrote about various editing techniques, notably montage, and gave it new meaning because of their emphasis on the hidden meanings that certain kinds of cutting conveyed to the audience. Today, even when the word is not used in a film editing context, it means a *collection* of thematically connected things edited together in an artistic way, as opposed to a logical one. School children create montages by gluing together magazine photos, clipped this way and that, to create a larger piece meant to leave the viewer with an *impression.*

Entire commercials are very often montage, especially those that are set to music and are meant, like music videos, to create mood and image rather than to tell a story. In a commercial for Dr. Pepper, singer Garth Brooks and a group of musicians jam on the stoop of a general store. People hear the music and drift over, including three beautiful young women. Everyone is smiling, chugging down Dr. Pepper, having a great time. We see close-ups of twinkling eyes, swaying hips, tapping feet, and great guitar fingering. There are more than twenty shots, cut on the beat. It's a feel-good commercial, associating the number one selling musical artist with a top soft drink brand. What is important to take away from this example is that the shots used in this montage could be reordered in ten different ways, and the message of the commercial would remain the same: "Garth Brooks and a whole slew of really attractive people drink our product. Shouldn't you?"

Within any commercial, there could be some combination of continuity and montage. The editor selects the shots, and the order, pacing, and transitions between them to either tell a story as in continuity editing, or to create emotion and mood, as in montage. She constructs the offline edit, and outputs it to tape for the agency.

AGENCY REVIEW AND FINAL OUTPUT

Once the creatives directly involved with the project are satisfied with the offline edit, they present it to their bosses for comments. After input from this level, they go back to the editor and make adjustments. The next offline edit will be presented to the client service staff and then to the client, usually by the agency producer and creative director. At each presentation, requests for adjustments can be made. The creatives may or may not accept the requests and, on occasion, there is a creative impasse. If there is a downside to the enormous flexibility provided by digital postproduction, it is the opportunity for rather dramatic changes to be made rapidly and often with little effort and at nominal cost. There is a tendency to overproduce.

After all parties, right up to the client, have approved the offline edit, the editor performs the online edit, if necessary, to make any last-minute changes. Then the final version of the commercial is output to digital tape for distribution. The offline edit may be good enough, so it is transferred to a medium for distribution. In effect, it becomes the online final commercial.

SUMMARY

Postproduction is the important final step in the creation of the television commercial. Visual and audio elements that are meaningless by themselves are combined and composited to form a persuasive message within a fixed time frame—:15 or :30. Most postproduction takes place at post houses, where the agency creative and an editor work with digital tools to edit the elements together, making decisions about what shots to use, the order the shots should appear in, pacing, transitions, and decisions about sounds.

The art and craft of editing has not changed since the beginning of film editing and the development of what we call the visual language. The basic skills are still needed by the commercial editor and the creative director to tell a visual story. Videotape and digital technology have provided the industry with certain benefits, including speed and flexibility.

Computer technology has made it possible to correct, modify, and even create new visual and audio material for commercials, and these tasks are now part of the postproduction process. Compositing two visual elements, for example, is done digitally during postproduction rather than optically at the film lab, as it had been in the past. Digital media has all but replaced analog media in postproduction, and the technology has made the work faster and better, if not cheaper. Technology has given creative people many more tools and the latitude to produce visually stunning commercials.

DISCUSSION QUESTIONS

1. Even though digital technology has introduced more and better tools into the editing process, the essential skill of the editor is still storytelling. Explain the power the editor has to tell a story. What does she have control over?

2. If the skill of the editor is still important, do you choose to use one postproduction house over another based on what equipment it has?

3. Why is nonlinear editing superior to linear editing? What problems does it solve?

4. Is there a danger in having too much control, too many toys, and plenty of time to work on a commercial during postproduction? What are some of the outcomes?

RECOMMENDED READINGS

Browne, Steven E. *Video Editing: A Postproduction Primer,* 4th ed. Boston: Focal Press, 2002.

Clark, Barbara, and Susan Spohr, eds. *Guide to Postproduction for TV and Film: Managing the Process,* 2d ed. Boston: Focal Press, 2002.

Dmytryk, Edward. *On Film Editing.* Boston: Focal Press, 1984.

Katz, Steven D. *Film Directing Shot by Shot: Visualizing from Concept to Screen.* Boston: Focal Press, 1991.

NOTES

1. Katz, p. 145.
2. Ibid., p. 148.

CHAPTER ELEVEN

THE WRAP

The commercial is now "in the can" and the client and the agency love it. So what's next? Plenty. For example, two important matters that outlive the design and production of the commercial are distribution to the media and talent reuse payments. At the agency, the traffic department must get the spot to the media (airing on television is only one form of presentation in this day and age), and the production department has to tend to all of the backroom management tasks. In this short chapter, we outline the process of getting the commercial to the media, what the various business tasks to wrap things up are, and some of the issues surrounding reuse payments to talent.

TRAFFIC

Traffic is the distribution of the commercial to the media. Up until twenty years ago, this consisted mainly of the three major networks and individual broadcast stations. Today, it includes the cable network; or the cable interconnect head-end; the satellite distributor; the cinema service distributor (for theatrical exhibition); Internet broadcaster—client Web site; or direct exposure at a retail site, perhaps in a kiosk; and so on.

Rest assured that no matter how long this list is now, it will expand even more because of new media and advances in telecommunications technology. Palmpilots and cell phones are being explored as possible receivers of *television* commercials. Regardless of media, the basic idea of trafficking is analogous. The media department has purchased a spot, and the advertising agency has to get the commercial to the facility that will disseminate the message.

Typically, the media department sends a *buy list* to the agency traffic department identifying the networks, stations, cable channels or providers, Web sites, and other media it has purchased for the spot, and when the commercial is scheduled to air. Customarily, after a commercial is approved and ready for distribution, the agency transfers a master copy of the commercial to a print procurement company. The traffic department orders duplicate copies of the commercial to be made and stored in inventory. This print procurement company then ships the materials, as instructed by the agency, to the purchased media. The company either makes duplicate copies for physical shipment or uses an *electronic distribution* method.

Shipment from the procurement company to the media was, at one time, an actual film print and later a videotape; they actually used the postal service or an air freight service. Today, most commercials are sent via satellite to distribution points where they are copied to tape or into a digital file server and stored until needed.

Separately, the agency traffic department sends scheduling instructions to the purchased media. For network spots, these instructions contain specific details as to which commercials should run in what timeslot. For spot and local media, the instructions may be a rotation schedule for possibly two or three commercials.

WRAPPING UP BUSINESS

In addition to distribution there are other tasks that have to be tended to after production is complete. Historically, a broadcast business department is responsible for most of the tasks, even though they may be assigned to other departments such as the media or the legal department. The broadcast business department is usually responsible for the talent reuse budget and for making residual payments to the talent, which is necessary if the commercial was shot using union talent. The department may also order and send materials (tapes and films) to purchased media (networks or cable channels) and submit materials for network clearance. At small agencies, all of this may be done by the producer, owner, or office manager.

The following are some of the tasks that remain to be done after the commercial has been produced and sent to the media.

- *Review and approval of all final billings*—There will be a pile of bills from vendors, contractors, travel agents, and others who participated in the production. The producer must approve these invoices before they can be paid.
- *Reconcile final client billing with the production estimate, including any applicable revisions*—This means the agency producer must match the actual expenses (bills) with the client estimate and *reconcile* them (find out why there are differences). During production, the client or the producer approved any requested overages, for example, and there must be a signed document or note about this.
- *Check to make sure all other paperwork is in order*—The producer must review the job files to ensure that all the proper paperwork is accounted for, including all purchase orders, releases, affidavits, substantiations, network clearances, copyright agreements, contracts with contractors and talent, as well as any special paperwork germane to the specific job.
- *Make sure all talent is properly credited and paid*—Lots of things happen during the shoot and during the edit that may change talents' *grading*—someone who was originally thought to have a major role may be edited out; someone else now may have a line or two. The producer must reconcile all talent reports so that they accurately reflect who is in the final edit. The producer has to forward to broadcast businesses notices about talent downgrade/outgrade for payment. A downgrade occurs when someone's face doesn't show in the final commercial. An outgrade occurs when talent is edited out of the commercial altogether. Both have implications for holding fees and residuals described in the next section.

- *Send things back to their owners*—The producer must follow through with all storage or disposal requirements for props, products, wardrobe, rigs, and other things that were used on the job.

All of these tasks have to be done carefully so that down the road the file can stand up to scrutiny on its own with regard to any audit or legal questions.

TALENT RIGHTS

Producers have to be aware of union rules, and deals made with nonunion talent, that will impact the commercial's life, and the rights the agency will have to reuse the commercial or parts of it in the future. Agencies do not even own the rights to images from the commercials for use in this book's figures. The authors had to get permission to use their pictures from the talent who appeared in the commercials in this book, which is considered a *commercial purpose.*

Commercials have only a 21-month maximum life if produced under the SAG Commercials Contract because that is the length of time that the advertiser can obtain rights to the talent. Most of the time, this is not a problem because most commercials do not run that long. But remember the "Crying Indian" PSA we spoke of in chapter 1. That one ran for more than ten years. If an agency produces a commercial that will air for as long as 21 months, there are certain renegotiation procedures to follow. It's up to the performer or his or her agent to contact the agency prior to the end of the 21-month period. They have 60 to 120 days (two to four months) prior to the end of the period to send in a renegotiation notice. If they don't send in a notice, the ad agency can roll over the commercial for another 21 months at the same rate that the performer was paid for the first 21 months, without having to renegotiate.

Sometimes older commercials are used for special purposes, such as in television programming or in special client exhibits, or other uses beyond normal broadcast commercial exposure. The talent must be contacted and a deal needs to be struck for use of their pictures.

HOLDING FEES AND RESIDUAL PAYMENTS

Most national and regional television commercials are produced under the Screen Actors Guild (SAG) Commercials Contract. In some cases, they are produced under the American Federation of Television and Radio Artists (AFTRA) contract, but terms and conditions are virtually the same. These contracts are negotiated between AFTRA and SAG jointly with a committee of the American Association of Advertising Agencies (4As) along with participation of the Association of National Advertisers (ANA). The 4As committee is made up of Agency people with very strong backgrounds in the broadcast business. It is this contract that not only dictates terms and conditions about how union member talent is paid for services during commercial production, but also dictates talent payments based on the use of the commercial.

During production, principal union talent are entitled to a number of payments, including being paid for interviews and auditions (although the first two interviews are not paid for) and for the sessions (shooting days). The daily rates for talent vary depending on whether they are principals, extras, or off-camera. The daily rate for an on-camera principal is currently $500.00; voiceover talent is paid $375.95. After production, and during the life of the commercial, there are two categories—holding fees and residuals—of payments that may be due the talent.

Holding fees are paid to talent beginning immediately after the session, and continuing every thirteen weeks during the commercial's run; these payments hold the talent as exclusive to the product. In other words, talent that appears in a commercial for Cheerios cannot appear in a commercial for Kellogg Corn Flakes while being paid holding fees by the Cheerios' agency.

Residuals (also called *program use* or *reuse* payments) are paid to talent when the commercial they appear in is broadcast or cablecast. The commercial contract categorizes commercials based on whether the commercial "sponsors" a program, is shown on the networks or on "wild spots," is shown in individual markets, and other criteria. There is a sliding scale of payments, and even a ceiling on payments when the commercial is shown on cable.

Because the contract between SAG, AFTRA, and advertising agencies is renegotiated periodically, the best current source for specific contract terms and conditions is available at the http://www.sag.org/contract2000/commercial_com_faqs.html Web site. The important point here is that talent will be entitled to payments of various kinds during the commercial's run, and possibly afterwards, if the commercial is used for other purposes.

SUMMARY

In this chapter we tied up the loose ends—paid people for their efforts, filed away all of the paperwork, sent things back to their rightful owners, and made certain that union contracts were honored. At the agency and the client, everyone now watches to see how well the commercial does its job.

4As (American Association of Advertising Agencies) Trade association for advertising agencies that subscribe to membership and are accepted based on association criteria.

Advertising agency departments

> **Account services department account executives** Provides liaison between agency and client. Will work on account planning and will work with creative department to sell advertising campaigns to clients. Will also provide clients with services as required.

> **Accounting department** Handles all invoicing from vendors and suppliers and handles all client billing.

> **Broadcast business department** Functions may vary somewhat by agency; however, this department is responsible for talent administration and may be responsible for procurement and trafficking of broadcast materials, reuse payments and reuse budgets, continuity clearance and contract administration related to talent. At some agencies these functions may be assigned to other departments.

> **Creative department** Fulfills creative assignments for client needs. Conceives ideas for specific advertising in accord with strategy previously determined. Executes the advertising to usable finished form along with the contributions of the production department (production department may be a part of the creative department depending on agency structure and organization).

> **Legal department** Some agencies have an internal, in-house legal department whereas other agencies rely on outside counsel. The legal department will work with other departments to ensure the legality of advertising, secure copyright clearance, prepare talent or music contracts, and perform any other tasks required by specific contracts. Will approve all basic business contract forms and purchase orders and will perform trademark and copyright searches. Will respond to any legal actions raised by third parties as a result of the advertising created by an agency.

> **Media department** Will devise media plans based on research that will best meet client's overall strategy. The media department will conduct research on effectiveness and will plan media purchases in accord with this strategy. Will purchase time on media to run advertising.

> **Production department** Will work with creative department to physically produce the client-approved television commercial.

> **Research department** Will manage all research projects at the agency for both client and agency needs in areas other than media. This can include target audience research, motivation research, and copy research.

Advertising research A function to analyze elements of the advertising process. Examples of this include advertising copy testing, effectiveness of a media purchase, determination of target audiences, and analysis of numerous other elements of the advertising process, measuring and quantifying these elements to determine efficiency and effectiveness of an advertising message.

Affidavit A legal document attesting to a statement or observation made.

Affiliated stations Organizations, businesses, and stations that are independently owned but have a contractual relationship with a supplier. Typically, a network in the broadcast world can carry program material distributed by the network, but these stations are not owned by the network or network parent company.

AFTRA (American Federation of Television and Radio Artists) The union that has jurisdiction over primarily live television and radio production but will usually have jurisdiction over recorded material produced at a facility that will produce the live material such as a television station or network production facility. Also has jurisdiction over portions of the recording industry. Primarily covers vocals and speech as music produced in the United States is under the American Federation of Musicians.

Agent In the entertainment business, a person who represents *talent* primarily for the purpose of getting them work. Can also represent directors, writers, directors of photography, makeup people, hairstylists, and others who have specialized talents and need representation to the purchasers of production services.

AICE (Association of Independent Commercial Editors) The trade association for the editor/post production part of the production business.

AICP (Association of Independent Commercial Producers) The trade association of the actual production companies and associated services in the production business.

ANA (Association of National Advertisers) A trade association of national advertisers that works in the common interest of advertising issues. They are part of the group along with the 4As that negotiates the talent and music union contracts on behalf of the advertising business community.

Analog A continuous reproduction of material rather than a sampling of the material as in digital. The amount of sampling is in direct proportion to quality. While more complete a representation of original, it can also have technical limitations that are overcome using a digital format. Analog material tends to degrade with generational copying while digital copies retain original quality much better.

Animatronic A device, usually a character like a puppet figure that is computer operated and usually functions at a specific venue; examples of this would be the characters that appear within a Walt Disney Theme Park venue in *Pirates of the Caribbean.*

Animatic Still pictures given motion through a technique similar to how animation is generated; used primarily for testing purposes.

Answer print The final finished assembled first print of a commercial (or any other production).

Antithetical Something that is against normal standards but not necessarily illegal.

Art director Responsible for the overall look of commercial; designs sets, dresses locations (*see* production designer).

Artifact An undesirable and degrading element that can be introduced through technical processing. These elements usually can not be totally eliminated, but can be minimized.

Audio Sound elements of a commercial.

Audition Screening of potential talent for a role in a commercial; may include recording of script.

Available households Number of television sets in the universe to be measured for research. Multiple sets in a household with possible multiple simultaneous viewing can create research complications with determining this base figure.

Best boy The second electrician on any production.

Bid A financial proposal used to execute a project for the money quoted, if the business is contracted to do so based on specifications supplied to it.

Blocking Setting up a shoot.

Booking Confirming employment of talent or crew and binding them to a contract.

Business model A plan for a project to be financially successful.

Buy out To pay talent, or sometimes other production materials, for the right to use the talent or material without any additional payments. This can be restricted to geographic area, length of use, or in some cases, occurs without restrictions.

Call An official time to report for employment on a production. It can also refer to being hired for the production.

Campaign A structure of advertising messages with a cohesiveness to further and reinforce an intended overall message.

Casting The process of looking at and selecting talent for performances; may be on-camera or voiceover.

Cel animation Traditional animation where drawings are made on acetate cels for later photography in sequence to give motion.

CGI Computer-generated images.

Chroma key A photographic process that allows different elements of a picture to be photographed separately and then composited. The object that is to be inserted into another image is photographed against a background that has color that is not in the final composition. It is important to remember that the image will "bleed" if the key color is in the background of the original photograph. This is a process of creating a matte, or overlay, of the image to be inserted using the missing color of the background and then removing that area of the background picture and "keying" in the element to be inserted, allowing creation of a composite image of the two separate images.

Clearance The process of obtaining approvals from appropriate authorities—legal departments, network continuity departments, or any other responsible authority that must grant approvals. (*see* continuity clearance.)

Color-corrected packaging Packaging designed to reproduce the best photographically; sometimes extraneous material, such as net weights, are removed to make for a cleaner and more generic look.

Color-corrected product Adjusting product for best photographic representation within legal bounds.

Color-correction Adjusting picture elements for best picture transmission.

Commercial use A legal definition that categorizes advertising materials for business purposes. By doing so, this creates certain restrictions in areas of right of privacy, requirements for releases, and other restrictions that must be addressed to ensure that the advertising can be presented unencumbered and free from possible legal actions by third parties or governmental jurisdictions.

Concept   The creative idea at its earliest point; often high-level, requiring tweaking and fine-tuning.

Conflict of interest   Being employed by a competitor.

Consolidation   The merger or acquisition of companies that had been competitors into one company. Many media companies and advertising agencies have consolidated recently, creating a few very large companies.

Consumer sovereignty   The idea that the customer has ultimate control over final decisions. In this book's context, the reference can be to viewing programming or purchase decisions, consumers' basic motivations, and buying behaviors.

Continuity clearance   Getting a proposed script approved by a specific organization, usually a television network.

Contract (standard)   A contract spells out general terms and conditions; if a specific contract is issued, all the terms of the general contract will also apply.

Copyright   The legal right of an author to protect his or her creation.

Cost plus   A contracting arrangement in which a purchaser agrees to pay all actual costs plus a percentage fee agreed on in the original bid. Both the costs and the final fee, comprising overhead and profit, will be adjusted to the actual costs.

Cost-plus-fixed fee   A contracting arrangement in which the purchaser agrees to pay all actual costs that he agrees to plus a fixed amount of money to cover contractor's overhead and profit.

Demo   Normally a demonstration element used for decision making rather than for final media distribution.

Demographic   Breakout of population by specific factors, such as age, sex, education, with or without children, geographic distribution, and so on.

Digital   A method of representing sounds, pictures, text, and data by using binary numbers; normally can be controlled, adjusted, manipulated by computer or similar device.

Disclaimer   A statement (usually a legal statement) that fulfills a specific requirement to inform the viewer of information that may be germane to understanding specifically what she is seeing.

Documentation   Backup for material that supports a claim or production demonstration. (For example a testimonial.)

DP (director of photography)   The crew person responsible for the camera and final look of the photographed-recorded image.

Dress   To embellish an area, set, or location with materials and props to enhance the look of the area.

Dual revenue streaming   When media has income from both advertising and subscriptions (or pay-per-view), as cable does.

Dubbing   Copying of an element (usually a sound element) or adding new material to an existing element through the copying process.

DVD (digital versatile disc)   Also digital video disc, but do not say this to any computer people.

Edit   To cut, rearrange, assemble, and reassemble as it applies to film and videotape in this book.

EFX   The acronym for special effects (*see also* SFX).

Endorsement   A testimonial statement giving a positive opinion about something or someone.

Ethographics   The study of an audience's lifestyle.

Exposure sheet   A breakout reference frame by frame of a soundtrack so that animated pictures can be blocked for exact action. For example, the animator will know on exactly which frame a character utters a specific sound or where a specific sound effect takes place.

FCC (Federal Communications Commission)   U.S. Government Agency that regulates broadcast and cable. It also has other regulatory responsibilities over phone companies.

FTC (Federal Trade Commission)   The U.S. government agency that regulates advertising and has some shared responsibilities over antitrust issues shared with U.S. Justice Department.

Firm-fixed bid   A contracting arrangement in which purchaser and contractor agree to a firm-fixed payment for services and materials delivered as long as there are no changes in the job specifications.

Frame   One single still picture of a production. Although commercials contain motion, they are made up of individual still frames. They are recorded in such a way that the human characteristic of image retention allows the series of recorded still frames to be viewed as continuous motion. Recording higher number of frames per second can enhance motion quality, and the ratio of frame recording speed to frame playback speed is used to create all kinds of effects such as slow motion and sped-up motion.

Freelancer   An independent contractor who works on a job-by-job basis for various agencies.

Frequency   A research and media sales term reflecting how many times an individual viewer will see the same message.

Gaffer   The chief electrician on any production.

General audience   The overall viewing public with no qualification for demographic breakout.

Generic master   A master element with the specific identifications, such as titles, omitted, so that commercials can be easily remade for use in foreign countries.

Glamour shot   The photograph of the most important element of the scene, most often the product, usually alone, with the shot designed to make the object look its absolute best.

Greeking   Removing specific identifications, usually from signs and so on, that can be seen in a background.

Grip   Person on set responsible for nonelectrical lighting instruments such as reflectors; responsible for rigging and camera platforms such as dollies.

HUT (households using television)   Refers to the number of households that have their television turned on during a particular part of the day.

Independent contractor   A nonemployee who works only under the direction of a general contractor, usually on a project only basis; normally brings very specific talents to a project. For example, the studio producer, director of photography, or the location scout. (In some instances though, all of these people could be employees.)

Infringement   A violation of another individual's or company's specific legal rights.

Intellectual property   Material created by an individual or company in which they have specific vested rights.

Interpretation   The individual translation of an idea to a finite produced element. It can also be a camera or voice-over talent rendering a specific performance based on directed or individual input.

Interstitial   The time between the end of one program and the beginning of the next.

JPC (Joint Policy Committee)   This group is made up of representatives of the 4As and ANA.

Leadman   Top person on the set-location dress and/or set build crew.

Library music   Music available for purchase and use by paying a license fee from existing prerecorded files.

License   A permit for a fee to use something—a location, a musical composition, and so on.

Location   An existing place or facility to photograph (shoot) a commercial—a house, a park, a highway.

Location release   A document executed by the owner or a responsible party granting permission to photograph property under his or her jurisdiction.

Lock up   The process of mechanically or electronically adjusting different equipment to maintain perfect or near perfect synchronization. For example, a motion picture camera and a sound recorder are locked up so that even though these are two separate pieces of mechanical equipment, the picture frame will match the sound element for that frame and maintain exact accuracy throughout the recording take.

Locked off   In photography, this normally refers to a camera being placed in a fixed position over the whole length of the take. This is normally done because this image will be used in such a way with other images that any motion will prevent proper integration or compositing to be accomplished with the other images.

Marketing research   A broad term that refers to the acquisition, development, and analysis of new information used for marketing, advertising, or marketing communication decisions.

Markup   Overhead and profit on a job, as opposed to direct costs.

Media   The disseminators of the advertising messages. Examples include television networks, stations, and cable services.

Media buy   The purchase of specific media by an advertising agency to carry an advertisement that it created. This can be the total list of all media that have been purchased to carry the advertising message.

Mixing   Typically referring to combining individual sound elements and adjusting all levels to make a balanced composite track. Usually the elements will consist of the sync-to-picture voice track, the voice-over announcer track, the music track, and any other sound effects. Mixing can also refer to combining individual elements of a music track, using various instruments, combining musical sections and vocals, and doing overdubs of individual sections to make the finished music track.

Mnemonic device   A visual or audio element that usually leads to nearly instant recognition, message reinforcement, or memorability. The last drop of coffee pouring into a cup or the straw going into the orange could be considered devices.

Normally, a slogan or a trademark such as "The Ultimate Driving Machine," "Like a Rock," or the Nike "swoosh" are not usually considered mnemonic devices even though they can trigger memorability in the same way.

NAB (National Association of Broadcasters) A broadcast station and network trade association.

Original music Music created for a specific project. Normally the advertiser purchases all rights from the composer and owns this music for use anywhere. However, sometimes a purchase agreement between composer and purchaser contains limitations, so this needs to be checked carefully to ensure that the advertiser has purchased all the rights needed.

Overhead Nondirect expenses associated with a business, such as rent, telephone service, office staff, and so on.

Owned and operated Stations that are owned by the network or the network parent company and carry network-distributed material.

P & W (pension and welfare) benefits Employ-er's responsibility payments for specific taxes, union contract fees, and other contributions for talent and crew.

Paper trail The process of maintaining records of the complete process of a project. It is designed so all steps and elements of the project can be documented for use at a later date.

Poster Close to perfect display of an individual or total element for the best possible impression on the intended audience.

Primary research Original research conducted directly by a company with research subjects.

Producer The person at the advertising agency or production studio who has overall responsibility for bringing together all elements needed to produce and for executing everything necessary to accomplish a production.

Production designer Responsible for the overall look of a production—set design, location, dress (*see also* art director).

Production notes A narrative usually written by the creative staff of an agency describing all of the elements of the commercial as they conceive it.

Property master Chief person responsible for all props on a shoot.

Props Any item that can be handled or placed within a film scene; normally not germane to a specific production, but helps establish atmosphere.

PSA (public service announcement) A commercial designed to advertise something in the public interest; usually, time is donated by the broadcaster to air a PSA.

Psychographic Refers to the psychological profile of a group of consumers; used by researchers to define and find an audience for a particular product or service.

Public domain Something that no person can claim a right of authorship to that would restrict use by others.

PVR (personal digital recorder) A device that allows the user to record television programming in digital format.

Rating A number that represents the total estimated number of viewing households expressed as a percentage of the total number of HUTs; a way of expressing what television shows people are watching.

Reach A research and media sales term reflecting how many total viewer and audience impressions are made by a particular advertising message.

Reconciliation Analyzing and categorizing all expenses back to the original budget so a status or budget position can be established. A good paper trail is required to do an effective reconciliation.

Redress Right of action for a violation of a specified legal right such as violation of a copyright.

Render The final computation of a computer-generated image—the step in which the final picture is created with lighting and texture.

Rigging Mechanical connections to objects so that they can be manipulated, hung, displayed, and so on.

Secondary research Finding and using the results of other, previously existing, research results.

SAG (Screen Actors Guild) The trade union that has major jurisdiction on film, most high-end commercial production, and some television production; shared and sometimes conflicting interests with AFTRA (*see also* AFTRA).

Sale Transfer of ownership (but not necessarily all rights) in a commodity. (You can sell a photograph of Tony the Tiger, but this does not give you an intellectual property right in the character.)

Scale The base minimum payment for a service as defined in a union contract.

Sets The constructed environment to use for shooting a scene on a stage.

Share Refers to the estimated number of households tuned in to a program, expressed as a percentage of households with televisions turned on at that particular time.

SFX (1) Sound effect—An audio embellishment to provide a certain atmospheric feeling such as a door slam or a car horn sounding. (2) Special effect—A picture element that is created to emulate realism but is not real; a computer-generated element or a matte painting—matte insert would be one of an infinite number of special effects.

SMPTE (Society of Motion Picture and Television Engineers)   A group that, among other activities, sets industry standards for engineering areas of television and motion pictures.

Stat   Short for Photostat, which is a photographic process that makes positive or negative reference prints directly from original materials. These stats are commonly used to copy storyboards and are also used in animation and live action title photography. Although there are other, newer techniques to achieve the same results, the stat continues to be the predominant one.

Stock footage   Normally, footage that previously exists and is available to be integrated into a new commercial; for example, a film of a plane taking off from an airport. Usually the footage will be used for an atmosphere shot. It saves producers a lot of time and money because a use fee usually costs much less than it would cost to shoot the same picture.

Stock music   Same idea as stock footage, but for music instead of pictures.

Storyboards   The creative artist's visual representation, scene-by-scene, of his concept for the commercial to be produced.

Stylist, food   Also known as the *home economist* who prepares the food required but more important makes it appear appetizing and very desirable; appearance must be in accord with legal requirements for presentation.

Stylist, wardrobe   Selects and supervises purchase or rental of wardrobe with input about overall commercial look from the director.

Substantiation   Providing legal backup for claims or demonstrations made in a commercial.

Super   A printed message over a visual element of a commercial that gives additional information, reenforces information, or gives a disclaimer for legal information.

Sync   Maintaining a perfect relationship between picture and sound in a production.

Take   One filmed version of a shot or scene.

Testimonial   A statement of how an individual feels about a product or service, usually very positive; designed to motivate potential customers about the value of the product or service.

Theme   The format of a commercial, such as stand-up presenter, testimonial, slice-of-life, and so on.

TiVo   A device that digitally records incoming television programming and plays it back on a time delay or on demand; a type of personal digital recorder (PVR).

Track   The audio—sound element of a commercial.

Trademark   The exclusive right and ownership of a design; can be a product, package, logotype, or any other device in commerce as defined by law. Mickey Mouse is trademarked by the Walt Disney Company, as is the package for Kellogg's Corn Flakes.

Treatment   A summary narrative description of how a creative work, such as a commercial, will be executed; usually the director's verbalized concept.

Trickle down   When a secondary person can benefit from the actions of a primary person. For example, a director of photography will specify what chief electrician (gaffer) he wants, and the gaffer will specify what assistants he wants.

USP (unique selling proposition, or unique selling point)   The one main thing that can be said or communicated about a product that differentiates it and sets it apart from the competition.

VALS Typology.   A system of classifying consumers into values and lifestyle groupings, which helps researchers understand target audiences and what would motivate them to buy a product.

Vertical integration   When one company owns or controls the entire production and distribution chain; Disney is vertically integrated because it owns the intellectual property (Mickey Mouse), the production studio (Walt Disney Studios), the distributor (Buena Vista), and the television network (ABC).

Visualization   Translating an idea into an actual picture or graphic representation.

Visual language   The use of the camera, lights, sound, editing, and other visual elements that the filmmaker controls to create a specific message or meaning.

Voiceover (VO)   The unseen vocal elements of a commercial; normally the announcer.

WebTV   A device and service introduced by Microsoft that allows consumers to use the Internet on their television sets.

Workers' compensation   Payment for an injury, medical treatment, and so on if an incident occurs while on the job, in lieu of legal action against an employer to recover expenses; coverage needs to be purchased for all productions.

Abrams, Bill. *Observational Research Handbook: Understanding How Consumers Live with Your Product.* New York: McGraw Hill/NTC Books, 2000.

Atchity, Kenneth, and Chi-L. Wong. *Writing Treatments That Sell.* New York: Owl Books. 1997.

Baldwin, Huntley. *How to Create Effective TV Commercials.* Lincolnwood, IL: NTC Business Books, 1988.

Bendinger, Bruce. *The Copy Workshop Workbook.* Chicago: The Copy Workshop, 1993.

Brown, Blain. *Cinematography Image Making for Cinematographers, Directors, and Videographers.* Boston: Focal Press, 2002.

Browne, Steven E. *Video Editing: A Postproduction Primer,* 4th ed. Boston: Focal Press, 2002.

Burton, Phillip Ward. *Advertising Fundamentals,* 3d ed. Columbus, OH: Grid Publishing, 1988.

Carter, David E., ed. *Creativity 30: Bright Ideas in Advertising and Design from 40 Countries Around the World.* New York: HBI, 2001.

Clark, Barbara, and Susan Spohr, eds. *Guide to Postproduction for TV and Film: Managing the Process, 2d ed.* Boston: Focal Press, 2002.

Cook, Albert C., and C. Dennis Schick. *Fundamentals of Copy and Layout.* Chicago: Crain Books, 1984.

Davis, Michael H., Arthur Raphael Miller, and Michael H. Davis. *Intellectual Property: Patents, Trademarks, and Copyright* (Nutshell Series). Belmont, CA: Wadsworth, 2002.

Dmytryk, Edward. *On Film Editing.* Boston: Focal Press, 1984.

Dominick, Joseph R., Barry L. Sherman, and Gary A. Copeland. *Broadcasting/Cable: An Introduction to Modern Electronic Media.* New York: McGraw-Hill, 1996.

Fortini-Campbell, Lisa. *Hitting the Sweet Spot: How Consumer Insights Can Inspire Better Marketing and Advertising.* Chicago: The Copy Workshop, 1992.

Goebert, Bonnie, and Herma Rosenthal. *Beyond Listening: Learning the Secret Language of Focus Groups.* New York: John Wiley & Sons, 2001.

Goulekas, Karen E. *Visual Effects in a Digital World: A Comprehensive Glossary of Over 7,000 Visual Effects Terms, 1st ed.* New York: Morgan Kaufmann Publishers, 2001.

Gross, Lynne S., and Larry W. Ward. *Electronic Moviemaking.* Belmont, CA: Wadsworth Publishing, 2000.

Haley, Eric, Margaret A. Morrison, Kim Sheehan, and Ronald E. Taylor. *Using Qualitative Research in Advertising: Strategies, Techniques and Applications.* Newbury Park, CA: Sage Publications, 2002.

Head, Sydney W., Thomas Spann, and Michael A. McGregor. *Broadcasting in America.* 9th ed. New York: Houghton Mifflin Company, 2001.

Herlinger, Mark. *The Single Camera Director.* Denver: Western Media Products, 2000.

Jamieson, Kathleen Hall. *Everything You Think You Know About Politics and Why You're Wrong.* New York: Basic Books, 2000.

Jewler, Jerry, and Bonnie Drewniany. *Creative Strategy in Advertising.* Belmont, CA: Wadsworth, 2001.

Jones, John Phillip. "The Unique Selling Proposition and Usage-Pull." In John Phillip Jones, ed., *The Advertising Business: Operations Creativity Media Planning Integrated Communications.* Thousand Oaks, CA: Sage Publications, 1999.

Kanner, Bernice. *The 100 Best TV Commercials: And Why They Worked.* New York: Random House, 1999.

Katz, Steven D. *Film Directing Shot by Shot: Visualizing from Concept to Screen.* Boston: Focal Press, 1991.

Kuperberg, Marcia. *Guide to Computer Animation for TV, Games, Multimedia and Web.* Boston: Focal Press, 2002.

Laybourne, Kit. *The Animation Book,* rev. ed. New York: Three Rivers Press; 1998.

Marra, James L. *Advertising Creativity: Techniques for Generating Ideas.* Englewood Cliffs, NJ: Prentice Hall, 1990.

Meeske, Milan D. *Copywriting for the Electronic Media: A Practical Guide,* 4th ed. Belmont, CA: Wadsworth, 2003.

Messaris, Paul. *Visual Persuasion: The Role of Images in Advertising.* Thousand Oaks, CA: Sage Publications, 1997.

Meyer, Trish, and Chris Meyer. *After Effects in Production,* 1st ed. Southampton, UK: CMP Books, 2000.

Morgan, Adam. *Eating the Big Fish: How Challenger Brands Can Compete Against Brand Leaders.* New York: John Wiley & Sons, 1999.

Ogilvy, David. *Ogilvy on Advertising.* New York: Vintage Books, 1985.

Phillips, William H. *Film: An Introduction.* Boston: Bedford/St. Martins, 1999.

Rose, Jay. *Producing Great Sound for Digital Video* (book/CD ed.). Southampton, UK: CMP Books, 2000.

Simon, Deke, and Michael Wiese. *Film & Video Budgets,* 3d rev. ed. Studio City: Edmond H. Weis, 2001.

Steel, Jon. *Truth, Lies and Advertising: The Art of Account Planning.* New York: John Wiley & Sons, 1998.

Sullivan, Luke, and Hey Whipple. *Squeeze This: A Guide to Creating Great Ads.* New York: John Wiley & Sons, 1998.

Sutherland, Max, and Alice K. Sylvester. *Advertising and the Mind of the Consumer.* Crows Nest, Australia: Allen & Unwin, 2000.

Swartz, Tony. *The Responsive Chord.* Garden City, NY: Doubleday, 1973.

Twitchell, James B. *Adcult USA.* New York: Columbia University Press, 1995.

Viera, Dave. *Lighting for Film and Electronic Media.* Belmont CA: Wadsworth Publishing, 2000.

Walker, James, and Douglas Ferguson. *The Broadcast Television Industry.* Needham Heights, MA: Allyn and Bacon, 1998.

White, Hooper. *How to Produce Effective TV Commercials.* Lincolnwood, IL: NTC Business Books, 1994.

Wright, Steve. *Digital Compositing for Film and Video,* 1st ed. (with CD-ROM). Boston: Butterworth-Heinemann, 2001.

Zeigler, Sherilyn, and Herbert H. Howard. *Broadcast Advertising.* Ames, IA: Iowa State University Press, 1991.

Zettl, Herbert. *Television Production Handbook.* Belmont, CA: Wadsworth Publishing, 2000.

INDEX